Fair Value in Accounting

Fair Value in Accounting

From Theory to Practice

The Complete Handbook for Fair Value Measurement (IFRS & US GAAP)

Shlomi Shuv
Yevgeni Ostrovsky

ANTHEM PRESS

Anthem Press
An imprint of Wimbledon Publishing Company
www.anthempress.com

This edition first published in UK and USA 2022
by ANTHEM PRESS
75–76 Blackfriars Road, London SE1 8HA, UK
or PO Box 9779, London SW19 7ZG, UK
and
244 Madison Ave #116, New York, NY 10016, USA

British Library Cataloguing-in-Publication Data
A catalogue record for this book is available from the British Library.

Library of Congress Cataloging-in-Publication Data
Names: Shuv, Shlomi, author. | Ostrovsky, Yevgeni, author.
Title: Fair value in accounting : from theory to practice /
Shlomi Shuv, Yevgeni Ostrovsky.
Description: New York, NY : Anthem Press, 2022. |
Includes bibliographical references. |
Identifiers: LCCN 2022000090 | ISBN 9781839984198 (hardback) |
ISBN 9781839984204 (pdf) | ISBN 9781839984211 (epub)
Subjects: LCSH: Fair value–Accounting.
Classification: LCC HF5681.V3 S48 2022 | DDC 657/.7–dc23/eng/20220107
LC record available at https://lccn.loc.gov/2022000090

ISBN-13: 978-1-83998-419-8 (Hbk)
ISBN-10: 1-83998-419-8 (Hbk)

Cover image: Double exposure of the city, graph, display of stocks and money for finance and business concept. By Number1411/Shutterstock.com

This title is also available as an e-book.

CONTENTS

PREFACE

Fair value, currently a very significant measurement base in financial statements, and a commonly used term in itself, is, somewhat surprisingly, a relatively new term in the world of accounting. Just to illustrate, the *Framework for the Preparation and Presentation of Financial Statements*, originally published in 1989 by the International Accounting Standards Board (IASB), makes no reference whatsoever to this term. This is despite the fact that measurement bases having similar or overlapping principles, such as present value or realizable value, are, indeed, mentioned.

The term "fair value" was first mentioned in US Generally Accepted Principles (US GAAP) in Statement of Financial Accounting Concepts No. 7 regarding *Using Cash Flow Information and Present Value in Accounting Measurements*, published by the Financial Accounting Standards Board (FASB) in 2000, although parts of the definition itself but not the term "fair value" were already used in Statement of Financial Accounting Concepts No. 6 regarding *Elements of Financial Statements*, originally published in 1985.

Over the years, fair value has been used increasingly by the world's leading accounting standard-setting bodies, both for measurement and for disclosure purposes. Thus, for example, using fair value as a measurement base is currently widespread in measurement of financial instruments and business combinations, and under International Financial Reporting Standards (IFRSs), fair value is also employed to measure investment property. As fair value became an increasingly used measurement base, the need to formulate a uniform and consistent rationale for fair value measurement has arisen, along with the need to put in place comprehensive disclosure principles that will provide financial statements' users with additional information, among other things, about the reliability of fair value estimates. This rationale was first reflected in US GAAP in Statement of Financial Accounting Standards No. 157—*Fair Value Measurements* (SFAS 157) and thereafter in the provisions of IFRS upon publication of IFRS 13—*Fair Value Measurement*, which, in effect, converged with the American standard.

This book aims to serve as a comprehensive guide to fair value measurement. In this book, we gradually unfold a comprehensive framework of fair value measurement from a detail-oriented and practical standpoint, both pursuant to IFRS 13 and Accounting Standards Codification (ASC) 820. This is done while referring to subtle nuances between the two accounting standard systems, including with regard to disclosure. In many cases, we opted to focus on theoretical and practical issues stemming from the Standards by providing further examples and analysis, referring to the Standards' explanatory notes and to existing practices. The chapter dealing with disclosure provisions includes a full review of the disclosure provisions and relevant examples, as well as summaries in tabular format as to the nature of the required disclosure, and includes a comparison between the Standards' disclosure provisions.

The first part of this book (Chapters 1 and 2) covers the definition of fair value as well as various scope issues. The second part (Chapters 3–8) discusses core principles in fair value measurement. The third part (Chapters 9–12) deals with issues of application to assets and liabilities and valuation techniques. Chapter 13 discusses in detail the related disclosure requirements.

The book is intended as an essential tool not only for professionals involved in preparing or auditing financial statements—such as accountants and financial managers—but also for practitioners in related domains, such as appraisers and preparers of valuations for legal proceedings based on fair value. We believe the book's instructive and user-friendly structure and its many practical examples could also make it highly useful for students (specifically, accounting students as well as individuals preparing to take the CPA exams) as well as for other academic purposes.

The accounting definition of fair value focuses on the notional price at which an orderly transaction to sell the asset or to transfer the liability would take place between market participants at the measurement date. Over the years, this definition became a universal convention. Among other things, it entails the use of methods that had already been commonly used in finance and appraisal theories, since it focuses on market prices. Nevertheless, the actual application of fair value measurement is not always straightforward. Firstly, as is the case in most economic calculations, measurement of fair value may be subject to a fair amount of uncertainty and subjectivity. Secondly, in quite a few theoretical accounting issues, judgment exercised by the entity may lead to a dramatic change in the way the measured item is perceived, and this might result in a significantly different fair value measurement. These issues pertain, among other things, to questions such as distinguishing between the characteristics of the measured item and the characteristics of the reporting entity itself, the unit of account in the light of which the measurement is carried out, the ability or the necessity to select or change different measurement approaches as well as the measurement parameters used in those approaches, issues pertaining to unique or complementary assets, dealing with restrictions placed on the transfer of the measured asset or liability and more. In that context it is important to note that the difficulty in understanding fair value stems, among other things, from the fact that the definition does not necessarily focus on the reporting entity itself. Thus, for example, restrictions or advantages that would have surely been taken into account by investors in a specific reporting entity would not necessarily be reflected in the measurement of the fair value of the assets it holds. This may be relevant, for instance, for economies or diseconomies of scale, the reporting entity's asset mix or number of assets and so forth.

The relevant Standards list three widely used valuation approaches: the market approach, the cost approach and the income approach, and they include a significant conceptual depth. It is, therefore, interesting to note that the role of accounting theories dealing with fair value may go beyond the classical boundaries of financial statements and permeate into related content worlds—such as economic opinions issued as part of legal disputes, tax issues or opinions issued for transaction purposes.

Generally, it may be said that the many dozens of academic studies published in the past decades reached the conclusion that using fair or current value in financial statements supports their relevancy despite the cost of applying fair value in accounting. Over the years, this trend was also clearly reflected in policies of standard-setting bodies worldwide, which increased the use of fair value in financial statements. It is important to emphasize that along the potential benefits arising from the use of fair value, the key disadvantage of such use naturally pertains to the level of subjectivity or reliability of some fair value measurements. Accounting standards currently deal with these issues in the form of disclosure requirements whereby main assumptions and the estimate's level within the fair value hierarchy (levels 1–3) should also be disclosed in the financial statements.

The gradual transition from historical cost accounting to fair value accounting is a prominent trend in accounting in the past few decades. The impact of this transition may even permeate into the real world and have an actual impact thereon rather than just describe it. Thus, for example, one of the concerns regarding frequent use of fair value is that such use may encourage companies to sell assets at times of crisis, since they wish to avoid recognition of additional future losses that may be caused by a further future decrease in fair values. The underlying argument of this concern is that fair value supposedly has a procyclical impact since it increases supply and causes further price decline in times of crisis; another example pertains to companies' ability to "unlock value" by revaluating investment property under IFRS, which is not allowed under US accounting standards—this might encourage US-based real estate companies or funds to issue their shares or units in other jurisdictions in order to be able to apply IFRS and improve their level of leveraging reflected in their financial statements compared to what it would have been under US GAAP. Another behavior that may be impacted by the use of historical cost accounting rather than fair value accounting is the potential tendency to dispose of assets (or even dispose of assets and repurchase similar assets, as in the case of wash sales of financial assets measured at amortized cost), in order to recognize the profits accrued from increase in value.

A significant advantage of fair value accounting is the fact that it is easy to understand and apply in financial statements, assuming that fair value can be reliably estimated. This advantage is particularly prominent when comparing fair value accounting to other measurement bases, such as amortized cost, the equity method, consolidation, best estimate and so forth. The consistent improvement in capabilities of machine learning systems may make the process of determining fair value shorter, more efficient and less expensive to perform; this, together with the increasing use of fair value in financial statements, will perhaps make it possible to publish financial statements more frequently. However, using such techniques may also have the adverse effect of reducing financial statements' transparency, since it is difficult to track the method employed in determining the result under the model used, which sometimes serves as a "black box."

We are very grateful to Mr. Gil Rosenstock (CPA), for his valuable professional insights. We would also like to extend our gratitude to Ms. Ella Bashan, for her instrumental linguistic editing.

We hope that readers will benefit from reading this book.

Chapter 1

BACKGROUND

1. Overview

While the rule-based US Generally Accepted Accounting Principles (US GAAP) do not widely adopt fair value as a measurement basis, this is not the case with the International Financial Reporting Standards (IFRSs). The latter currently use fair value quite extensively, both for measurement and for disclosure purposes, with one of the key differences lying in the revaluation of investment property and property, plant and equipment (PPE) allowed only under IFRS.

However, fair value as a measurement basis is a relatively new accounting concept, at least from a historical perspective. Interestingly, the *Framework for the Preparation and Presentation of Financial Statements* (for International Accounting Standards (IASs)), originally published in 1989, made no mention of the term. It did mention several other possible measurement bases, such as historical cost, present value, current cost and realizable value. However, the conceptual difference, if any, between the various measurement bases—other than historical cost—was not clearly explained.

Over the years, the IASs underwent significant changes, with one of the most important presumably being the growing use of fair value as a measurement basis. Fair value also sometimes doubles as an acceptable basis for disclosure. However, prior to the formulation of IFRS 13—*Fair Value Measurement*, other IASs offered no unified definition of this measurement basis, nor did they provide a consistent framework for its estimation. Consequently, certain IASs that made use of fair value (for several current examples, see Section 2), as well as the related practice, were not always consistent in applying the measurement principles and even in its basic definition. In addition, some of the Standards, such as IAS 39—*Financial Instruments: Recognition and Measurement*, which was later superseded by IFRS 9—*Financial Instruments*, included a relatively detailed set of guidelines regarding the measurement of fair value, while other Standards, such as IAS 41—*Agriculture*, only included limited guidelines.

Originally published in 2000, US GAAP Concepts Statement 7 did discuss the fair value basis of measurement, but a similar phenomenon of multiple definitions and limited guidance was also the case under US GAAP prior to the publication of Statement of Financial Accounting Standards No. 157—*Fair Value Measurements* in 2006 (SFAS 157). The US national accounting standard-setter, the Financial Accounting Standards Board (FASB), was the first of the two accounting standard-setters to address this problem, with the publication of SFAS 157. The aim of SFAS 157 was to increase the consistency of fair value measurement and to expand related disclosures. This Standard was later codified to become Accounting Standards Codification (ASC) Topic 820 and, after further amendments, served as the basis for the current versions of IFRS 13 and ASC 820.

Finalized in 2011, IFRS 13 and the corresponding version of ASC 820 (hereinafter—the "Standards") were developed jointly by the International Accounting Standards Board (IASB) and FASB. One of the objectives of this joint effort was to unify the meaning of fair value across the world's two leading financial accounting frameworks. Practically speaking, it can be said that while fair value is not used as often under US GAAP as under IFRS, both Standards are very similar, with few minor differences. For more information, see Section 4. The Standards share, among other things, their illustrative Examples. However, the FASB separately developed a Basis for Conclusions (explanatory notes) summarizing its considerations in formulating the current version of ASC 820. SFAS 157 had its own Background Information and Basis for Conclusions.

The purpose of the Standards was to define—in a principled manner—what fair value is, to provide a uniform framework for measuring fair value and to establish the disclosure provisions to be applied when using this measurement basis. The Standards describe how fair value should be measured wherever another IFRS (or US GAAP accounting standard) requires or allows the fair value basis to be used. In other words, they do not specify under which circumstances and to which items fair value should be applied, nor do they address the question of where to recognize changes in fair value from one period to another, as these questions are answered by the relevant Standards using the said measurement basis. The Standards establish general principles, which apply to both financial and nonfinancial items. The Standards also include specific provisions applicable to nonfinancial items alone. Generally speaking, when IFRS 13 (or SFAS 157) came into force, the specific provisions regarding fair value measurement and related disclosure included in the various other Standards were deleted or amended.

It may be said that, as opposed to other accounting measurement bases such as historical cost or value in use, one of the main characteristics of the fair value basis under both IFRS and US GAAP is that it is intended to serve as an objective, market-based measure that is nonspecific to a particular reporting entity. Fair value is defined by IFRS 13 and ASC 820 as the price that would be received to sell an asset or paid to transfer a liability in an orderly transaction between market participants at the measurement date. Thus, whether or not there are observable transactions for the appraised item, the objective of measuring fair value is to estimate the potential price of the item in an ordinary (hypothetical) transaction between market participants at the measurement date, under existing market conditions. Thus, for example, the reporting entity's intention to hold the asset (rather than sell it) is irrelevant to the measurement. It is also important to note that, at times, estimating the fair value of specific items (such as the fair value of investments in start-up companies) may require considerable judgment and may also be subject to significant uncertainty and a relatively wide range of possibilities.

The following sections of this handbook provide a thorough explanation of the definition, principles and accounting issues associated with fair value measurement and disclosure in accounting in US GAAP and IFRS.

2. Use of Fair Value in IFRSs Compared to US GAAP

The IFRSs make extensive use of the fair value basis compared to US GAAP. In many cases, the use of this basis is mandatory, and in others, its use is an accounting policy choice. At times, it is only required to disclose the fair value in the notes to the financial statements.

Following are some examples of the use of fair value in IFRSs:

Example A—Financial Instruments

Historically speaking, fair value has mainly been used to measure financial instruments, for which, consequently, there were detailed measurement guidelines. Under IFRS, the Standards that deal with financial instruments—IAS 32—*Financial Instruments*: *Presentation*, IFRS 9—*Financial Instruments*, and IFRS 7—*Financial Instruments: Disclosures*—use fair value extensively for measurement and disclosure purposes. The same holds true for ASC Topic 825—*Financial Instruments* and Topic 815—*Derivatives and Hedging*.

Following are several key examples of how fair value is used to measure financial instruments under both systems:

a. Measurement at initial recognition: The guiding principle in IFRS 9 is that assets and liabilities should be measured at fair value at initial recognition. As a side note, the said Standard includes various restrictions that apply to situations where the transaction price at initial recognition is different from the fair value (a minimum reliability threshold approach of sorts where only Level 1 or Level 2 valuations are accepted with regard to immediate revaluations). In addition, in certain classes of financial instruments, at initial recognition, the transaction costs incurred by the reporting entity should be added to the fair value upon the instrument's origination or purchase. Under US GAAP, derivatives are generally measured at fair value at initial recognition, with any difference between the transaction price and the fair value recognized immediately without any minimum reliability threshold.

b. Subsequent measurement: Pursuant to IFRS 9, a reporting entity is required (and sometimes entitled) to measure financial assets or financial liabilities at fair value through profit or loss and financial assets only at fair value through other comprehensive income. A similar logic exists under US GAAP ASC Topics 825 and 815, which includes a so-called fair value option.
c. Fair value disclosure of financial assets and financial liabilities: As a rule, according to IFRS 7, the notes to the financial statements should include a disclosure of the fair value of financial assets and financial liabilities as at the reporting date, especially if the instruments are not measured at fair value in the statement of financial position. A similar requirement exists under US GAAP ASC Topic 825.

Example B—Business Combinations

IFRS 3—*Business Combinations* establishes a guiding principle whereby, except for a number of specified exceptions, the acquirer in a business combination shall recognize the acquiree's identifiable assets and liabilities and measure them at their fair value as at the acquisition date. This is also generally the case under US GAAP ASC Topic 805—*Business Combinations*.

Example C—Property, Plant and Equipment, Investment Property and Intangible Assets

Under IFRS, the Standards dealing with PPE, investment property and intangible assets allow the use of fair value as a relevant measurement alternative following the item's initial recognition. Thus, IAS 16—*Property, Plant & Equipment* allows for each class of PPE to be measured at subsequent dates at either amortized cost or fair value (the revaluation model). However, it is noted that the said Standard permits the revaluation model to be applied only if an item's fair value can be reliably measured. Similarly, IAS 38—*Intangible Assets* allows for a choice of the subsequent measurement of intangible assets for which there is an active market (as defined in IFRS 13; for more information, see Chapter 12, Section 2.2) between an accounting policy under which the assets are measured at amortized cost and one in which they are measured at fair value (the revaluation model).

IAS 40—*Investment Property* provides a choice between the amortized cost model and the fair value model as an accounting policy for the subsequent measurement of investment property. As a rule, under the fair value model, periodic measurement of the fair value of an asset shall be made while recognizing fair value changes in profit or loss. In addition, IAS 40 requires the fair value of investment property to be disclosed in the notes to the annual financial statements if the fair value model was not chosen.

It is important to note that one of the key differences between IFRS and US GAAP is that US GAAP does not treat investment property as a separate class of assets, nor does it generally permit the revaluation of PPE. Therefore, investment property is generally accounted for under US GAAP on a historical cost basis. This is also the case for intangible assets under ASC 350—*Intangibles—Goodwill and Other.*

Example D—Impairment of Assets and Noncurrent Assets Held for Sale

Under IFRS, the Standards dealing with impairment of assets use fair value as a measurement stage (rather than necessarily as the final outcome). Thus, under IAS 36—*Impairment of Assets*, when testing an asset for impairment, the recoverable amount is defined as the higher of its fair value less costs to sell and its value in use. To determine the fair value for the purpose of the test, the provisions of IFRS 13 should be applied, after which costs to sell should be deducted. It should be noted that value in use as a measurement basis possesses certain aspects that are similar to fair value but is not within the scope of IFRS 13, since it is measured in the specific context of the reporting entity (for more information, see Chapter 2, Section 2).

Similarly, IFRS 5—*Non-Current Assets Held for Sale and Discontinued Operations* prescribes the accounting treatment of a noncurrent asset or group of assets that the reporting entity intends to dispose of when a sale is highly probable. Subject to the conditions set forth in the said Standard for the classification as held-for-sale of a noncurrent asset or held-for-sale disposal group, the measurement rules at the time of the classification and on subsequent dates determine that the value of the asset (or of the disposal group, as relevant) will be measured at the lower end of the carrying amount and fair value less costs to sell. Here too, when determining fair value for the purpose of the test, the provisions of IFRS 13 should be applied, net of the costs to sell.

While US GAAP prescribes a two-step approach for impairment testing—where a recoverability test on an undiscounted cash flow basis is performed first—if it is determined that an asset is irrecoverable, it is written down to its fair value, as defined in ASC 820.

Example E—Assets of an Employee Benefit Plan

According to IAS 19—*Employee Benefits*, the plan assets of defined benefit postemployment plans shall be measured at their fair value (subject to the asset ceiling and several exceptions). This is also the case under ASC Topic 715—*Compensation—Retirement Benefits.*

Example F—Fair Value as Deemed Cost

IFRS 1—*First-Time Adoption of International Financial Reporting Standards* allows a reporting entity adopting the IFRS for the first time to measure—at the transition date—PPE items, investment property or intangible assets (under certain conditions) at fair value as deemed cost (i.e., as an initial value on the adoption date), even if in subsequent measurements, the reporting entity chooses to apply the cost model to such items. IFRS 13 applies to fair value measurement when the reporting entity has chosen the alternative of fair value as deemed cost.

3. Key Principles

The Standards include several key principles, which generally relate to the fair value basis and apply to all types of items within their scope. It may be said that the relevant guiding principle for measuring fair value—which is common to most of the Standards' provisions—is that fair value should serve as an objective criterion, which is largely unrelated to the reporting entity. Thus, IFRS 13 and ASC 820 formalize the following principles:

a. Fair value is based on the characteristics of the appraised item rather than on those of the holding entity, subject to the unit of account. Thus, for example, the fair value estimate may not take into account unique advantages (entity-specific synergy) or disadvantages (legal or tax-related restrictions) applicable to the reporting entity alone rather than to the item (for more information and examples, see Chapter 3, Sections 2 and 3, and Chapter 9, Section 2.1).

b. Fair value reflects the assumptions of a market participant regarding the appraised item rather than the reporting entity's subjective inputs. Specifically, IFRS 13 and ASC 820 clearly prioritize assumptions supported by observable inputs rather than unobservable inputs (for more information, see Chapter 12, Section 8.4).

c. Fair value may be calculated using more than one appraisal technique (e.g., the discounted cash flow technique or the multiples technique). Specifically, due to the broad scope—which ranges from derivative and nonderivative financial instruments, through tangible assets such as investment property or biological assets, to intangible assets—the Standards do not purport to extensively discuss the existing appraisal techniques or the finance theories underlying these techniques. Nevertheless, the purpose of each technique used is the same—to measure fair value—and the choice of technique is made while taking into account all relevant facts and circumstances and maximizing the use of market inputs (for more information, see Chapter 12, Section 2).

d. Fair value measurement prioritizes more observable inputs to the selected valuation technique. In this sense, the Standards define a hierarchy regarding the inputs used in a valuation (so-called Level 1, Level 2 and Level 3 inputs) based on their level of observability, with Level 1 being the most observable. The fair value hierarchy is important for two reasons: firstly, in situations where a particular input can be estimated in more than one method, the hierarchy assigns the highest priority to observable inputs. Secondly, when a reporting entity uses unobservable inputs, which are more subjective, it will be required to provide more extensive disclosures about the valuation in the notes to the financial statements than in a situation where no unobservable inputs were used (for more information, see Chapter 12).

4. Differences between IFRS 13 and ASC Topic 820

As outlined in Section 1, there is much similarity between IFRS 13 and ASC 820—*Fair Value Measurements and Disclosures*, the equivalent US GAAP Standard. Following are several specific differences between the Standards:

a. When a reporting entity has investments in hedge funds, private equity funds, venture capital funds, nontradable real estate investment trusts (REITs) and so forth, there may be practical difficulties in determining the fair value of the reporting entity's holding. These difficulties may stem from a lack of sufficient information about the fair value of the fund's investments and from the need to determine the necessary valuation adjustments required at the fund level due to characteristics such as the fund's liquidity, management costs, deferred taxes and so forth (for more information, see Chapter 3, Section3). Such funds sometimes publish information about their net asset value (NAV) per unit or share. Even then, it may still be difficult to determine whether or not the reported value meets all the applicable fair value measurement provisions and whether additional adjustments are needed. As a rule, IFRS 13 does not include provisions that make it easier to determine the fair value of the abovementioned type of investments. ASC 820, on the other hand, includes a practical expedient whereby, if there is no readily determinable fair value for the investment at the fund level (see Chapter 12, Section 2.2), and subject to the fund being an investment company as defined by the US GAAP or a real estate fund reporting in a similar manner, and the fund applies the US GAAP provisions for investment entities (ASC Topic 946), an investor may estimate the fair value of the investment as a whole according to the NAV per share reported by the fund under said rules, without making any additional adjustments. As aforesaid, the practical expedient is relevant only in cases where there is no readily determinable fair value. Under US GAAP, this applies in cases where there are no quoted prices for the fund, including ask and bid prices, in US capital markets or in markets of comparable depth, and there is no unit price for the fund (such as a mutual fund), which serves as the basis for performing transactions in its shares or units. ASC 820's disclosure provisions were also adapted to the said practical expedient. Specifically, reporting entities are required to disclose the nature and risks of investments in such funds that were subject to the practical expedient and whether the investments, if sold, may be sold at amounts different than the NAV per share. Additional requirements focus on the redemption frequency and mechanisms of such funds. However, there is no requirement to categorize these investments within the fair value hierarchy for disclosure purposes.

b. Under IFRS 13, the fair value of a financial liability with a demand feature, such as a demand deposit, may not be lower than the amount payable, discounted from the earliest demand date. In certain cases, however, the fair value may be higher (for more information, see Chapter 10, Section 7). This issue is relevant, among other things, to financial liabilities that do not have a defined repayment date, such as current accounts or demand deposit accounts. According to US GAAP, on the other hand, the fair value of a financial liability with no defined repayment dates is generally the amount payable on demand as at the reporting date.

c. There are several differences between IFRS 13's and ASC 820's disclosure requirements. Specifically, the US Standard includes several disclosure exceptions for nonpublic reporting entities. In addition, the US Standard does not include an obligation to carry out a quantitative sensitivity analysis, which IFRS 13 requires for certain financial instruments. In August 2018, ASC 820's disclosure requirements were further amended, introducing several additional differences, such as a difference in the disclosure objectives, elimination of several requirements and so forth. For more information, see Chapter 13, Section 7 (j). For a detailed comparison of the requirements, see Chapter 13, Section 6.

Chapter 2

DEFINITION AND SCOPE OF FAIR VALUE

1. Definition of Fair Value and the Fair Value Measurement Approach

International Financial Reporting Standard (IFRS) 13 and Accounting Standards Codification (ASC) 820 define fair value as the price that would be received to sell an asset or paid to transfer a liability in an orderly transaction between market participants at the measurement date. Despite the fact that this definition is relatively short, each of its components (exit price, orderly transaction, market participants and the measurement date) is of great significance. First, it is explicitly noted in the definition that the theoretical transaction is carried out on the measurement date, thereby emphasizing that the market conditions to be taken into consideration for the purpose of determining the valuation should be those at the valuation date rather than past market conditions or market conditions that may exist in the future. Furthermore, the definition means that to determine fair value, the reporting entity is required to refer to several issues:

a. Identify the item to be measured (in view of the unit of account) (for more information, see Chapter 3).
b. Identify the principal market (and in some cases, the most advantageous market) for the asset or the liability (for more information, see Chapter 4).
c. For nonfinancial assets, identify the highest and best use of the asset, subject to existing restrictions (for more information, see Chapter 9).
d. Identify and select the appropriate valuation techniques while maximizing the use of available market input and taking into consideration the assumptions of market participants (for more information, see Chapter 12).

2. Items within the Scope of the Standards

2.1. Overview

Generally speaking, the scopes of IFRS 13 and ASC 820 are considerable, which make them relevant to most cases where fair value measurements are made.

Formally, the Standards apply when another IFRS or US Generally Accepted Accounting Principles (US GAAP) topic requires or allows fair value measurements to be carried out. The Standards also apply in cases where measurements are based on fair value, that is, whether the fair value is the final outcome or an intermediate stage. Under IFRS, a case where fair value serves as the final outcome is the measurement required by International Accounting Standards (IAS) 40, in which the reporting entity opts to measure investment property at fair value on subsequent dates (for more examples, see Chapter 1, Section 2). Examples of fair value measurements as an intermediate stage under IFRS are when measuring fair value less costs to sell pursuant to IFRS 5 or when measuring fair value of biological assets less costs to sell, in accordance with IAS 41. A similar logic applies to the scope of ASC 820. The latter applies when another Topic (such as ASC Topic 805 or Topic 715 mentioned above) requires or allows fair value measurements or disclosures about fair value measurements to be made (and measurements, such as fair value less costs to sell, based on fair value or disclosures about these measurements).

In certain cases, a reporting entity is required to measure fair value at each reporting date (periodically), while in other cases, measurement is needed only when an event or significant change occurs, such as indications of impairment as defined by IAS 36 or if there have been significant changes to the value of property, plant and equipment items measured according to the revaluation model, as defined by IAS 16. Sometimes fair value is not measured periodically but rather only once. A case in point is the allocation of the consideration transferred in a business combination in accordance with the provisions of IFRS 3 (or ASC 805) or when a reporting entity settles a financial liability by issuing equity instruments within the scope of International Financial Reporting Interpretations Committee's Interpretation 19 (IFRIC 19).

It should be emphasized that, at times, accounting standards distinguish between measurement at the initial recognition date and at subsequent dates. Some Standards, such as IAS 40, make such a distinction and state that the fair value basis applies only to dates following the initial recognition date. In such cases, IFRS 13's provisions shall not apply at the initial recognition date but rather only on subsequent dates at which the fair value is measured, which may be adjacent to, or even coincide with, the initial recognition date (for a related issue, see Chapter 6, Section 3). Other Standards, such as IFRS 9, state that the item should already be measured at fair value or at fair value plus transaction costs at the initial recognition date. In such cases, the provisions of IFRS 13 shall already apply to the initial measurement of the item.

The Standards, including some of their disclosure provisions (for more information, see Chapter 13, Section 10), are applicable even when other IFRSs or Topics, respectively, allow or require (only) disclosure of the fair value in the notes to the financial statements. According to IAS 40, for example, when a reporting entity applies the cost model, it should also provide disclosure in the notes to its investment property's fair value, other than in exceptional cases. Similarly, according to IFRS 7, a reporting entity shall disclose the fair value of its financial instruments, even if the instruments are not measured at their fair value in the statement of financial position (but rather at amortized cost). Under such circumstances, IFRS 13's provisions regarding measuring the fair value shall apply for the purpose of the note, in addition to IFRS 13's relevant disclosure provisions.

2.2. Exceptions to the measurement and disclosure requirements of IFRS 13

While ASC 820 and IFRS 13 are almost identical in their instructions and definitions (for more information, see Chapter 1, Section 4), they differ in scope.

IFRS 13 includes relatively few exceptions in which the measurement and disclosure guidelines do not apply and others in which the disclosure provisions are not mandatory but the measurement guidelines are, as detailed later.

IFRS 13's measurement and disclosure guidelines do not apply to the following transactions or measurements:

A. Share-Based Payment Transactions

IFRS 2—*Share-Based Payment* uses the term "fair value" but is excluded from the provisions of IFRS 13. Fair value is defined in IFRS 2 as the amount for which an asset could be exchanged, a liability settled, or an equity instrument granted could be exchanged, between knowledgeable, willing parties in an arm's-length transaction. It is therefore obvious that the definition of fair value in the two Standards is very similar in nature (for IFRS 13's definition, see Section 1). According to IFRS 2, a reporting entity that grants its employees an equity-settled, share-based payment shall measure the fair value of the services received from the employees based on the fair value of the equity instruments granted. IFRS 2, however, also states that vesting conditions or reload features of the equity instruments granted are not taken into account in measuring the fair value but rather in the amount of equity instruments expected to vest. When developing IFRS 13, the possibility of changing the terminology used in IFRS 2 to a term other than fair value, such as market-based measurement, was considered. However, due to the wish to avoid distinctions between measurement bases on the one hand and undesirable consequences (due to the supposed change in the measurement basis) on the other hand, it was ultimately decided not to apply IFRS 13's provisions to fair value measurements performed pursuant to IFRS 2.

In certain cases, where the provisions of IFRS 2 apply, in our view, the provisions of IFRS 13 may also be relevant, at least by way of analogy. Thus, for example, according to IFRS 2, a reporting entity purchasing goods as part of an equity-settled, share-based payment transaction is required to measure the goods received as well as the resulting increase in equity at the fair value of the goods, unless that fair value is not reliably estimable. If the increase in equity is indeed measured at the fair value of the goods and there are no additional related conditions, it would be difficult to justify a distinction between the measurement principles of the asset received among the said Standards. Thus, for example, in our view, the goods received will also be measured according to IFRS 13's highest and best use assumption (see Chapter 9, Section 2).

When an equity-settled, share-based payment transaction with employees is settled by way of granting share options, IFRS 2 includes relatively detailed provisions regarding measuring the grant's fair value, including the various criteria and considerations to be taken into account in the option pricing models used. In this context, it should be noted that IFRS 2 also allows taking into consideration assumptions regarding the early exercise of stock options by employees, due to the employees' risk aversion or lack of investment asset diversification, among other things. However, the early exercise of stock options may be a behavior that is economically inefficient, since under certain assumptions and circumstances, it reduces the value of the exercised options due to loss of their time value. In addition, early exercise is sometimes due to risk exposure, inherent in a larger unit of account than a single option. According to IFRS 13, fair value is measured under the assumption that market participants are acting in their economic interests. Neither does IFRS 13 include in the measurement of fair value characteristics that are not part of the unit of account. Hence, in our view, except for specific cases, it would be difficult to assume early (and economically inefficient) exercise of options where the transactions are not within the scope of IFRS 2.

B. Leases

According to IFRS 16—*Leases*, leases are excluded from IFRS 13. It should be noted that in IFRS 16, fair value is defined—from the lessor's perspective—as the amount for which an asset could be exchanged or a liability settled in a transaction between knowledgeable, willing parties in an arm's-length transaction. However, the Standards fail to explain the differences in the meaning of fair value between them.

C. Measurements Similar to Fair Value That Do Not Constitute Fair Value

IFRS 13 excludes measurements similar to fair value that are not formally defined as fair value. In this context, IFRS 13 includes examples such as the measurement of value in use according to IAS 36 and of inventories' net realizable value according to IAS 2—*Inventories*.

Regarding value in use, it is our view that the most significant differences between the fair value basis and the said measurement basis are the way they relate to an entity-specific synergy (see Chapter 5 and Chapter 9, Section 2.1), as well as to capital expenditures required to improve or increase the performance level of an asset or cash-generating unit. In particular, according to IAS 36, the future cash flows shall be estimated for the asset in its current condition, to determine value in use, that is, the cash flow estimates shall not include estimated future cash inflows or outflows that are expected to arise from a future restructuring to which the reporting entity is not yet committed or improving or from enhancing the asset's performance. In particular, according to IAS 36, the future cash flows shall be estimated for the asset in its current condition, to determine value in use; for example, in most cases, it is not assumed that the reporting entity will add a floor to a shopping mall in order to estimate its value in use, even if adding such a floor is the highest and best use of the property from a market participant's perspective and is physically, legally and financially feasible. IFRS 13 does not include a similar limitation.

In terms of inventories, IFRS 13, its explanatory notes and IAS 2 do not specify the notional differences between net realizable value and fair value. In our view, one of the obvious differences is the fact that net realizable value should be calculated after deducting expected costs to sell as opposed to fair value. And indeed there appears to be additional differences. Thus, for example, in our view, the net realizable value should be calculated from the perspective of the reporting entity rather than from a market participant's perspective. Thus, in our view, net realizable value should also include factors that are unique to the reporting entity, such as:

a. Location, type and price level in the ordinary course of business in the reporting entity's stores or sales channels;
b. The reporting entity's existing contracts and supply agreements that are not necessarily in accordance with current market conditions; and
c. The unique synergetic or operational capability specific to the reporting entity.

In addition, in our view, net realizable value does not necessarily take into account, as part of the completion costs, the time factor and developer's risk factor (also referred to as "developer's margin") in the same way these two factors are taken into account under regular circumstances when measuring fair value of items under construction or in process within IFRS 13's scope. Thus, for example, let's assume that a reporting entity holds a real estate project that includes an inventory of apartments under construction. The project's selling price per square meter is CU 10,000, and the completion costs per square meter are CU 7,000, including the borrowing cost estimate for discounting for the remaining life of the project. In this situation, to determine the project's fair value in its current state (as is) from the perspective of a market participant (such as another construction company), it is reasonable to assume that a total of less than CU 3,000 per square meter (= 10,000 − 7,000) will be paid in the project. This may be partially explained by the existence of a certain developer's margin required by the buyer, that is, the buyer would not agree to pay a price that would reflect his assuming all the project's risks without adequate compensation. Another potential reason for such a shortfall is that disposing of all the apartments may take a significant time, which is not adequately reflected in the borrowing cost taken into account in the completion costs estimate. On the other hand, regarding the net realizable value, it should be noted that IAS 2 allows the reporting entity to assume that the asset will be sold as a finished asset rather than as is. For this reason, the reporting entity is required to deduct the completion costs estimate. In other words, if the selling price (without the discount factor) less the completion costs (including the reporting entity's remaining finance costs but excluding the developer's margin or discounting the amounts to present value) is CU 3,000 per square meter, then if the costs of disposal are ignored, the example will show that the land's net realizable value will be higher than its fair value.

It should be emphasized that when allocating the acquisition costs for a business combination, inventory is not an exception to the measuring rule in IFRS 3; therefore, inventory should always be measured on the business combination date at fair value (i.e., in accordance with the provisions of IFRS 13) rather than at the net realizable value. One of the examples included in IFRS 13 shows that in order to estimate the fair value of finished goods in a retail outlet store, the fair value measurement represents the price that would have been received in a transaction for the sale of the inventory to another retailer that would have completed the required sales efforts. In other words, the sales margins (which are the equivalent of the developer's margin in the above example) should be deducted. Alternatively, IFRS 13 notes that the inventory could have been measured according to the wholesale price for retailers in a wholesale market, adjusted (upward) in respect of factors such as location (transport costs) and condition, all according to the type of measurement that requires the least amount of subjective adjustments.

2.3. Exemptions applicable only to the disclosure requirements of IFRS 13

Under IFRS, the measurement requirements of IFRS 13 will apply in the following situations, but its disclosure requirements will not:

a. Measurement of fair value of plan assets, within the scope of IAS 19. In view of IAS 19's disclosure requirements, it was determined that due to cost-benefit considerations, the application of IFRS 13's disclosure requirements will not be mandatory;
b. Measurement of the fair value of retirement benefit plan investments, which are measured at fair value according to IAS 26—*Accounting and Reporting by Retirement Benefit Plans*;
c. Measurement of fair value of assets whose recoverable amount is their fair value less costs of disposal according to IAS 36. Here too, the reasoning for the said exemption is that when the recoverable amount is based on fair value less costs of disposal, IAS 36 requires in any case to provide a relatively comprehensive disclosure on the valuation technique, all the key assumptions and how they were made, changes made to the valuation technique and the reasons for making those changes, as well as the level of the measurement in the fair value hierarchy. It should also be noted that the disclosure requirements of IAS 36 have been extended as part of the development of IFRS 13 in order to enhance the correlation between these Standards.

2.4. Exceptions to the measurement and disclosure requirements of ASC 820

Under US GAAP, and similarly to the scope exclusions of IFRS 13, Topic 820 does not apply to the accounting principles that address share-based payment transactions (this includes all subtopics in Topic 718 except for 718–40, which are within the scope of Topic 820). According to the explanatory notes of the original SFAS 157, which excluded SFAS 123(R) from its scope, although some measurements in SFAS 123(R) are fair value measurements and not only based on fair value, the scope exclusion is for "practical reasons."

Additionally, ASC 820 does not apply where measurements are required or allowed and are similar to fair value but are not intended to measure fair value, such as standalone selling price for inventories under ASC Topic 330—*Inventory*, which is "vendor-specific" entry price (as referred to in SFAS 157's Basis for Conclusions). Neither does it apply to the recognition and measurement of revenue from contracts with customers in accordance with Topic 606 (for instance, to variable consideration) and to the recognition and measurement of gains and losses upon the derecognition of nonfinancial assets in accordance with ASC Subtopic 610–20.

It should also be mentioned that ASC 820 explicitly states that it does not eliminate the practicability exceptions to fair value measurements that exist within other US GAAP Standards. This seems to be more of a clarification than a scope exclusion. For instance, the use of transaction entry price to measure the fair value of a guarantee at initial recognition; the exemption to the requirement to measure fair value if it is not practicable to do so for financial instruments; or the exemption to the requirement to measure fair value if fair value is not reasonably determinable for Asset Retirement Obligations (AROs), nonmonetary assets, restructuring obligations and so forth. Similar logic applies under IFRS, where certain Standards explicitly include practical expedients to fair value measurement. For instance, IAS 40 requires investment property to be measured using the cost model (even when the fair value model is applied), in exceptional cases where its fair value is not reliably determinable. Another example is IFRS 9, which states that under limited circumstances, cost may be an appropriate estimate of the fair value of an equity instrument or a related derivative.

Chapter 3

IDENTIFYING THE ASSET OR LIABILITY TO BE MEASURED

1. Overview

Before measuring the fair value, it is first required to identify the item whose value is to be measured, since the type of item to be measured may impact the outcome of the valuation. To identify the item to be measured, the reporting entity should take into account the specific characteristics of the asset or the liability that market participants would have also taken into account when determining the transaction price. These characteristics will be taken into consideration when determining the fair value, unlike characteristics specific to the reporting entity, which are not transferred along with the asset or liability and which are not to be taken into consideration when determining the fair value. The question of the item to be measured is closely related to the unit of account question, which is relevant to the asset or liability (for more information, see Section 3). The unit of account is the level at which the asset or liability is aggregated or disaggregated, that is, the unit of account will determine whether the item is measured on a standalone basis or in combination with a group of items that may include either assets or liabilities or both assets and liabilities. It should be clarified that even when the unit of account is defined as an individual asset, it is still possible that the valuation premise will be that, from the perspective of a potential market participant, the asset will be operated with other assets or liabilities, even if those assets or liabilities are not part of the unit of account and are not part of the relevant transaction (for more information, see Chapter 9, Section 3).

2. Characteristics of an Asset or Liability versus Characteristics of the Entity Holding the Asset

Fair value measurement is carried out from a market participant's perspective and relates to a specific asset or liability (i.e., while taking into account relevant characteristics of the asset or liability). As a rule, fair value measurement should take into consideration characteristics of an asset or a liability if and only if market participants would have done so. The extent to which the influence of a certain characteristic should be taken into consideration is the extent to which it would have been attributed to that characteristic by market participants.

International Financial Reporting Standard (IFRS) 13 and Accounting Standards Codification (ASC) 820 provide several examples of characteristics of an asset or a liability that may be taken into consideration by market participants when determining the transaction price:

a. The condition of the asset—obsolescence, wear and tear, maintenance and so forth;
b. The location of the asset—an attractive location, the need for transportation and so forth;
c. Restrictions on the sale of the asset—sale to certain buyers, prohibition on sale for a certain period of time and so forth;
d. Restrictions on the use of the asset—conditions imposed by donors, regulators, antitrust authorities and so forth.

Based on the examples provided in the Standards, it may be said that the most appropriate rule of thumb for deciding whether a certain characteristic should be taken into account when determining the fair value is whether a certain characteristic can be separated from the unit of account of the asset or the liability or whether this characteristic is an integral part thereof and will be transferred with the asset or liability in an orderly transaction. The answer to the question of whether certain characteristics are an integral part of the item may be dependent on the unit of account and on various legal questions (such as whether it is possible to transfer an asset without transferring a related obligation) and may involve exercise of judgment.

Set forth below are several examples in connection with the distinction between types of restrictions:

Example A—the Planning Status of a Plot of Land

A reporting entity holds a plot of land whose sole lawful use (subject to planning laws) is housing development. In this case, the building rights in the land are an integral part of its characteristics and will be transferred to the buyer along with the land. Therefore, this characteristic will also be taken into consideration by market participants when determining the price that they would have agreed to pay for the plot of land; therefore, when measuring the fair value of the plot, the reporting entity should take the building rights into consideration.

A related example involves a certain real estate asset (e.g., a plot of land), which is subject to a government's easement to run power lines across it. Clearly, this issue can definitely impair the asset, whether due to the need to take the restriction into account when planning the construction of a building on the asset or due to the fact that the restriction may have environmental implications (such as radiation). In this situation as well, the easement right is a specific characteristic of the asset and would be transferred to market participants along with the plot of land. Therefore, the fair value measurement of the plot of land would reflect the influence of the right to run power lines across it. The extent of the influence will naturally depend on all facts and circumstances that are relevant to the highest and best use of the land from the perspective of market participants. In our view—as in the case of the right to run power lines across the plot of land—when there are other planning restrictions such as easements granted to the public or to other parties (such as the obligation to provide right of way), those restrictions should be taken into consideration when measuring fair value, as well as other issues related to the plot of land that would have been taken into account by market participants, such as the planning of adjacent properties, the view and transportation.

When illegal construction has taken place on a certain asset, which raises concerns regarding future demolition orders, levies imposed due to nonconforming use or future betterment levies (when the use of the asset is approved), these characteristics will, in most cases, form an integral part of the asset as far as market participants are concerned and will accordingly be taken into consideration when determining the transaction price. Therefore, it is customary to include such characteristics in the fair value of real estate assets, such as investment property under IFRS. On the other hand, if illegal construction work had previously taken place on a certain asset and the illegal construction issues were resolved prior to the reporting date—but there are legal proceedings still pending against the reporting entity that may result in a fine—the said fine will not form part of the asset, provided that the fine, lawsuit or legal proceeding will not be transferred to a potential buyer with the asset (whose use has already been approved) but will continue to lie with the owners of the asset on the date in which the illegal construction work was carried out. In other words, in most cases, fines or lawsuits that relate to past periods are not a characteristic of the asset and are usually accounted for within a separate provision.

Example B—Existing Leases

According to the provisions of IFRS 16—*Leases* and International Accounting Standard (IAS) 40—*Investment Property*, existing leases should be considered an integral part of the asset for the purpose of measuring its fair value. This means that when a real estate asset is under long-term leases with stable lessees paying rent that is higher than market rent rates, these parameters should be taken into consideration when measuring the asset's fair value. Therefore, it is reasonable to assume that the fair value of the said asset will be higher than that of an identical unoccupied asset (where it may take some time before its unoccupied areas are leased out) or than the fair value of an identical asset that is leased for less than market rent rates at the time of the valuation (such that it will take time until the term of the existing lease contracts will end and before the rent can be raised). It should be noted, however, that in accordance with ASC Topic 805 and related customary practice under US Generally Accepted Accounting Principles (US GAAP), leases are usually accounted for separately from tangible assets, such as assets held for use (income-generating properties). In other words, the property is usually valued based on an as-vacant basis, where any contribution from existing leases, including above- or below-market rent leases, is accounted for separately.

Example C—Restrictions on a Charity

A reporting entity, which is defined as a nonprofit organization, holds land donated for use as a playground. The donor donated the land on the condition that it will be used as a playground for an indefinite period of time. A review of the (legal and other) documentation shows that the restriction regarding the use of the land will not be transferred to a buyer of the land if the land will be put up for sale by the reporting entity. This means that the restriction on the use of the land is only imposed on the reporting entity and is not a restriction that is specific to the asset. In addition, there is no restriction on the sale of the land by the reporting entity, and the land has an alternative use—housing development. In this case, since the restriction applies to the reporting entity rather than to the asset, the restriction will not be transferred if the land is sold to market participants. Accordingly, the fair value of the land will be the higher of its value when used as a playground (which reflects the assumption that the use of the land will be made in combination with other complementary assets, such as a nearby residential complex whose attractiveness to buyers will increase due to its proximity to the playground) and its use as a housing development site (such a use reflects an assumption that the asset will be used separately from other assets rather than in combination with them), and the restriction placed on the use of the land will not be taken into consideration when measuring its fair value.

It should be noted that this example, which is based on a similar example included in the Standard, emphasizes the legal assessment of the asset, which determines that the restrictions on the use of the asset are separate from the asset itself (so that when, for example, the land is transferred, the buyer cannot be forced to use it as a playground). In our view, when the legal restrictions themselves are imposed on the asset (i.e., it is impossible to separate the restrictions from the right to the asset—such as in the case of restrictions that were imposed as part of the lease by virtue of which the asset exists, including restrictions that require the buyer to undertake the seller's obligations in connection with the asset), those restrictions should be taken into consideration when measuring the fair value. Furthermore, in the example provided in IFRS 13 and ASC 820, it is specifically noted that according to the legal documents, the nonprofit is not prohibited from selling the asset (which is then unrestricted from the buyer's perspective). In doing so, the example provided in the Standards avoids the question of what would have been the fair value of the land if, on the one hand, the use of the land is unrestricted as far as a market participant is concerned, but if the land is sold (which will come into effect and be irrevocable), the nonprofit will be exposed to claims for damages that may be filed by the donor for breach of contract. Assuming that the sale transaction will come into effect and that it will be impossible to impose any restrictions on the buyer, it may be said that the fair value of the land should still reflect the price that may be received for it, which does not reflect the said claims, since they do not apply to the buyer (see also Example E, concerning a related issue).

Example D—Restrictions Placed on a Real Estate Investment Trust (REIT)

A reporting entity is defined as a Real Estate Investment Trust (REIT) for tax purposes. The tax status of the reporting entity entitles it to pay a reduced transfer tax as well as transparency for tax purposes (such that the income tax in connection with the fund's activity is imposed directly on its shareholders). To retain its status for tax purposes, the fund is required to meet certain criteria. Among other things, the fund may not exceed a certain debt ceiling, is not allowed to construct projects beyond a certain scope and may not dispose of certain types of assets if it has held them for less than 20 years. Noncompliance of the fund with those requirements may cause it to lose its tax status, and for some requirements, this may mean a higher capital gain tax when the trusts' assets are sold. This begs the question: Is the fund required to take these restrictions into consideration when measuring the fair value of its assets? Thus, for example, let us assume that the fund has a plot of land that is designated for building. However, for reasons of economic viability, the fund is prevented from developing the land so that it will not exceed its debt ceiling or the maximum threshold of projects under construction. In this case, the economic constraints placed on the fund will not be taken into consideration in determining the fair value of the asset if, from a market participant's perspective, the highest and best use will be to begin the construction, assuming that the relevant market participants are able to fund the construction. Similarly, the fact that the fund may not sell certain assets for a period of 20 years (otherwise it will be subject to higher taxes) does not impair the fair value of those assets from the perspective of a market participant that acquires the said assets.

Example E—Restriction on the Sale of an Equity Instrument

A reporting entity holds a share of another entity (from the reporting entity's perspective, it is a financial asset). The sale of the said share is restricted for a defined period of time, under a legal or contractual provision. An example of such a restriction is the temporary lockup restriction placed on buyers of securities in a private offering by virtue of the securities laws or an underwriter lockup agreement. According to the said restriction, the holder of the share is prohibited from selling it on the stock exchange throughout the lockup period and may only do so in an off-floor transaction. In other situations, the restriction is reflected by the fact that the security may only be sold to institutional investors.

In such cases, and if the restriction is placed on the security itself and will be transferred to the buyer with the security (e.g., the buyer will also be prohibited from selling the security on the stock exchange), then the lockup or restriction is a characteristic of the asset and will be taken into consideration when measuring its fair value.

In the abovementioned scenario, the fair value of the instrument will usually be measured based on the fair value of a quoted price of a similar yet unrestricted instrument and will be adjusted (i.e., reduced) to reflect the effect of the restriction placed on its sale. The adjustment made to the quoted price should reflect the amount that market participants would have demanded in respect of the risk deriving from the inability to access the public market for the specified period. The adjustment would vary subject to the following:

a. The nature and the duration of the restriction. In this context, it is reasonable to assume that the more comprehensive the restriction and the longer the restriction period, the greater the discount needed;
b. The effectiveness of the restriction. In this case as well, the more effective the restriction, the more significant the discount. Thus, for example, the

security may be under lockup when it comes to selling to nonclassified investors, but the number of classified investors in the market is too high to result in a significant discount in the sale price, if any. Another example of a situation requiring a smaller discount in the sale price is when the market has mechanisms in place that enable to effectively bypass the lockup provisions, such as when the market conditions enable a market participant who would have purchased the restricted share to carry out a short sale in a quick, inexpensive and efficient manner; and

c. Qualitative and quantitative factors specific to both the instrument and the issuer. In this context, and consistently with the guiding principle, the characteristics of the issuer (as opposed to those of the holder) are relevant to the fair value. As a result, the lockup restriction may not be as effective for some types of issuers as for others. Thus, for example, a certain issuer may be characterized by a very large number of restricted shares, where the lockup on all the said shares is expected to expire at once, such that there is a concern that there will be an increased supply of shares when the lockup expires. In such a case, the lockup restriction may result in a more significant discount in the fair value of the instrument than in a situation where the issuer did not have a significant number of shares that are expected to be unlocked at the same time. Similarly, securities that are typically held by investors for relatively long periods, such as shares of a young startup, may be impacted to a lesser extent by such restrictions.

This indicates that when the fair value of the instrument should reflect a discount in respect of a lockup, the discount is made after taking into account all the specific facts and circumstances of the case; it is our view that, in most cases, a fixed discount will be inappropriate (among other things, since the remaining lockup period is usually shorter from one period to the next). In practice, determining the effect of a sale restriction is carried out in most cases either by using empirical models (i.e., the discount in similar cases, such as private offerings in which restricted securities were issued) or by using theoretical models, which are often based on option pricing models.

Another example of a characteristic that is specific to shares and is transferred to a buyer along with the shares upon their sale is when the shares are not tradable on a stock exchange. Let us assume, for example, that Company A holds shares of Company B as a financial investment. The characteristics of those shares are identical to those of other Company B shares, which are traded on the stock exchange, except for the fact that Company A's holdings are not listed for trading; to complete their listing, Company A is first required to resolve a legal dispute with company B, which prevents the listing of the said shares. In this case, in our view, the fact that the shares in question are not listed for trading will lead to a discount to their fair value compared to the quoted price of ordinary Company B shares that were actively traded on the stock exchange. The reason is that the fact that the shares are not listed for trading is a specific characteristic of the shares that is transferred to the buyer along with the shares.

It may be said that IFRS 13 and ASC 820 do not include specific provisions regarding the criteria for determining whether or not the restriction is a characteristic of the measured item or of the holder of that item, except the question of whether the restriction will be transferred to the buyer along with the item. At times, the reporting entity will be unable to dispose of the item, instrument or asset at all, in which case it will still be required to determine whether or not the restriction is a characteristic of the item itself. Following are additional considerations that may be relevant in order to determine the above:

a. Does the restriction form part of the contractual or legal terms that create the instrument or item itself? or
b. Is the restriction (whether regulatory or contractual) separate from the valued instrument?

For example, let us assume that a reporting entity may not sell another entity's shares that it holds and that are traded in an active market, because the said shares are pledged as collateral to secure a loan taken by the reporting entity. In this case, the fair value of the shares held by the reporting entity should not reflect the said restriction, since the latter would not be transferred to a buyer in a hypothetical sale. This is the case despite the fact that the reporting entity is unable to sell the shares.

Similarly, our view is that when the reporting entity is barred from selling another entity's shares over a certain period of time due to the existence of an underwriter contractual lockup agreement or inside information concerning the other entity, this factor will not be reflected in the fair value of the tradable equity shares held by the reporting entity. This stems from the fact that this restriction will not be transferred to the buyer along with the shares. Based on a similar rationale, it can also be concluded that when the reporting entity enters into various agreements (such as financing agreements, investment agreements or trust arrangements), under which it is prohibited from changing its shareholding rate in an investee without first obtaining approval, this condition is not taken into consideration when measuring the fair value from the perspective of a market participant who buys or sells the shares.

3. The Unit of Account of the Asset or Liability

The second characteristic that should be taken into consideration at the stage of identifying the measured asset or liability is the unit of account of the said asset or liability. A unit of account is defined as the level at which an asset or a liability is aggregated or disaggregated for recognition purposes. In other words, the objective of measuring fair value is to estimate the value relating to the sale of the unit of account in its entirety, which is why identifying the appropriate unit of account is critical.

The unit of account should be determined in accordance with the Standards, which require or allow the measurement of fair value, except for the exemptions set out in IFRS 13 and ASC 820 (for more information, see Chapter 11). It should be noted that IFRS 13 (and ASC 820) expressly acknowledges that in situations where transactions are carried out at a unit other than the unit of account, the transaction price may not reflect the fair value as of the date of initial recognition (for more information, see Chapter 8, Section 1).

It can, therefore, be said that IFRS 13 and ASC 820 refrain from determining the relevant unit of account, under the assumption that the unit of account should be evident from the provisions of the other IFRSs or US GAAP standards. However, this is not necessarily the case, and sometimes the identification of a unit of account may require reporting entities to exercise judgment. The IFRSs seldom refer to the unit of account in an orderly manner, and one of the few references that do exist is found in the revised *Conceptual Framework for Financial Reporting* published in March 2018. Indeed, much like other standards, the IFRS Conceptual Framework does not determine the unit of account for specific types of items—a matter that should be taken into consideration when developing and implementing specific standards. The Conceptual Framework explains that at times, it may be appropriate to define the unit of account differently for recognition and measurement purposes (e.g., a group of contracts in which each contract is recognized separately, and in subsequent periods, each contract is measured as part of the group). Sometimes, the unit of account can change, for example, due to derecognition or partial transfer of rights or obligations. According to the IFRS Conceptual Framework, the unit of account should provide relevant information. Therefore, it lists several relevant considerations that may assist in determining whether a group of items can be a single unit of account, subject, of course, to any specific provision included in other IFRSs:

a. Is it possible or reasonable that the components comprising the group may be the subject of separate transactions?

b. Is it possible that the rights or obligations comprising the group will expire differently?
c. Do the components of the group share similar economic characteristics and risks?
d. Are the components comprising the group used together for the purposes of the activity?
e. Does the group create a faithful representation of the nature of the event?

Nevertheless, the IFRS Conceptual Framework refrains from ranking the aforementioned factors in terms of their importance.

It is important to distinguish between identifying an item's unit of account and the question of whether a nonfinancial asset's fair value is based on the assumption that the asset is used on a standalone basis or in combination with other assets and liabilities. Thus, for example, even when the unit of account is a single asset, it may sometimes be assumed, when measuring its fair value, that the highest and best use of the asset will be in combination with other assets or liabilities (for more information, see Chapter 9, Section 3).

Below is a discussion of several issues that are relevant to the identification of the unit of account under IFRS:

A. The Unit of Account of Financial Instruments

IFRS 9 and IAS 32, which deal with financial instruments, state (at least implicitly) that the basic unit of account of financial instruments is derived from the contractual source of the financial instrument. In the said Standards, the unit of account is relevant, among other things, to issues such as designation of financial instruments as at fair value through profit or loss, designation of an investment in equity instruments as at fair value through other comprehensive income, issues of derecognition of financial assets and financial liabilities, offsetting financial assets against financial liabilities and more.

When the financial instruments under question are "discrete," such as ordinary shares or bonds, the basic unit of account is usually defined separately under IFRS for each instrument. This is because in most cases, it is possible to sell, pledge, distribute as dividend or transfer the holding in the instrument separately from other instruments of the same type, and the holding represents a separate legal right. ASC Topic 825 is more explicit about the unit for account as for the fair value option and has several guidelines in this respect.

According to IFRS 13 (and ASC 820), when the reporting entity holds a position comprising a number of identical assets or liabilities, and the assets or liabilities are traded in an active market (Level 1), the fair value of the position will be measured as the product of the quoted price for the individual asset or liability and the quantity held by the reporting entity. This type of measurement is sometimes called P × Q (Price × Quantity) (for more information, see Chapter 12, Section 2.2). Furthermore, no adjustment in respect of a blockage factor for a quoted price may be made, even if the market's normal daily trading volume is incapable of absorbing the quantity held by the reporting entity, such that the sale of the entire position in a single transaction may impact the quoted price (for more information, see Chapter 12, Section 7.2). Thus, IFRS 13 and ASC 820 effectively prescribe the unit of account for some financial instruments.

In view of the above provisions, when the reporting entity needs to estimate the fair value of items that are traded in an active market and that are within the scope of other standards that are relevant to financial instruments, the fair value shall be measured according to the quoted price as of the measurement date while ignoring the number of instruments held by the reporting entity. It may, therefore, be said that ignoring a discount made in respect of a large block of shares held by the reporting entity is due to the fact that the holding is an entity-specific characteristic rather than a characteristic of each and every one of the shares that comprise the holding. In addition, the timing and manner of disposal of the block in its entirety is a characteristic that is specific to the reporting entity rather than to the components of the block. Therefore, it is certainly possible that when the reporting entity expects to sell a large block of shares (which are traded in an active market) at a certain discount (due to the size of the block) in an off-floor transaction, the discount will not be reflected in the measurement of the shares' fair value, and the loss attributed to the discount will be recognized by the reporting entity only when the transaction is actually carried out.

Similarly, when the reporting entity purchases a large block of shares listed for trading at a certain discount in relation to their quoted price in an active market (a discount that is explained, for example, by the distribution efforts involved in marketing the shares), it will recognize a profit already upon initial recognition of the purchased shares, due to the difference between the unit of account of the actual transaction (the entire block) and the unit of account of the purchased assets (which is separate for each and every share).

Indeed, when the unit of account of a financial instrument is larger (e.g., a single commercial loan of CU 2 billion), it may not be artificially split into smaller units of account in order to apply IFRS 13 or ASC 820 (e.g., into 20 loans of CU 100 million each). Therefore, there may be differences between the fair value of the single instrument and the total valuations of its notional components (i.e., there may be a difference between the fair value of a single large loan and the fair value of several smaller loans with an identical aggregate amount). Such differences may arise from factors such as a small number of participants in the relevant market (a factor that usually increases the discount arising from the absolute size of the instrument), various illiquidity premiums and so forth.

Other related issues deal with the unit of account under IFRS of a financial liability of the reporting entity, which includes third-party credit enhancement (for more information, see Chapter 10, Section 3.2), and the unit of account of investments in subsidiaries, associates and joint ventures (see below).

B. Unit of Account of a Cash-Generating Unit

According to IAS 36, a reporting entity is required to identify the cash-generating unit (CGU) to which the asset that is being tested for impairment belongs. A CGU is defined in the said Standard as the smallest identifiable group of assets that generates cash inflows that are largely independent of the cash inflows from other assets or groups of assets. The testing for impairment on the described level in fact identifies that the economic substance of the asset is its holding in combination with other assets rather than as an individual asset that is unable to generate cash flows on its own. Therefore, when a certain asset belongs to a CGU that includes other assets or liabilities in the financial statements and the fair value of that CGU is measured (net of costs to sell), the purpose of the measurement of the fair value will be the estimation of the price that would be received from a market sale of the entire unit as of the measurement date rather than necessarily from a sale of the specific asset that belongs to that CGU. In such a situation, although there may be market prices for some of the unit's components, the relevant question when carrying out the measurement will be the price that would be received for the entire CGU. It should be clarified that even when a specific asset is tested for impairment independently, it is still possible that, from the perspective of a market participant, the highest and best use of this asset will be in combination with other assets or liabilities. In such a situation, the objective of the valuation would be to estimate the proceeds that would have been received from the sale of such asset, with the working hypothesis being that the buyer will have in mind the proceeds from the asset when the asset is being used as part of a defined group of assets (for more information, see Chapter 9, Section 3).

When the CGU is an operation, it is our view that the appropriate question is the price that would have been received on the sale of the entire operation rather than the price that would have been received on disposal of separate parts of the operation. Thus, for example, the reporting entity may have a holding in a real estate fund that holds several real estate assets. In such a situation, it is possible that the aggregate fair value of all real estate assets that are held by the fund, net of the value of the allocated liabilities (net asset value—NAV) will not necessarily be identical to the fair value of the holdings in the fund, since certain adjustments are required, such as adjustments in respect of management quality or excess management costs, ownership structure, the scope or composition of the portfolio and so forth. It is our view that under such circumstances, it will not be appropriate under IFRS to measure the fair value of the operation in its entirety as the aggregate amount of each of its parts, without taking into consideration the required adjustments (due to the size of the fund, its composition, management quality, etc.). This is because the abovementioned adjustments form a part of the unit of account and would have been taken into consideration by market participants when pricing the holding. On the other hand, had each of the assets been defined as a unit of account, it would not have been required to take into consideration additional adjustments at the operation level. While US GAAP has a similar concept to a CGU (i.e., the reporting unit), it should be noted that, under certain circumstances, US GAAP allows to rely on the reported NAV as an estimate of fair value, even without making the abovementioned adjustments. However, this matter is one of the points of difference between the IFRS and US GAAP (for more information, see Chapter 1, Section 4).

C. Unit of Account of Investment in Subsidiaries, Associates and Joint Ventures

IFRSs sometimes require the reporting entity (or give it the option) to measure investments in subsidiaries, associates and joint ventures (hereinafter in this section, "investees") at fair value. Measuring investees at fair value (net of costs to sell) may be required when the investee is a disposal group, which is measured according to the provisions of IFRS 5, or when the investee is a CGU, and it is required to measure its recoverable amount in accordance with the provisions of IAS 36. In addition, such measurement is required when the reporting entity is defined as an investment entity according to the provisions of IFRS 10—*Consolidated Financial Statements* and can be applied to investees that are associates or joint ventures if the reporting entity is a mutual fund or a similar entity and selects an accounting policy according to which investments will be measured at fair value, in accordance with the provisions of IAS 28—*Investments in Associates and Joint Ventures*. Similarly, under US GAAP, investment companies also measure their holdings at fair value, pursuant to ASC Topic 946 (see Chapter 1, Section 4).

As a rule, and unlike the case of the unit of account of investment in financial instruments (see Section A above), the unit of account of an investment in investees includes the holding in its entirety, even if the said holding is composed of, or arises from, several identical financial instruments, such as ordinary shares of the investee. Indeed, IFRS 13 and ASC 820 appear to include contradictory provisions regarding the manner of measuring an investment in an investee, when the investee's shares are quoted in an active market. This ambiguity has significant implications, and in our view the accounting policy that is applied shall conform to one of the following two approaches.

Under IFRS, on the one hand, the provisions of IFRS 13 may be interpreted so that, for investees, the P × Q rule (see Section A above) will necessarily apply, and as a result, when there is an active market for the investees' shares, characteristics such as control premium, significant influence premium, discount for lack of tradability or a blockage factor shall not be taken into account (even though the investment cannot necessarily be sold in a straightforward manner like a single share), and the fair value of the entire holding should be estimated on the basis of the quoted price of a single share multiplied by the relevant number of shares (the first approach). Although this approach relies on the most objective measurement, it may lead to absurd results, especially when the factors that are being ignored in the measurement of the fair value are actually facts from the perspective of market participants. Thus, for instance, let us assume that a reporting entity that is defined as an investment entity under IFRS pays a control premium for the acquisition of a controlling interest in a public company (as is the practice in certain markets). In such a situation, under the first approach, the buyer will recognize a loss (under the assumption that the quoted share price has not changed) in respect of the difference between the quoted share price and the price that includes the paid control premium. At the same time, when an agreement is to be signed for the sale of the investment at a price that reflects a control premium, the investment itself will continue to be measured in accordance with the quoted price, until the investment is derecognized and the proceeds are received (with a profit that is explained by the control premium).

According to the second approach, IFRS 13 can be interpreted such that the P × Q rule is relevant only when the unit of account as a whole has a quoted price in an active market. Under this approach, when the investment in question is in an investee, the unit of account will be the entire investment, and therefore, there is no quoted price for such an investment (i.e., the quoted price relates only to the price of a single share). Therefore, it is not necessary to estimate the fair value of the holding on the basis of the quoted price without making any adjustments. According to this approach, relevant characteristics shall be taken into consideration such as a control premium, lack of tradability of the block of shares, the size of the holding (which may impact the number of potential buyers) and so forth, provided that such characteristics would have been taken into consideration by market participants. Furthermore, it is our view that, according to this approach, it is possible to measure investments in investees by using multiple valuation techniques, such as the discounted cash flow (DCF) method or the multiples method (for more information, see Chapter 12, Section 3), and there is no requirement to estimate the fair value based on the quoted share price with adjustments (such as adjustments in respect of a control premium or lack of tradability), even though this method is based more significantly on objective assumptions.

Under US GAAP, it seems that noninvestment companies will be subject to the P × Q rule when measuring the fair value of their holdings (including controlling shares) based on Level 1 inputs. However, it seems that existing practice and the wording of ASU 946 allow investment companies to use a single unit of account for controlling interests and to consider control premiums, even when there are Level 1 inputs available for the share price.

D. The Unit of Account When Measuring the Fair Value of Investment Property

One of the most common types of valuations for financial reporting purposes under IFRS is the measurement of the fair value of investment property assets, which are accounted for in accordance with the provisions of IAS 40. Indeed, when determining such fair value, questions relating (among other things) to the unit of account often arise.

As a rule, IAS 40 notes that in determining the fair value of investment property, a reporting entity should avoid double-counting assets or liabilities that have been recognized as individual assets or liabilities. Thus, for example, equipment such as elevators or air conditioners are often an integral part of a building and are generally included in the fair value of the investment property rather than recognized separately as property, plant and equipment. Similarly, if an asset is leased on a fully equipped basis (e.g., a furnished office or a fully equipped nursing care ward in an assisted living facility), the fair value of the office or the ward generally includes the fair value of the furniture or the equipment, since the rental income relates to the equipped item. According to the said Standard, the fair value of investment property excludes prepaid or accrued operating lease income, because the reporting entity recognizes it as a separate liability or asset (for more information regarding incentives given to lessees, see below).

Indeed, except for the aforementioned provisions, IAS 40 does not include explicit provisions as to the issue of aggregating or disaggregating investment property assets for the purpose of determining their unit of account. This issue may have implications on the fair value of real estate assets, concerning, among other things, the question of whether a deduction in respect of size is required in connection with the said assets.

Generally, a deduction (or premium) in value in respect of size is required when the specific circumstances indicate that market participants will not be willing to pay for certain assets the same price (per area unit or per unit of building rights) that they would be willing to pay for assets with a smaller area or less building rights. A deduction in value in respect of size may be explained by factors such as difficulties in the construction or financing of the project (due to its scope), the need to construct the project in several stages (which causes some of the proceeds from the project to be deferred), difficulties to sell or occupy the project and so forth. Indeed, before reducing the fair value in respect of size, a reporting entity is required to decide whether or not the unit of account includes the asset in its entirety (in which case such a deduction will be required), or whether the unit of account relates to smaller parts of the asset (in which case, it will not necessarily be required to make a deduction in respect of each and every part, and the relative price may reflect a premium). In connection with this issue, our view is that—for the purpose of determining the unit of account—a reporting entity will be required to exercise judgment while taking into consideration circumstances such as the planning and legal status of the asset (whether, for example, the land has been parcellated), as well as the manner in which the asset will be disposed of or its optimal use. Thus, for example, when the asset in question is land, it is our view that a reporting entity should take into consideration the legal ability to sell the plots of land separately and independently. If it is possible to carry out such a sale in practice, our view is that it would be possible to claim that each and every one of the plots of land should constitute a unit of account, and therefore, holding multiple plots of land is an entity-specific characteristic rather than a characteristic of the asset in question. Of course, when determining the transaction price, market participants may still take into consideration the fact that there are other plots of land available for sale or that there are additional building rights in the area, but this matter will not necessarily be reflected in a price that is identical to that of a scenario in which all plots of land are sold to a single buyer. Indeed, a practical question may arise in the opposite direction, where the reporting entity may legally sell each of the plots of land separately, but the highest and best use of those plots will be achieved by combining the building rights of those plots and constructing a joint project or selling them to a single buyer. It may be concluded from the explanations in IFRS 13 and some of the examples it provides that, as part of the valuation premise, a reporting entity may assume that when selling an asset, a market participant will wish to dispose of it in an optimal manner, even if this means selling the item together with complementary assets or liabilities and even if those assets or liabilities are not part of the same unit of account (for more information, see Chapter 9, Section 3). Indeed, there appears to be a difficulty in such a premise in cases where the complementary assets or liabilities themselves are relatively unique assets or liabilities, which constitute independent units of account. Theoretically, it is possible to claim that the ability to use all the plots jointly is not a characteristic of each of the plots but rather of the entity that holds them and that the ability to dispose of all the plots of land at the same time will not be available to another market participant (since unlike other complementary assets and liabilities, each of the plots of land is unique and cannot be complemented by another market participant). However, on the other hand, it may be said that a measurement that ignores the combined potential of the plots of land held by the reporting entity may lead to results that are irrelevant to the user of the financial statements and that such a measurement also contradicts the highest and best use premise (see above for a discussion of the matter in the IFRS Conceptual Framework). Thus, for example, let us assume that the reporting entity holds a certain plot of land and purchases an adjacent plot at a price that reflects a premium (relative to the economic benefit arising from using each of the two plots separately), with the intention of constructing a single joint project on the two plots. In this case, measuring the plots as if one of them will be sold to a separate buyer with the other still being held by the reporting entity may lead to an impairment loss for the reporting entity in respect of the paid premium. Even if the reporting entity follows an approach whereby unique synergetic characteristics should not be taken into account—as is the case in the aforementioned example—it is our view that given the lack of clarity in IAS 40, the unit of account may be redefined to include both plots of land, provided that the specific facts and circumstances lead to the conclusion that a redefinition of this type is appropriate and relevant.

Under IFRS, when an investment property that is initially recognized as part of a business combination is measured at fair value on the business combination date and subsequently at amortized cost, it is sometimes required to allocate its fair value among the various depreciation components (such as the land and building), which form separate units of account. This may also be relevant to real estate assets that are classified as property, plant and equipment and are measured according to the revaluation model. In such a situation, there is no practical way to carry out a transaction involving one component without the other, despite the fact that the unit of account of the building is separate from the unit of account of the land. In limited situations as above, the fair value is estimated under the assumption that the components will be sold as a single unit, and thereafter, the result is allocated to the relevant components. Nevertheless, IFRS 13 does not provide details as to how to allocate the fair value to the various components as aforesaid.

Another issue related (among other things) to the unit of account of investment property under IFRS deals with a situation where such investment property measured at fair value is subject to incentives that are paid or granted to lessees, such as reimbursement of specific renovation costs of stores in a shopping mall or granting an incentive in the form of a limited period with lower or zero rent (free rent). In that context, the question arises of whether the investment in an incentive is a separate asset or an integral part of the real estate asset itself. In that context, it is worthwhile noting that at least in economic terms, the granting of the incentive cannot be separated from the real estate asset since immediately after the incentive is granted, the fair value of the real estate asset reflects the additional cash flows arising from the investment in the incentive; this is also true from the perspective of a market participant acquiring the asset. Thus, for example, if as a result of granting a rent-free period, the rent payable in a subsequent period is higher than the rent that would have been paid uniformly over the two periods, at the end of the first period, the fair value of the asset will, indeed, be higher than the fair value of an equivalent asset, for which rent was uniform over the two rent periods. This will be the case until the end of the second period, at which point the rent will revert to the market rate. Similarly, when the rent paid by a certain lessee is higher than the rent that would have been paid otherwise, due to the reporting entity's reimbursement of the construction or renovation costs of the lessee's offices or stores, as the case may be, then immediately after the reimbursement, the fair value of the asset will, indeed, be higher. In that respect, the reimbursement of the lessee's specific costs is an investment in the asset (in practice, it increases the cash flow from the asset), in a similar (and even more explicit) way to other betterments such as replacing the air-conditioning system or even extending the asset. Therefore, it is normal practice among appraisers to measure the fair value of the entire asset, taking into consideration the remaining future cash flows from the asset, without separating the additional cash flows arising from the incentives granted to lessees. There are those who believe that in order to achieve a more appropriate classification for rental income and gains or losses from changes in fair value in each period, the reporting entity should split the overall fair value between the asset that reflects the depreciated balance of incentives granted to lessees (where the depreciation in respect of the asset reduces the rental income) and the balance of fair value that will be the investment property line item.

An issue similar to the one presented above deals with a situation where an investment property measured at fair value under IFRS is subject to various restrictions by virtue of government grants accounted for in accordance with the provisions of IAS 20—*Accounting for Government Grants and Disclosure of Government Assistance*. Thus, for example, the reporting entity may have received a loan under preferred terms (e.g., a noninterest-bearing loan that is extended for a very long repayment period), subject to the condition that throughout the term of the said loan, an apartment building, which is held by the reporting entity, will be leased for supervised rent to tenants who are eligible for such a benefit. In principle, if the said restriction is already taken into consideration as part of the fair value measurement of the real estate asset (e.g., as part of the calculation of the asset's representative income), in our view the reporting entity should not recognize an additional liability (in the form of deferred income or a further discount to the asset's carrying amount) in respect of the restriction, since this will lead to double-counting of the restriction. On a practical level, with respect to the aforementioned example, it is our view that on the date of receipt of the preferred loan, the difference between the fair value of the loan and the cash amount received shall be recognized as a decrease in the asset's fair value. Of course, the asset will be revalued at the next reporting period so that this decrease will only affect the revaluation gain or loss. Under hypothetical market conditions, this difference (deduction) would be equivalent to the decrease in the fair value of the asset due to the imposition of further restrictions in connection with the use of the asset.

Another practical question in this context is whether the unit of account of an investment property (and real estate properties in general) under IFRS should also include the fair value of related operating or management activities. Thus, for example, commercial assets, such as malls, quite often also include management activity and may generate additional gains (or losses) from management activity (in addition to rent). Generally speaking, gains or losses from management activity include the effect of management fees collected from lessees (and sometimes also include other payments, such as for electricity) and net of the management costs (such as security, cleaning, maintenance, insurance, municipal taxes and electricity for shared spaces). In such situations, it should be borne in mind that from the lessees' perspective, the management fees and rent are substitutable, which allows for cross-subsidization of the amounts. It should also be borne in mind that the management activity is a relatively simple one, and it is reasonable to assume that assets characterized by a profitable management activity will be sold at a higher price than assets whose management activity has led to a deficit (and therefore requires injection of funds by the holder, or an increase of the management fees, which may lead to an adverse effect on the rent in the long term). Therefore, the practice is to include the (positive or negative) value of the management activities in the fair value of investment property assets. Indeed, it is our view that in most cases, the fair value of the unit of account of investment property does not include profits arising from more complex or material operating activities. In such cases, the practice is to isolate the value attributed to the real estate component, that is, the amount that would have been received from selling the asset without selling the asset's related activity. Let us assume, as a relatively extreme example, that a standard residential apartment is being used as a profit-generating dental practice. In this situation, discounting the dental practice's profits in order to calculate the fair value of the apartment would have resulted in overestimating the apartment, since from the perspective of a market participant, these profits are not attributed to the apartment but rather to the activity of the dental practice. It is clear that when determining the appropriate rent payable in respect of the apartment, the potential lessee (e.g., the dental practice) will also take into consideration the rent in alternative residential apartments, and therefore, the fair value of the apartment will not take into consideration its use as a dental practice, even though it is used for that purpose by the reporting entity itself (when the asset in question is a property, plant and equipment line item that is measured at fair value). Indeed, in more complex situations, where the assets in question are relatively unique operating assets (such as hotels, gas stations, server farms or refrigeration facilities), it is clear that from a market participant's perspective, the rent that will be received from these assets will be closely linked to the operating performance of the lessee. For such assets, how to allocate the value attributed to the operating activity and to the fair value of the real estate property will involve the exercise of judgment and will also depend on factors such as the operator's expected profitability in relation to the rent, to what extent the asset is unique (or substitutable) in relation to the uniqueness (and expertise) of the potential lessee, the construction costs of an alternative asset and so forth.

For a related discussion of the unit of account of real estate and in-place leases under US GAAP, also see Example B above.

Chapter 4

DETERMINING THE MARKET IN WHICH THE TRANSACTION WILL TAKE PLACE

Fair value is defined as "the price that would be received to sell an asset or paid to transfer a liability in an orderly transaction between market participants at the measurement date." This definition requires to characterize the relevant market under the current conditions of which the transaction will be conducted and the identity of the participants in that market (for more information, see Chapter 5). This is required since the market in which the transaction is conducted may impact the transaction price.

However, it should be noted that the term "market" is not expressly defined. In certain situations, such as in the case of financial instruments that are traded on several stock exchanges, the term appears to be sufficiently understandable, and the issue in question is which stock exchange's quoted prices should the instrument's fair value be based on. However, at times, the term may take on a more abstract meaning. Thus, for example, under International Financial Reporting Standard (IFRS) and according to the provisions of International Accounting Standard (IAS) 41—*Agriculture*, a reporting entity selling agricultural produce (e.g., apples) is required to measure the fair value of its produce at the point of harvest (under US Generally Accepted Accounting Principles (US GAAP), agricultural products are measured using historical cost until harvested). The apples are sold by the reporting entity in many markets (e.g., in wholesale markets as well as in retail markets), and they definitely have the potential of being exported to numerous countries worldwide, whose markets are characterized by different price levels. Here, according to the provisions of IFRS 13 (and Accounting Standards Codification (ASC) 820), in order to determine the fair value, it is essential to first select the market in which the measurement will take place.

Other cases in point include products such as cars. When determining the fair value of cars, it is first essential to identify the market in which the transaction will take place. Thus, for example, market sale prices in transactions between car importers and leasing companies (the leasing market) may be lower than the sale prices for private customers. Furthermore, the prices of cars sold by international car manufacturers to car importers are even lower and do not include the economic burden arising from import taxes. Similarly, used cars can be sold for scrap to be dismantled for use as spare parts (or melted), or alternatively, sold as secondhand cars.

It should be clarified that the market that is relevant to the fair value measurement should be determined regardless of whether the price in the different markets is observable or is estimated using a different valuation technique. Mapping all the different markets may be exhaustive and may even result in a fair value measurement that is irrelevant from the reporting entity's perspective. Thus, for example, as described above, there may be many potential markets for products such as apples, apparel, cars or machinery. Therefore, IFRS 13 and ASC 820 significantly limit the various alternatives and also improve the relevance of the financial statements by determining that only markets to which the reporting entity has access are relevant for purposes of fair value measurement. However, they do not clarify the meaning of the term "access"; however, it is emphasized that although a reporting entity must be able to access the market, it does not need to be actually able to sell the particular asset or transfer the particular liability on the measurement date to be able to measure their fair value on the basis of the price in that market. It is our view, then, that the term "access" should be viewed from a broader perspective.

Thus, for example, if there is no trading on the measurement date on a specific market (e.g., on Saturday), it is our view that the level of prices in the said market can still be taken into account for the purpose of the fair value measurement. Similarly, when the reporting entity holds pledged securities, which are traded on a specific stock exchange, the fact that the reporting entity is unable to dispose of the pledged securities on the measurement date due to contractual restrictions will not prevent it from relying on the quoted prices on the said stock exchange when determining the fair value in a notional sale.

In other words, the identification of the market is very much an issue that may be entity-specific. Accordingly, a certain reporting entity may not have access to certain markets, but other reporting entities may have access to those markets, the result being that different reporting entities may set a different fair value for the same item. Cases in point are securities markets where only dealers can trade, markets requiring mutual agreements with other parties, markets where access requires physical infrastructure, such as logistic infrastructures and electricity or gas transmission infrastructures, and markets where access entails complex regulatory and licensing procedures. In addition, under certain circumstances, it is possible that reporting entities belonging to the same group or controlled by the same party will vary in terms of the markets to which each of them has access.

The relevant market for fair value measurement purposes should be selected from among the markets to which the reporting entity has access, based on the following order of priority:

a. The principal market—which is defined as the market with the greatest volume and level of activity for the asset or liability rather than necessarily for the reporting entity. This means the market in which the asset or liability is traded in the greatest volume and level of activity should be sought rather than necessarily the market in which the reporting entity conducts most of its transactions; followed by
b. The most advantageous market—which is defined as the market that maximizes the amount that would be received on the sale of the asset or minimizes the amount that would be paid to transfer the liability, after taking into account transaction costs and transport costs. For more information about transaction costs and transport costs, see Chapter 6, Sections 2 and 4.

Where there is a principal market, the fair value measurement assumes that the transaction will take place in that market, even if the reporting entity does not conduct most of its transactions in the said market (but only under the assumption that the reporting entity has access to that market). IFRS 13 and ASC 820 thus give some precedence to the objective aspects. In our view, the principal market should be assessed in terms of the turnover or volume of trading for the specific item being estimated rather than for different types of items. Thus, for example, a certain stock exchange may have an overall higher volume of trading compared to another stock exchange, but trading volumes for a specific share are actually higher on the other stock exchange. Under such circumstances, it is our view that the other stock exchange would be defined as the principal market for the said share.

It is only when there is no principal market (e.g., if all potential markets have a similar level of activity, in terms of total trading volume or relevant quantities) that the reporting entity is required to determine what is the most advantageous market and to assume that the transaction will take place on that market. It should be noted that if the reporting entity is able to identify a principal market, the prices in the most advantageous market should not be taken into account, even if it is clear that the prices in the most advantageous market are higher.

A reporting entity need not undertake an exhaustive search of all possible markets to identify the principal market, and it should take into account only information that is reasonably available. Mostly, reporting entities routinely carry out a process of identifying markets as part of their ongoing business activities and business development. Therefore, the Standards state as a practical presumption that in the absence of evidence to the contrary, the market in which the reporting entity would normally enter into a transaction to sell an asset or to transfer a liability is presumed to be the principal market or, in the absence of a principal market, the most advantageous market. This presumption comes from the assumption that reporting entities that act rationally will wish to act in a market that maximizes the amount that would be received to sell an asset or minimizes the amount that would be paid to transfer a liability. The Standards do not specify the period of time during which a reporting entity should assess what the principal or most advantageous market is or when the reporting entity is required to reassess the market. However, given that they do not require a reporting entity to undertake an exhaustive search to identify the markets, it is our view that reassessment will not be required for every reporting period, unless there is evidence that may contradict the previous market selection.

Example—Determining the Market in Which a Transaction Takes Place

A certain asset held by the reporting entity is sold in two markets (which are defined as active markets) at different quoted prices. The reporting entity normally carries out transactions in both markets and—as of the measurement date—has access to each of the said markets.

Below are further details regarding the level of prices in each market as of the measurement date (in CU):

	Market A	**Market B**
Quoted sale price	26	25
Transaction costs	(3)	(1)
Transport costs	(2)	(2)
Net proceeds	21	22

In such a case, if the reporting entity determines that Market A is the principal market, that is, the market with the greatest volume and level of activity for the asset, the fair value of the asset will be CU 24, which reflects the transaction price net of transport costs only (for more information, see Chapter 6, Sections 2 and 4). If the reporting entity has determined that there is no principal market for the asset (e.g., the markets are characterized by similar volumes of activity), it should assess which market is the most advantageous one by comparing the net amount that would be received from the sale. In this case, Market B is more advantageous than Market A, since the net amount that would be received in Market B is CU 22 versus CU 21 in Market A. Accordingly, in this scenario, the fair value will be CU 23, which reflects the transaction price net of transport costs only. It should be noted that transaction costs are taken into account in determining the most advantageous market but are not weighted when measuring the fair value after determining the relevant market for the measurement. This may sometimes lead to a result (as in the above example), where the fair value determined for the most advantageous market will be lower than the fair value determined under other markets.

Chapter 5

IDENTIFYING MARKET PARTICIPANTS

Another significant key element of the definition of the fair value is the use of assumptions that would have been made by market participants when pricing an asset or a liability, since the measurement is not specific to the reporting entity. Accordingly, after the characteristics of the item and the relevant market are defined (for more information, see Chapters 3 and 4), the market participants in a specific market should also be identified, in a manner that is consistent with the nature of the asset or liability and with the preliminary identification of the market in which the hypothetical transaction will take place to sell the asset or transfer the liability being measured.

The reporting entity is required to identify the characteristics that are generally unique to participants in the market in which the measurement is being made, but it is not necessarily required to identify specific participants (e.g., to specifically identify the particular buyers that may participate in the relevant transaction).

Market participants are defined as buyers and sellers in the principal market (or most advantageous market, as the case may be) that have all the following characteristics:

a. They are independent of each other, that is, they are not related parties (as defined in International Accounting Standard (IAS) 24—*Related Party Disclosures* or Accounting Standards Codification (ASC) Topic 850—*Related Party Disclosures*, respectively), although the price in a related party transaction may be used as an input to a fair value measurement if the reporting entity has evidence that the transaction was entered into at market terms (for more information, see Chapter 7).
b. They are knowledgeable, having a reasonable understanding about the asset or liability and the transaction using all available information, including information that might be obtained through due diligence efforts that are usual and customary. The premise here is that the knowledge and understanding of the investors will be sufficient to enable them

to identify the relevant risk factors and take those factors into consideration when calculating the transaction price.

c. They are able to enter into a transaction for the asset or liability—that is, no restriction is placed on market participants that may prevent them from entering into the transaction (e.g., restrictions imposed by the Antitrust Authority or restrictions due to financial or operational capabilities).
d. They are motivated to enter into a transaction but not forced or otherwise compelled to do so—the objective of this premise is to ensure that no pressure or necessity to enter into the transaction is taken into consideration when measuring the fair value (e.g., when a party sells an asset due to financial difficulties, or alternatively, when an asset is sold for a certain price due to exercise of an option that has been previously granted).

The underlying premise of the process of identifying the market participants is that market participants will act in accordance with their economic interest, that is, to maximize the amount that would be received to sell an asset or minimize the amount that would be paid to transfer a liability.

It should be noted that fair value is not defined as the price that would be received in a transaction on the market between the reporting entity and another market participant but rather as a price that would be received in a notional transaction involving typical market participants (i.e., the selling or transferring party, and the buying or receiving party, as the case may be). It is thus possible that the reporting entity would not have agreed, or would not have been able, to sell the asset or transfer the liability, whether due to restrictions, preferences or assumptions that are different than those of market participants (e.g., the reporting entity predicts a growth in a certain market, whereas it is generally assumed that the market is declining). Another example is when the reporting entity benefits from a unique entity-specific synergy, which is unavailable to other market participants, and therefore, the reporting entity would not be able to receive sufficient economic consideration for the asset from another market participant. Such considerations should not be taken into account when measuring fair value. The underlying premise is that fair value is an objective value, and therefore, the assumptions that would have been made by typical market participants should be identified and taken into consideration.

In certain cases, there may be a practical issue in determining the fair value of a unique asset or operation, due to the fact that their highest and best use (for more information, see Chapter 9, Section 2) can only be achieved by a single market participant (such as a competitor of the reporting entity or an acquirer that owns a complementary operation to that of the reporting entity). Hence, it is only that market participant who is able to optimally utilize the synergy arising from the acquisition of the unique operation. In the absence of several other market participants who will boost competition on the price on the one hand, and on the other hand, an absence of similar operations on sale, the transaction may be advantageous in economic terms both to the buyer and to the seller over a broad range of prices, and the price agreed upon for the transaction will depend on the relative bargaining power of the seller and the buyer. In our view, when measuring fair value, a possible approach would be not to take into account the value from the perspective of market (or markets) participants with unique characteristics. Therefore, it is possible that, in the above example, the fair value will be calculated from the perspective of other market participants, such as a buyer who will continue using the operation on a standalone basis. A similar practical issue concerns the fair value measurement of unique assets such as schools, rail links or other governmental assets. In such cases, there may be a question of whether the fair value should be calculated from the perspective of a market participant that is the government (e.g., what benefit the government derives from the existence or lack of a certain road or rail link) or whether the fair value should be calculated from the perspective of a market participant who will receive the assets without the right to operate them (e.g., for the purpose of dismantling the iron from the railway tracks, selling the iron for melting or selling the locomotive fleet) or with a certain theoretical right to operate the assets.

Following are several other examples to illustrate the market participant principle:

Example A—Synergy When Selling a Supermarket Branch

A reporting entity holds 12 supermarket branches, with joint logistics, headquarters and procurement functions. The reporting entity is required to measure the fair value of a single branch. It is reasonable to assume that if the branch will be operated on a standalone basis, its cash flow would be lower than the cash flow that would be generated by the branch had it been operated in combination with others. The reason for the difference is the economies of scale arising from the costs shared with other branches (synergy). The question is whether this means that the fair value of the branch will be calculated while discounting the cash flows that do not take into account the cost savings. Firstly, the mere fact that the reporting entity benefits from cost savings does not necessarily mean that this cost saving will be relevant from the perspective of a market participant. In order to determine the appropriate assumptions from the perspective of a market participant, the reporting entity should first map the market participants for whom buying the branch is relevant. It is thus possible that if the potential market participants are supermarket chains that are similar to the reporting entity, they will also be able to benefit from the synergy. Therefore, if there are several market participants that compete for a hypothetical purchase of the branch, it is reasonable to assume that the price that will be paid for the branch will reflect a typical level of synergy. In another situation (e.g., if the reporting entity is a monopoly protected by a law that allows other market participants to operate only single supermarket branches), the relevant market participants will not benefit from a synergy, and therefore, it may be argued that this synergy will not be taken into account when calculating the fair value. It should be noted that the branch's value in use, as defined by IAS 36, may also take into account an internal synergy that is specific to the reporting entity, such as the synergy described in the last example, if such synergy is expected in the future—in our view, this is one of the most significant conceptual differences between fair value and value-in-use under International Financial Reporting Standards (IFRS).

Indeed, it is interesting to note that the market participant principle works in both directions. This means that even if the reporting entity does not benefit from any synergy whatsoever (e.g., if it has a small number of branches or is prohibited—by virtue of law, contract or its financial position—from carrying out a particular move that other market participants may make), it is possible that a typical market participant will be able to benefit from a typical synergy, and therefore, the fair value of the branch may be even higher than its value in use, assuming that the reporting entity continues to hold the branch.

This example illustrates the importance of mapping the characteristics of the relevant market participants, particularly where there is no quoted price in an active market. One of the examples included in the Standards demonstrates that, in situations where a particular asset or activity is characterized by several types of market participants that are potential acquirers (e.g., potential strategic acquirers who wish to merge the operation into another operation vs. buyers who are expected to operate the asset or operation on a standalone basis), it will be best to make a separate calculation from the perspective of each type of market participant, unless the answer is already clear. Such calculation would determine the price from the perspective of the participant for whom the value will be optimal while taking into account specific factors for each type of market participant, such as the relevant rates of return and typical investment amounts.

Example B—A Reporting Entity That Avoids Performing a Reasonable Due Diligence

A reporting entity holds a large shopping mall that is classified as an investment property and measured using the fair value model prescribed by IAS

40. Normally, the reporting entity determines the fair value of the mall based only on current lease rates and general rates of return in the market. For efficiency and time-saving reasons, the reporting entity does not take into account factors that may be relevant to market participants when determining the price of the mall, such as its physical condition, turnover data and changes in the turnovers of the leased shops (which may cause changes in rent in the mid to long term) or rent trends on renewal of leases (which may indicate expected future changes in leases that have not yet been renewed). In this situation, it is our view that the measurement method used by the reporting entity does not necessarily comply with the definition of fair value. This is because the Standards expressly stipulate that when measuring fair value, the assumption is that the price will be determined, at the measurement date, in an orderly transaction between market participants who have access to the information needed in order to determine the price that can be obtained through usual and accepted means, such as conducting a due diligence procedure. Since the asset in question is a significant one, it is reasonable to assume that toward its acquisition, the acquirer will examine the issues described above as well as other relevant aspects and risks. Therefore, it is our view that further assessments of reasonable scope should be performed, which would have been performed by market participants when selling or buying the asset, for the purpose of measuring its fair value.

Chapter 6

DEFINING THE TRANSACTION PRICE

1. Exit Price

Fair value is the exit price, which is defined as the price that would be received to sell an asset or paid to transfer a liability. It is apparent from this definition that the exit price takes into account the perspective of the selling market participant, whereas the entry price, which is the price paid to buy an asset or the price received to assume a liability, takes into consideration the perspective of the buying market participant.

Certain International Financial Reporting Standards (IFRSs) (such as IFRS 3 or IFRS 9) stipulate that upon initial recognition, certain assets or liabilities should be measured at their fair value or based on their fair value. Similar provisions also exist within Accounting Standards Codification (ASC) 805 and ASC 815. In other words, for the purpose of measurement at initial recognition, the fair value is, in fact, calculated under the notional sale assumption. That is to say, the question of whether the reporting entity intends to hold the asset or the liability is irrelevant to the definition of fair value, which is measured under a sale assumption. The issue of the price that best represents the fair value was discussed during the development of IFRS 13 and ASC 820 in the context of selecting the entry price as a potential alternative to the definition of fair value upon initial recognition. Indeed, it was decided to reject this alternative, among other reasons, on the grounds that when the buying and selling are performed in the same market, in the same manner and on the same date, the exit price from the perspective of market participants equals the entry price (for more information, see Chapter 8). Nevertheless, the cases for which the exit price is not necessarily the price that best reflects the objective of the measurement were excluded from the scopes of IFRS 13 and ASC 820 (for more information, see Chapter 2, Sections 2.1–2.4).

2. Transaction Costs

IFRS 13 and ASC 820 refer specifically to adjustments to the transaction price and stipulate that the price in the principal (or most advantageous) market used to measure the fair value of the asset or liability shall not be adjusted for transaction costs. In other words, the transaction price should not be reduced when the transaction involves an asset, and it should not be increased when the transaction involves a liability.

Transaction costs are defined as the costs to sell an asset or transfer a liability in the principal (or most advantageous) market for the asset or liability that is directly attributable to the disposal of the asset or the transfer of the liability. Transaction costs should also meet both of the following criteria:

a. They result directly from and are essential to that transaction.
b. They would not have been incurred by the reporting entity had the decision to sell the asset or transfer the liability not been made (under IFRS, this may be similar to costs to sell, as defined in IFRS 5).

Common examples of transaction costs include due diligence costs, fees and commissions (e.g., costs of buying or selling on the stock exchange), registration fees, professional fees paid to advisors, travel costs and so forth. The Standards explain that such costs are not taken into consideration when determining fair value, because transaction costs are not specific to the measured asset or liability but rather to the transaction. Thus, there may be significant differences in transaction costs between different reporting entities, and the costs may also differ depending on how the reporting entity enters into a transaction for the asset or liability.

Since fair value is not adjusted to reflect the transaction costs, those costs should be accounted for when incurred according to the relevant standards. Thus, for example, according to IFRS 3, transaction costs relating to business combinations shall be recognized as an expense in profit or loss. Another example is IFRS 9, which stipulates that when financial instruments are classified as measured at fair value through profit or loss, the relating transaction costs are recognized in profit or loss at initial recognition. On the other hand, according to the said Standard, when financial assets or financial liabilities are classified as measured at amortized cost, the transaction costs are added to, or deducted from, the fair value, respectively, at initial recognition. It should be noted that IFRS 5 excludes finance costs and income tax expenses from the definition of costs to sell. This means that those costs are not deducted from the fair value when calculating the fair value less costs to sell and are accounted for in accordance with other standards (IFRS 9 and International

Accounting Standard (IAS) 12). Therefore, in our view, fair value should also not be adjusted in respect of finance costs and income tax expenses.

In that context, the distinction between the manner of determining fair value and the manner of identifying the most advantageous market (for more information, see Chapter 4) should be emphasized. As mentioned above, in order to identify the most advantageous market, a reporting entity should select the market in which the net price after deduction of transport costs and transaction costs is the highest. Nevertheless, when measuring fair value, it is only transport costs, and not transaction costs, which should be taken into consideration, since transport costs are a characteristic of the asset based on its location.

3. Transfer Tax and Other Transaction Costs Relating to Investment Property (IFRS Only)

According to IAS 40, at initial recognition investment property shall be measured at cost, which also includes the transaction costs incurred on buying the asset. One of the most common costs that may be incurred as part of the purchase of such assets are property transfer taxes. Other common costs include registration fees, real estate agent commissions, legal fees, economic assessments or due diligence procedures. Where it is the reporting entity's accounting policy to measure investment property at fair value subsequent to initial recognition, IFRS 13's provisions apply to subsequent measurements. As detailed above (for more information, see Section 2), the transaction price should not be adjusted in respect of transaction costs. Therefore, if the reporting entity measures the fair value of the investment property close to the date of initial recognition based on the purchase transaction price, it may be claimed that this price should not include the transaction costs (and property transfer taxes), and therefore, the reporting entity shall recognize a loss from a negative change in the fair value, which is attributed, as aforementioned, to the various transaction costs incurred by the reporting entity on purchasing the asset. Nevertheless, in certain cases, where the transaction costs will clearly lead to cost savings for a future buyer (such as the cost of performing a complex legal evaluation that the buyer will not be required to conduct since it had already been conducted), in our view, such costs should be taken into consideration as an adjustment to the transaction price. This is because those costs actually change the nature of the asset and are thus similar in nature to transport costs.

It should be noted that when a potential transaction takes place, transaction costs may also be incurred by the seller (rather than only by the buyer). In other words, while fair value should not include transaction costs that will be paid by the buyer, transaction costs that will be paid by the seller should not be deducted from the fair value. Thus, let us assume that the price of a plot of land purchased by the reporting entity in an orderly transaction was CU 1 million. As part of the transaction, each of the parties—the reporting entity and the selling party—paid real estate agent commission of 1 percent. In this case, the initial cost of the asset from the perspective of the reporting entity is CU 1.01 million, and the net proceeds from the sale of the asset from the perspective of the seller are CU 0.99 million. However, the fair value of the asset will be CU 1 million from the perspective of both participants. In another market, where the asset would have been sold for CU 0.99 million, plus a CU 20,000 commission that would normally be paid by the buyer alone, the fair value would be different than the fair value in the first case described above and will amount to CU 0.99 million from the perspective of both parties, even though the net proceeds and the net cost of the land for each of the parties in both cases are identical. In our view, the conclusion from this example is that the method and significance of the measurement and quotation of the fair value also depend on the normal method of attributing transaction costs in the relevant market.

4. Transport Costs

Transaction costs do not include transport costs. Transport costs are defined as the costs that would be incurred to transport an asset from its current location to its principal (or most advantageous) market, as the case may be. If location is a characteristic of the asset (as might be the case, for example, for a commodity at a certain location, or for inventory in general), then market participants will also take into consideration transport costs in order to determine the price of the asset, and therefore, transport costs should be deducted when determining the fair value of the asset. It is our view that transport costs may also include factors such as loss or obsolescence of the asset in the course of transport, storage costs, insurance and customs costs, as well as other risk factors related to the transport process. However, IFRS 13 and ASC 820 do not discuss transport costs in the context of liabilities but rather only in the context of assets. The conceptual distinction between transport costs and transaction costs is explained in the explanatory notes of IFRS 13 by the fact that unlike transaction costs, transport changes the characteristics of the asset. The different treatment of transportation versus transaction costs can also be traced back to Statement of Financial Accounting Standards (SFAS) 157: according to its basis for conclusions, transaction costs are not an attribute of an asset or a liability, but if the location of an asset or liability is an attribute (e.g., in commodities), the price in the relevant market must be adjusted for transportation costs.

Example—Transport Costs of Coal

Company A needs to measure the fair value of its coal inventory, which includes 2,000 tons of coal located on a certain island. The Company has access to several potential markets and has determined the Chicago Mercantile Exchange to be its principal market. Indeed, in order to sell the coal in Chicago, it must be transported from the island, since the contracts are settled on a physical basis in the Chicago area. The transport costs of the coal (including costs such as insurance, physical loss, port taxes and customs) are expected to amount to $10 per ton, and its price as of the measurement date (according to the quoted price of the relevant type of coal) is $40 per ton. The transaction costs, which include costs such as brokers' fees, are expected to amount to $1.5 per ton. Therefore, the fair value of the inventory as of the measurement date will be $60,000 (= 2,000 × (40 − 10)), which does not take into account the transaction costs. As may be concluded from this example, assuming that all other factors remain unchanged, the fair value of the coal will gradually increase as it is transported to the principal market.

It should be noted that this example is based on commodity prices in active markets. A practical issue may arise concerning the question of whether, at the time of measuring the fair value of the inventory, prevailing market spot prices or future prices should be taken into account, as well as the period required to transport the inventory to the principal or most advantageous market, as the case may be. Some are of opinion that the prices that should be used to measure fair value are the spot prices at the target markets rather than future prices. On the one hand, this approach may result in theoretical fair value estimates, especially in situations where there is a temporary imbalance in the market; for example, when there is a specific shortage of goods, such as tomatoes, but the future price reflects the market's return to balance. However, such an approach may be justified to some extent by analogy to the way IFRS 13 and ASC 820 refer to the term "orderly transaction," since the premise is that even prior to the measurement date, the seller would have followed generally acceptable selling procedures for the item even if the reporting entity did not actually do so (for more information, see Chapter 7).

Example—Betterment Levies

In some jurisdictions, betterment levies are levied due to land value appreciation resulting from planning improvements, such as granting expedients, permitting nonconforming use or approval of a local master plan that includes preferential building rights. Let us assume that the levy is calculated as a percentage of the betterment value as of the betterment date, but the owner of land is only required to pay the levy when exercising the betterment right; for example, when the additional building rights are exercised by virtue of a building permit or when the asset is sold. As a rule, under IFRS the levy is within the scope of IFRIC 21 issued by the International Financial Reporting Interpretations Committee (IFRIC), and the reporting entity can avoid paying the levy by refraining from taking actions that will give rise to the obligation to pay the levy. Therefore, the liability in respect of the levy should only be recognized when payment of the levy becomes mandatory, that is, when the payment of the levy is no longer subject to the discretion of the reporting entity. As a result, prior to recognition of the liability, the question arises as to whether the potential payment of the levy should be taken into consideration when determining the fair value of an investment property on which the levy was imposed (i.e., to deduct the expected levy from the transaction price). On the one hand, it may be claimed that the payment of the levy is a specific characteristic of the holder of the asset rather than a characteristic of the asset itself, since from the perspective of a market participant, the asset that will be transferred will be free of levy payment obligations, and therefore, its price in an orderly transaction will be identical to the price of an identical asset, whose owners will not be subject to a levy payment obligation. In that sense, the nature of the levy is similar to that of transaction costs, which are not taken into account when measuring fair value. On the other hand, the payment of a betterment levy differs from transaction costs in that it triggers a change in the asset (in the form of the option to exercise the building rights), and in that respect, it is similar in nature to transport costs or to conversion costs required to bring an asset to its highest and best use. According to this approach, the betterment levy should be regarded as an integral part of the asset, and therefore, the fair value is calculated on the basis of a price in a (notional) transaction between market participants, which also includes an obligation to pay the levy (i.e., the asset would have been transferred with the obligation). Indeed, even under the second approach, a difficulty arises as to whether or not the betterment levy should be discounted by the reporting entity on the basis of its expected payment date or whether it should be assumed that the levy will have already been paid as at the measurement date. Practically speaking, in our view, some appraisers' opinions assume that the payment of a levy will be somewhat delayed. It is our view that the aforementioned approach may be supported by the abovementioned claim, whereby the levy is an integral part of the asset, even though a practical way to transfer the asset along with the obligation to pay the levy is not necessarily available.

Chapter 7

DEFINITION OF AN ORDERLY TRANSACTION

1. Guiding Principle

Fair value is the amount that would have been received in an orderly transaction. The term "orderly transaction" is defined as a transaction that assumes exposure to the market for a period before the measurement date to allow for marketing activities that are usual and customary for transactions involving such assets or liabilities; it is not a forced transaction (e.g., a forced liquidation or distress sale).

International Financial Reporting Standard (IFRS) 13 and Accounting Standards Codification (ASC) 820 recognize that the sale price that will be determined in a transaction between market participants may also depend on the extent of exposure to the market and on the situation of the parties to the transaction. As an example, let us assume that a reporting entity is required to measure the fair value of a large office building it owns. The selling process of such an office building may take time (e.g., six months), due to the size of the transaction, the need to find a suitable buyer, the performance of due diligence procedures (to evaluate financial, legal and physical aspects of the building and transaction) by potential buyers, conducting negotiations, raising funding by the buyer and so forth. If the reporting entity will be forced to dispose of the building quickly, this might be reflected in a lower transaction price, since under such circumstances, the reporting entity will be unable to find an optimal buyer or to allow buyers to complete sufficient due diligence procedures or raise adequate funding, which will increase the level of risk undertaken by the potential buyers and may lead them to offer a significantly lower price for the property in order to justify their undertaking of the risk. It is also recognized that the normal period of marketing efforts depends on the nature of the measured item. While a relatively long period of market exposure is required for the abovementioned office building, more standard assets, such as cars or apartments, usually require a shorter normal period.

The term "orderly transaction" is important for two main reasons:

Firstly, this term instructs the reporting entity to measure the fair value as the price that would have been obtained in a hypothetical orderly transaction, even if the reporting entity has not actually taken steps to sell the asset prior to the measurement date. In other words, the reporting entity is not required to estimate the price that would have been received in a forced transaction or in a transaction in which the item did not receive the exposure that is usual and customary in the market.

Secondly, determining whether a specific transaction observed in the market is an orderly transaction is important for the purpose of determining the weight to be given to the price achieved in that specific transaction when determining the fair value of the item being measured by the reporting entity. It should be noted that this question may even apply to a situation where the observed market transaction is the transaction in which the reporting entity itself bought the measured asset or assumed the measured liability (for more information, see Sections 2 and 3).

2. Identifying Transactions That Are Not Orderly

Generally speaking, it is possible to say that when a Level 1 input is available for the measured asset or liability (for more information, see Chapter 12, Section 8.5), identifying transactions that are not orderly is not of great significance, since the premise is that a quoted price in an active market is the best and most objective indication of the fair value of the measured item. However, when the volume of trading in a market is declining, such that the market is no longer an active market (for more information, see Section 3), or when there was no active market in the first place for the measured asset or liability (or for similar items), determining whether a transaction involving an asset or a liability (or a similar asset or liability) is an orderly transaction may be highly significant in terms of the weight given to that transaction when determining the fair value of the measured asset or liability.

IFRS 13 and ASC 820 explicitly state that even when there is no active market for an asset or a liability, and even when the volume of transactions in the market has decreased to the extent that it is no longer active, this in itself does not lead to the conclusion that all transactions in the market are not orderly. There is a (nonexhaustive) list of circumstances that may indicate that a transaction is not an orderly transaction:

a. There was no adequate exposure to the market for a period before the measurement date to allow for marketing activities that are usual and customary for transactions involving such assets or liabilities under current market conditions.

b. There was a usual and customary marketing period, but the seller marketed the asset or liability to a single market participant.
c. The seller is in or near bankruptcy or receivership (i.e., the seller is distressed).
d. The seller was required to sell to meet regulatory or legal requirements (i.e., the sale was forced).
e. The transaction price is an outlier when compared with other recent transactions for the same or a similar asset or liability.

Even if some of the aforementioned circumstances exist, a reporting entity should evaluate all facts and circumstances to determine whether, based on the evidence available, the transaction is orderly. In our view, sometimes a reporting entity will need to take into account more specific considerations, such as the ones listed below:

a. The extent of exposure of the sold asset or liability to the market. For example, has the sale of the asset been made public or have orderly brokerage or distribution services been used; has an orderly tender taken place; what is the number of potential buyers to whom the asset was marketed; what is the scope of the evaluations that potential buyers were able to conduct prior to the acquisition?
b. Understanding the parties' incentives to enter into the transaction. For instance, was one of the parties relatively indifferent to the price (due to the structure of the transaction); what was the extent of the financial pressure under which the transaction was carried out?
c. The difference between the transaction price and the price in other transactions or other reliable indications.
d. The degree of the transaction's complexity (e.g., a transaction that involved a complex legal procedure, taking over an asset or dealing with several sellers).
e. Is the transaction a negligible transaction? For example, is it likely that the parties did not invest considerable resources in analyzing its viability?
f. Was the transaction achieved by exercising an option, whose price was predetermined?
g. Was the transaction impacted by the existence of a special relationship, such as between related parties?

It thus appears that in certain cases, although an asset was sold to a single market participant, further analysis will show that there is no reason to assume that the price that was achieved does not reflect a price that would have been achieved in an orderly transaction. Similarly, even if a sale was required only for the purpose of complying with regulatory or legal requirements, it is possible that further analysis will lead to the conclusion that the price that was achieved reflects the price in an orderly transaction, since the said requirement has given the seller sufficient time to conduct a sufficiently normal selling process.

If an analysis of the above evidence indicates that the transaction is not orderly, when measuring the fair value, the reporting entity should place less weight, if any, on that transaction, compared with other fair value indications such as the use of pricing models. If, on the other hand, the evidence indicates that the transaction is orderly, the reporting entity shall take into account the transaction price. The weight to be placed on that transaction price when compared with other indications of fair value will depend on the facts and circumstances, such as the volume of the transaction, the comparability of the underlying item of the transaction to the asset or liability being measured and the proximity of the transaction to the measurement date.

IFRS 13 and ASC 820 do not stipulate that fair value should be based on a single transaction, particularly since it is possible that the transaction is not sufficiently recent or that it was not carried out in an asset and liability that are absolutely identical. Therefore, the weight to be placed on a specific transaction depends on all facts and circumstances. In our view, this range of weights can be reflected when transaction data are weighted alongside data of other transactions, such as for the purpose of implementing the multiples method or when determining the price per square meter for a certain asset. This range of weights can also be expressed by weighting both a valuation technique that is based on the transaction price and a valuation technique that is based on a different pricing approach, such as the present value technique (for more information, see Chapter 12, Section 3).

The analysis aimed at determining whether a certain transaction that was observed in the market is an orderly transaction may require the reporting entity to obtain many facts and data about the transaction. When the reporting entity is a party to a transaction (e.g., when the reporting entity has purchased a certain asset), it is presumed to have sufficient information to conclude whether or not the transaction is orderly. When the reporting entity is not a party to the transaction and does not have sufficient information to decide whether or not the transaction is orderly, it should still take into account the transaction price. In other words, the reporting entity cannot ignore the transaction price and not take it into account solely on the grounds that the reporting entity did not participate in it. However, since the transaction price may not represent fair value, it will not necessarily be used as the exclusive or principal basis for determining the fair value, such that the reporting entity will place little weight on the transaction price compared with other transactions that are known as orderly transactions. In our view, when there is a sufficiently reliable technique to determine fair value, which does not use the transaction data, the reporting entity can place less weight on the transaction compared to other indications of fair value. Thus, for example, let us assume that there is an active market for a share of a certain listed company. Furthermore, call warrants that are convertible into the company's shares are also listed for trading but are not actively traded, and it is unclear whether the few transactions that were carried out in the warrants close to the reporting date and whose trading volumes were immaterial are orderly transactions. A quoted share price is one of the most significant parameters for determining the fair value of the warrants. Additionally, it is possible to measure the expected volatility of the shares according to their historical volatility or by using other methods, such as sector surveys or, if possible, even according to the volatility of other warrants of the issuer for which there is an active market. The other inputs required for the pricing of the warrants according to accepted option pricing models, such as risk-free interest rate, the period to maturity or the exercise price, can usually be reliably estimated. Under these circumstances, in our view, it will be possible to give little to no weight to the quoted prices of the warrants in an inactive market, compared to the weight placed on results obtained by using an accepted pricing model.

3. Measuring Fair Value When the Volume or Level of Trading Activity for an Asset or a Liability Has Significantly Decreased

The global financial crisis, which started in 2007, led to situations where the liquidity that existed in markets for certain assets that had previously been characterized by significant trading volumes had dried out and even disappeared altogether. Aiming to implement some of the conclusions drawn from the crisis, IFRS 13 and ASC 820 include guidance regarding the measurement of fair value in markets where there has been a significant decrease in volume or level of trading activity for the asset, such that they no longer meet the definition of active markets.

It should be noted that even if the volume of activity for a certain asset or liability that is traded in the market has decreased, but the market still meets the definition of an active market (for more information, see Chapter 12, Section 8.5), the wording of the Standards and their explanatory notes imply that reporting entities should continue to rely on the quoted price of the asset or the liability (Level 1 input) as the sole indication of fair value. Furthermore, even when the level of liquidity in a certain market deteriorates, the objective of fair value measurement remains the same, and various considerations of the reporting entity, such as unwillingness to sell the asset under current market conditions, are irrelevant to the measurement. However, if the reporting entity concludes that there has been a significant decrease in the volume or level of activity for that asset or liability in relation to normal market activity, such that the market is no longer an active market, the reporting entity is required to further analyze the price quotations before using them. It is possible to say that, to some extent, the Standards prevent automatic use of price quotations, such as price quotes received from brokers in markets whose liquidity has dried out significantly. In addition, the guidance for such situations may also be relevant when the specific asset or liability being measured is not traded in an active market, but there has been a significant decrease in activity levels in markets for similar products, which are used for determining the fair value of the specific asset or liability.

IFRS 13 and ASC 820 include a (nonexhaustive) list of evidence that may be used to determine whether or not there has been a significant decrease in the volume or level of trading activity for an asset or a liability:

a. There are few recent transactions.
b. Price quotations are not developed using current information.
c. Price quotations vary substantially either over time or among market-makers (e.g., some brokered markets).
d. Indices that previously were highly correlated with the fair values of the asset or liability are demonstrably uncorrelated with recent indications of fair value for that asset or liability.
e. There is a significant increase in implied liquidity risk premiums, yields or performance indicators (such as delinquency rates or loss severities) for observed transactions or quoted prices when compared with the reporting entity's estimate of expected cash flows, taking into account all available market inputs about credit and other non-performance risk for the asset or liability.
f. There is a broad bid-ask spread or significant increase in the bid-ask spread.
g. There is a significant decline in the activity of, or there is an absence of, a market for new issues (i.e., a primary market) for the asset or liability or similar assets or liabilities.
h. Little information is publicly available (e.g., for transactions that take place in a principal-to-principal market).

Even when the reporting entity identifies a significant decrease in the volume or level of activity, this does not necessarily mean that the quoted price no longer represents fair value. In other words, even in a market that is characterized by low levels of activity, transactions may be orderly (and therefore give good indication of the fair value). Therefore, under circumstances where such significant decrease has taken place, further analysis is needed as to whether the transactions in the market are orderly (for more information, see Section 1). If the reporting entity determines that a transaction or a quoted price does not represent fair value, an adjustment to the transaction or quoted price will be necessary if the reporting entity uses those prices as a basis for measuring fair value. Adjustments may also be necessary because of differences between the assets that are the subject of the transactions and the measured asset or due to the passage of time. Such adjustments may be significant to the fair value measurement in its entirety. It, therefore, appears that the reporting entity will be required to take those adjustments into account to determine the fair value hierarchy of the fair value measurement of the asset or liability in their entirety, which, under such circumstances, will probably be categorized within Level 3.

The method used in the measurement of fair value in a situation where the market suffers from liquidity distress may require reporting entities to exercise significant judgment. Indeed, IFRS 13 and ASC 820 do not prescribe a methodology for making significant adjustments to transactions or quoted prices, but they do note that the reporting entity should include appropriate risk adjustments, reflecting the amount that market participants would demand as compensation for the uncertainty inherent in the cash flows of an asset or a liability. Furthermore, a significant decrease in the volume or level of activity for the asset or liability may justify a change in valuation technique or the use of multiple valuation techniques. Thus, for example, under such circumstances, the reporting entity may stop relying solely on the market technique (e.g., a quoted price) and start using an approach that combines the market technique and the present value technique, with the weightings determined by taking into account all the facts and circumstances (for more information, see Chapter 12). Too broad a range of fair value measurements may be an indication that further analysis is needed before determining the fair value.

As a rule, the use of quoted prices (in an inactive market) provided by third parties, such as pricing services or brokers, for the purpose of determining fair value is not precluded if the reporting entity has determined that the quoted prices provided by these parties have been developed in accordance with the principles of the Standards. Indeed, if there has been a significant decrease in the volume or level of activity for an asset or a liability, a reporting entity should evaluate whether or not the use of quoted prices is still appropriate.

In weighting a quoted price as an input to a fair value measurement, the reporting entity should place less weight on quotes that do not reflect the result of transactions (but are rather based, for example, on a model alone). Furthermore, the nature of a quote (e.g., whether the quote is an indicative price or a binding offer) will be taken into account when weighting the available evidence, with more weight given to quotes provided by third parties that represent binding offers.

Example—Measuring Fair Value When the Volume or Level of Activity for an Asset or a Liability Has Significantly Decreased

This example, which is based on a similar example provided in the Standards (with slight changes), is aimed to demonstrate the manner of measuring fair value when the volume or level of activity for an asset or a liability has significantly decreased.

A company invested in a junior AAA-rated tranche of a residential mortgage-backed security (RMBS) on January 1, 2016. In terms of seniority under the waterfall mechanism that is inherent to the securitization entity invested in, the junior tranche is the third most senior out of a total of seven tranches. As from the date of investment, the securities have not been listed for trading but were tradable through a brokered market. However, as from the date of investment through mid-2016, trading volume in that market was infrequent with only a few transactions taking place per month, and there was little, if any, trading activity through the nine months to the end of March 2017. At the same time, the credit rating of the instrument was lowered to A, and there has been some deterioration in the performance of the underlying mortgage portfolio. Taking into account the different circumstances, the company concludes that on the measurement date (March 31, 2017), the volume or level of activity of the securities has significantly decreased and, therefore, decides not to use a market technique (such as a quoted price) as the principal method for measuring the fair value of its investment. Instead, the company decides to use the income approach, that is, discounting the contractual cash flows from the security, using an appropriate discount rate. In order to estimate the discount rate, the company uses as a starting point a risk-free interest rate. The company needs to adjust this rate to reflect the various risk factors it identifies, including non-performance risk (specifically, the credit risk stemming from mortgage defaults or impairment of the apartments on which the mortgages taken were based) and a premium in respect of the liquidity risk.

The risk-free interest rate is developed by using observable market input, such as the yields on government bonds of the appropriate currency and country, and is estimated at 3 percent. The risk spread added to the risk-free interest rate is estimated at an additional 9 percent, as follows:

a. The original credit spread on the securities' issue date was 2.5 percent.
b. Add a credit spread rate of 7 percent, for the estimated change in the original spread over the period since the issuance of the security, based on a comparable index, which, in turn, is based on spreads of similar securities. These inputs are adjusted to reflect factors such as credit rating, the quality of the underlying assets, default rates, loan loss rates and early repayment rates in the mortgage portfolio, reports of analysts and rating agencies, the tranche's subordination level and so forth.
c. Subtract 3.5 percent from the credit spread, following a comparison between the implied yield from the most recent transactions for the security in June 2016 and the implied yield in the comparable index price on those same dates. There was no information available indicating that the relationship between the company's security and the index has changed.
d. Add 3 percent to the credit spread, to reflect the company's estimate of the additional liquidity risk inherent in its security as compared with the index. This estimate was developed taking into account liquidity risk premiums implied in current transactions for similar securities.

The above lead the company to conclude that the total yield is 12 percent. In addition, the company takes into account two nonbinding quotes provided by reputable brokers that imply yields of 15–17 percent. The company is unable to evaluate the valuation technique(s) or the inputs used to develop the quotes. The company concludes that 13 percent is the point within the range of indications that is most representative of fair value. The company placed more weight on its calculation according to the income approach, since it believes that its own estimate appropriately reflects the risks market participants would take into account. Furthermore, the quotes received from third parties were nonbinding, and the company was unable to obtain information about the valuation models and techniques used to develop the quotes.

This example, which, as aforementioned, is based on a similar example provided by the Standards, may indeed leave several unsolved technical questions regarding the method of calculation, such as the following: Was it possible to determine the price in reporting periods prior to March 31, 2017, solely based on price quotations of transactions, even though it was noted that there were very few transactions in the market even long beforehand? Does the original spread, used as a benchmark when determining the interest rate (on the issuance date in January 2016), refer to the index's spread at that time or to the tranche's spread (in our view, it refers to the index's spread on issuance date, since otherwise there might have been double-counting in the calculation)? How does this technique take into account the lowering of the tranche's rating (e.g., have the underlying securities of the index also deteriorated at the same time), and when did the lowering of the credit rating or deterioration of credit quality take place (e.g., did they take place before or after June 2016)? How did this technique isolate the liquidity risk from the credit risk for each and every one of the observation dates? When did the most recent transactions in the security take place (on the one hand, it is noted that the most recent transactions took place in June, and on the other hand, that very few transactions, if any, were carried out thereafter)? There are additional technical points that remain unsolved. Nevertheless, the example clearly illustrates the difficulty that may arise when pricing assets or liabilities in an environment that is characterized by few transactions. Furthermore, the example illustrates the significance of using observable market data whenever possible while exercising judgment as to the weight given to each input, with regard, among other things, to the level of the input's reliability and the information available about it. Thus, for example, in our view, had the company received binding quotes from a dealer (e.g., a binding offer for a sale and purchase transaction) regarding a significant number of securities of the relevant tranche, and the result of the company's internal estimate is not within the price range, then the company would have had to place significantly higher weight on such quotes and adjust the said pricing model (for more information, see Chapter 12, Section 8.3).

Chapter 8

FAIR VALUE AT INITIAL RECOGNITION

1. Does the Transaction Price Represent the Fair Value?

Under International Financial Reporting Standards (IFRS) and US Generally Accepted Accounting Principles (US GAAP), certain standards stipulate that assets or liabilities should initially be measured at fair value (or on the basis of fair value plus transaction costs). This applies particularly to financial instruments but also to assets or liabilities that are recognized in a business combination. Under IFRS, however, a day 1 gain or loss on a financial instrument is recognized only when the fair value of that instrument is evidenced by observable inputs or market transactions.

One of the basic questions IFRS 13 and Accounting Standards Codification (ASC) 820 deal with in this context is whether it is conceptually possible that the fair value at initial recognition will be different than the transaction price. The answer to that question is that the definition of fair value is based on the exit price, whereas the transaction price is an entry price. In other words, there are certainly circumstances in which the entry price will not equal the exit price, and the Illustrative Examples provided by the Standards even clarify explicitly that the Standards do not purport to suggest such a presumption. Statement of Financial Accounting Standard (SFAS) 157's Basis for Conclusions stated clearly that the fact that no such presumption exists was a departure from US GAAP Concepts Statement 7, which stated that cash and cash equivalents paid or received are usually assumed to approximate fair value in the absence of evidence to the contrary. On the other hand, the Standards note that, in many cases, the transaction price will, indeed, equal the exit price and will therefore also represent the fair value of the asset or liability (e.g., that might be the case when the transaction to acquire an asset takes place in the market in which the asset would be sold). Therefore, reporting entities should exercise judgment in order to determine whether the transaction price represents the fair value.

The Standards include a nonexhaustive list of examples for situations in which the transaction price might not represent the fair value of an asset or liability at initial recognition:

a. Related parties: In many cases, a transaction between related parties may not be entered into at terms that reflect fair value. Nevertheless, if a reporting entity has evidence that the transaction was entered into at arm's length, the price in the related party transaction may be used as an input in a fair value measurement. Thus, for example, it is possible that despite the fact that the transaction in question is one with related parties, another party took part in the transaction under the same terms and was interested in having the transaction be carried out under market terms. Thus, for example, let us assume that a public company acquires an operation from a private company that is held (60 percent) by the controlling shareholder of the public company and by a third party (40 percent) who has no holdings in the public company. In this situation, the existing interests may definitely increase the probability that the acquisition is carried out at a market price. Let us assume that the audit committee of the public company's board of directors approves the transaction, and so does the required majority of minority shareholders in the public company's general meeting of shareholders, who are interested in having the transaction carried out at not too high a price. The third party (the seller), on the other hand, is interested in having the transaction not be carried out at too low a price. In other situations, where the parties are relatively indifferent to the transaction price, such as in the case of transactions where assets are moved "from one pocket to another" and have no real-life implications, or transactions where there are unilateral interests to distort the price (such as transactions entered into solely for tax purposes), the price may, indeed, not be indicative of the fair value at initial recognition.
b. A transaction under duress or forced transaction (e.g., a so-called fire sale): When the transaction takes place under duress or the seller is forced to accept the price of the transaction, the transaction may not be indicative of the fair value—for example, if the seller is experiencing financial difficulty or if the transaction price is derived from the exercise of an option that was previously awarded to one of the parties. In practice, this section means that the transaction in question is not an orderly transaction. For more information regarding the considerations for identifying transactions that are not orderly, see Section 2.
c. A unit of account that is not identical: When the unit of account represented by the transaction price is different from the unit of account

for the asset or liability measured at fair value, there may be a difference between the transaction price and the fair value of the items included in the transaction. For example, that might be the case if the asset or liability measured at fair value is only one of the components of the transaction; the transaction includes unstated rights and privileges that are measured separately in accordance with another Standard, or the transaction price includes transaction costs, which should not be reflected in the fair value and should therefore be excluded (for more information, see Section 2). A prominent example of such a case is a business combination, where the unit of account of the consideration (in its entirety) is not identical to the (separate) unit of account of each of the assets or liabilities of the acquiree recognized in the business combination. Characteristics such as the quality of the acquiree's management or workforce, as well as other general characteristics, which may well have been given weight within the total transaction price, might not be recognized as separate assets or liabilities. This may lead to a difference between the consideration for the acquisition as a whole and the net assets recognized in the business combination. Other typical examples that may result in a difference due to a different unit of account are situations where a large "block" of separate financial instruments is purchased at a discount or at a premium compared to the price of each instrument when bought separately, or an acquisition of assets from third parties and the combination of those assets into a synergetic asset or operation (such as taking over land by purchasing portions of the land from different parties). For more information, see Chapter 3, Section 3.

d. The market in which the transaction takes place is other than the principal market (or most advantageous market, as the case may be): When the market in which the transaction takes place is different from the principal or most advantageous market from the perspective of the reporting entity, this may cause a difference between the entry price and the exit price. For example, those markets might be different if the reporting entity is a dealer that enters into transactions with customers in the retail market, but the principal (or most advantageous) market for the exit transaction is with other dealers in the dealer market to which the reporting entity has access as of the measurement date (see example below in this section).

The explanatory notes of IFRS 13 state explicitly that the transaction price may be indicative of the fair value even in an inactive market. However, such a market may require further analysis in order to understand the nature of the transaction price. It is, therefore, possible to see that the question of whether the transaction price at initial recognition constitutes fair value is closely linked to the question of whether or not the transaction is an orderly transaction (for more information, see Section 2).

It should be noted that when the reporting entity concludes that the transaction price reflects the fair value of the asset or liability, and such an asset or liability will also be measured at fair value in subsequent periods, it is important to calibrate the valuation technique to be used (for more information, see Chapter 12, Section 5). Moreover, even if a certain asset or liability (such as an investment property measured under the fair value model under IFRS) is measured at fair value only in subsequent periods, and as a result the question of whether or not the transaction price reflects the fair value appears to be irrelevant at initial recognition, a question may still arise as to the weight that should be given to the purchase transaction when determining the fair value close to the transaction date. In this context, in our view, in many cases, the price of an orderly transaction involving a real estate asset represents the fair value also on dates close to the transaction date, and such a value should be given a relatively high weight compared to a value that is determined in an appraisal. Therefore, when a transaction is an orderly transaction (based on its relevant characteristics), any deviation from the transaction price where the circumstances have not changed (such as a change in the market or a material change in the asset) will require the reporting entity to provide substantial evidence to support such deviation.

Example—Fair Value of an Interest-Rate Swap at Initial Recognition

Company A is a financial firm acting as a dealer with access to both the retail market and the dealer market. The retail market is a market for nonfinancial companies that require financial products, such as industrial companies that wish to enter into financial hedging transactions with a counterparty. The dealer market is the market for the financial companies themselves. Company B is an industrial company that does not have access to the dealer market. Company B enters into an interest-rate swap (IRS) with Company A. An IRS is a derivative used by entities to swap a certain interest rate with another interest rate, for example, to swap a floating interest rate with a fixed interest rate. According to the terms of the IRS, its value at initial recognition is zero. This means that at the time of entering into the engagement, neither of the parties was required to compensate the other party.

From Company B's perspective, the transaction price represents the fair value, since the company operates in the principal market for the IRS. If Company B were to transfer its rights and obligations under the IRS, it would do so in the retail market (i.e., by entering into engagement with another dealer operating in that market). The transaction price will not be adjusted in respect of incremental costs, such as transaction costs that would be charged by a dealer counterparty.

On the other hand, from Company A's perspective, it is possible that the principal market for the IRS (to which Company A has access) is the dealer market. In other words, if Company A were to transfer its rights and obligations under the IRS, the assumption might be that it will do so in the dealer market. Under this assumption, since the market in which Company A entered into the transaction is not Company A's principal market, the transaction price (which is, in fact, zero) will not necessarily reflect the fair value of the derivative at initial recognition. Thus, for instance, under IFRS, if there is a difference between the transaction price and the fair value of the IRS in the dealer market, Company A is required to apply the provisions of IFRS 9—*Financial Instruments*, in order to determine whether it should recognize that difference in profit or loss at initial recognition. Under US GAAP, the difference is recognized in profit or loss at initial recognition.

In this example, the main reason for the difference between the transaction price at initial recognition and the fair value from Company A's perspective stems from the fact that the transaction was not entered into in the principal market. It is also possible to see that the fair value at initial recognition may not necessarily be identical for both parties to a transaction.

Another reason mentioned in IFRS 13's explanatory notes, which may create differences between the cost and the fair value at initial recognition, is the difference between the price a prospective dealer is willing to pay for an instrument (the bid price) and the price at which a dealer would sell that same instrument (the ask price) in a dealer market. This difference is sometimes called the "bid-ask spread," which is mainly relevant to "over the counter" markets; for more information, see Chapter 12, Section 8.3. Thus, for example, when the industrial company (Company B) enters into the swap, and there are bid and ask prices offered by dealers, in order to measure the fair value of the derivative (including at initial recognition), the industrial company is required to select a point within that range that best represents its exit price (and not necessarily its entry price). Therefore, the difference between the bid prices and the ask prices may lead to a difference between the transaction price and the fair value already at initial recognition (from the perspective of Company B).

2. The Manner of Recognizing the Difference between Fair Value and Cost at Initial Recognition

When all the relevant considerations (for more information, see Section 1) indicate that the transaction price does not reflect fair value and the standard relevant to the item requires or permits a reporting entity to measure an asset or a liability initially at fair value, the manner of recognizing the difference between the transaction price and the fair value depends on the provisions of the specific standard that applies to the event or the transaction. However, if the relevant standard does not include provisions regarding the manner according to which this difference should be recognized, the reporting entity shall recognize it in profit or loss at initial recognition. Recognizing a profit or loss at initial recognition is sometimes called "day 1 profit or loss."

Listed below are several examples regarding the accounting treatment that should be applied according to IFRSs to potential differences between the transaction price and the fair value at initial recognition:

a. Business combinations: When there is a difference between the fair value of the consideration plus the amount that is attributed to noncontrolling interests and the fair value of the net identifiable assets of the acquiree, this difference is accounted for as goodwill (i.e., recognized as an asset) or as negative goodwill (i.e., immediately recognized as income from a bargain purchase), as the case may be. This is also similar under US GAAP.
b. Transactions with related parties: IFRSs do not deal extensively with related party transactions, and sometimes such transactions are even explicitly excluded from the scope of various standards and interpretations. Under these circumstances, the accounting treatment applied to the difference between the consideration and the fair value at initial recognition depends on the circumstances. Thus, for example, according to existing practices, when an asset is purchased in a related party transaction for consideration that clearly does not reflect the fair value of that asset, in our view, the asset should be recognized at fair value, and the difference between the fair value and the transaction price should be recognized directly in equity. This is generally also the case under US GAAP.
c. Biological assets: According to International Accounting Standard (IAS) 41—*Agriculture*, the difference arising between the fair value less costs to sell and the transaction price at initial recognition of a biological asset shall be recognized in profit or loss in the period in which it arises. Under US GAAP, biological assets are usually not measured at fair value.
d. Financial instruments: As mentioned in Section 1, as a rule, under IFRS the accounting treatment applied to the difference between the fair value and the transaction price at initial recognition of financial instruments depends on whether or not the fair value was determined by using unobservable inputs. Such a requirement does not exist in US GAAP.

Chapter 9

APPLICATION TO NONFINANCIAL ASSETS

1. Overview

The fair value basis is relevant, among other things, to the measurement of various classes of nonfinancial assets. Specifically, this basis is relevant, or may be relevant under International Financial Reporting Standards (IFRS), to investment property; property, plant and equipment; intangible assets; biological assets; cash-generating units; or noncurrent assets held for sale (for more details, see Chapter 1, Section 2). While discussing the provisions of the Standards, the International Accounting Standards Board (IASB) and Financial Accounting Standards Board (FASB) reached the conclusion that they should include specific measurement (and disclosure) provisions that are applicable only to nonfinancial assets. In principle, as described in detail below, it may be said that the said guidelines deal with the issue of the highest and best use of non-financial assets and with the related issue of the valuation premise. In practice, these or similar principles existed long before the current Standards were finalized, within general practices for valuation of nonfinancial assets (and within specific practices regarding land appraisal), and those principles were formally incorporated into the Standards. Among other things, the highest and best use principle is incorporated into International Valuation Standards (IVS), as well as into Royal Institution of Chartered Surveyors (RICS) Professional Standards ("Red Book"), which are widely accepted appraisal standards that adopted the IVS. It was also mentioned in Statement of Financial Accounting Standards (SFAS) 157 and in US Generally Accepted Accounting Principles (US GAAP) Concepts Statement 7.

The guidelines regarding the principle of highest and best use and the valuation premise are irrelevant to financial assets or financial liabilities, due to, among other things, the view whereby financial assets and financial liabilities (unlike nonfinancial items) do not have an alternative use, such that the manner in which they are used or utilized depends only on their contractual terms.

2. The Highest and Best Use Premise

2.1. Guiding principle

Generally, the fair value of nonfinancial assets is measured under the highest and best use premise. The Standards define the highest and best use as the use of a nonfinancial asset by market participants that would maximize the value of the asset or the group of assets and liabilities within which the asset would be used, such as a business or a cash-generating unit. Underlying this idea is the assumption that the price that will be determined in a notional transaction between market participants will also take into account the inherent potential of the asset's use. Specifically, the Standards recognize that while in many cases the current use of the asset is indeed the highest and best use, it is sometimes possible that the present use of an asset will not reflect the highest and best use, but the asset's price in an orderly transaction between market participants (and therefore also its fair value) will reflect the potential use from the perspective of a market participant. In our view, examples of situations where the highest and best use of an asset may be different from its current use include situations where the asset has not yet exhausted its potential (such as land whose rezoning has not yet been completed, or a building that has not yet been fully leased) or situations where the reporting entity does not wish or is prevented from using the asset in its highest and best use for a variety of reasons, including but not limited to its financial position, the availability of other resources, synergetic aspects, other investment alternatives available to the reporting entity, regulatory or licensing reasons and so forth.

According to the Standards, a fair value measurement of a nonfinancial asset takes into account a market participant's ability to generate economic benefits by using the asset in its highest and best use (including when the asset is not used in its highest and best use at the measurement date) or by selling it to another market participant that would use the asset in its highest and best use. In other words, as part of the measurement, a reporting entity is also required to assess the manner in which the asset will be used by a market participant. In that context, it is also worthwhile to note that the conclusion of this analysis needs to correspond to the relevant market participants who were identified by the reporting entity (for more information, see Chapter 5). Thus, for example, the highest and best use may assume a synergy that is available to other market participants. However, in our view, it cannot assume the existence of a unique synergy that is not part of the assets and liabilities included within the unit of account (for more information, see Chapter 3, Section 3) and that is unavailable to other market participants. Therefore, the fair value (under the highest and best use premise) may be higher, identical or sometimes even lower than the value that would have been obtained by the reporting entity under its current use.

Highest and best use is determined from the perspective of market participants, even if the reporting entity intends to use it otherwise. Nevertheless, in most cases, the reporting entity itself will have an obvious economic incentive to make the highest and best use of its assets. Indeed, the explanatory notes of IFRS 13 state that in many cases, it would be unreasonable for the current use of the asset not to be its highest and best use. Therefore, the reporting entity need not undertake an exhaustive search of all potential uses of a nonfinancial asset, and the reporting entity's current use of a nonfinancial asset is presumed to be its highest and best use unless the market or other factors suggest that a different use by market participants would maximize the value of the asset. Where it was assumed that the highest and best use of a nonfinancial asset is different from its current use, the Standards do not require to separate the fair value into components—that is, fair value under current use and incremental value as a result of the highest and best use. However, if the highest and best use of a nonfinancial asset differs from its current use, reporting entities shall disclose that fact and why the nonfinancial asset is being used in a manner that differs from its highest and best use; such disclosure will be provided within the notes to the financial statements (for more information, see Chapter 13, Section 11).

Indeed, the Standards (as well as the relevant publications that deal with real estate appraisal and valuations) restrict the types of assumptions that can be taken into account when determining the highest and best use of a nonfinancial asset. Specifically, the highest and best use of a nonfinancial asset may only take into account uses of the asset that are physically possible, legally permissible and financially feasible, as follows:

A. Physically Possible Use

A use that is physically possible takes into account the physical characteristics of the asset that market participants would take into account when pricing the asset, such as the location or size of a property. Other characteristics that are mentioned in the relevant literature that deal with real estate appraisal include physical restrictions, such as the shape of the asset or plot of land, the type of surface on which the asset is located (graded/flat), the accessibility of the asset, the natural risks to which the asset is exposed (such as an area with increased flooding or earthquake risks, which may limit certain uses of the asset), the directions of its façade, its visibility, the availability of infrastructure such as transportation and sewage and so forth. This means that a reporting entity should take into consideration the aforesaid restrictions as well as other similar ones when selecting the highest and best use and avoid considering a highest and best use that is impossible or unreasonable considering such restrictions. Thus, for example, a reporting entity should not entertain the idea of constructing a skyscraper on land that is unable to bear its weight.

B. Legally Permissible Use

A use that is legally permissible takes into account any legal restrictions on the use of an asset that market participants would take into account when pricing the asset, such as the provisions of a zoning plan, which are relevant to a specific plot of land. The professional literature regarding appraisals also mentions restrictions relating to environmental laws, conservation areas of special architectural or historic interest, building regulations, restrictions arising from lease contracts that establish the right to the land and so forth.

The restriction pertaining to legally permissible use may also be relevant to the measurement of the fair value of various operations or activities, especially regarding the laws that are relevant to such operations (such as labor and consumer protection laws, regulatory supervision and environmental laws).

The explanatory notes to IFRS 13 explain that the term "legally permissible" does not mean that the use being considered has to be legal as of the measurement date but rather that it must not be legally prohibited in the relevant jurisdiction. Thus, in our view, the Standards are making a distinction between well-based assumptions that would have been taken into account by a market participant and speculative assumptions. The explanatory notes include the example whereby a government has prohibited building on or development of an area declared a nature reserve. It will be impossible to assume that the highest and best use of a plot of land located within that nature reserve will be the construction of a shopping mall. Alternatively, let us assume that a zoning plan that applies to a certain plot of land (being used in the interim period as a temporary parking lot) permits the construction of a residential building on the land, subject to obtaining a building permit, the issuance of which (for the sake of the example) is merely a formality. In such a case, in our view, the reporting entity will be able to take into account using the land for the purpose of constructing the residential building, provided that this use is the highest and best use and provided that the risks relating to obtaining the permit (including the time factor) have been adequately taken into account. This will be the case even if as of the measurement date, it is impossible to begin the actual construction work.

Indeed, a range of intermediate cases may exist between the two clear-cut extreme examples described above. Since the basic rationale is that a reporting entity should take into account a use that would have been taken into account by a market participant, in our view, it will not be appropriate to give the principle too restrictive an interpretation. Nevertheless, in our view, in cases where the current legal status of an asset will need to change in order to obtain its highest and best use, the scope of objective evidence the reporting entity will need to provide in connection with the rezoning or other legal change will have to be substantial. In this case, assumptions such as the intentions of the reporting entity's management or its subjective expectations will usually not suffice. One of the examples included in the Standards (see below) illustrates the types of evidence required for the assumption of changing the zoning, such as similar and recent changes that have actually been completed in assets located in nearby areas and changes in the master plan that applies to the area. Existing professional literature also mentions other potential evidence, such as documents that are not legally binding (such as declarations of planning bodies), and in our view, plans that are in advanced stages can also be taken into account, as well as procedures that are acceptable in a certain area, such as expedients that allow adding building rights beyond the existing formal plan. In any case, when making a well-founded assumption that the legal status of an asset will change, a reporting entity should take into account the related risks when measuring the value of the asset, including the probability that the said assumption will not materialize.

Indeed, the Standards provide guidance with regard to situations where the highest and best use premise is expressly reflected in the valuation assumptions. However, the Standards seem not to provide much guidance for situations where this premise is only implicit, such as when a reporting entity uses a market technique (e.g., when applying the comparison technique to real estate). After all, sometimes the price level for a comparable property in the market embodies, in and of itself, the potential for the highest and best use, even if such a use is relatively speculative and is not supported by substantial evidence as required by the Standards. Thus, for example, the Standards' requirement that a reporting entity only take into account a use that is legally permissible may cause difficulties when pricing agricultural land with speculative characteristics. In certain situations, it is clear that the use of agricultural land according to its zoning (e.g., leasing it to farmers) will generate significantly lower yields than the actual prices of transactions involving land of this type in the area. This difference may be explained by the probability that the land will be rezoned and may also exist when the probability for such rezoning is not clearly supported by objective evidence. That may be the case when the profit generated as a result of the rezoning will be very significant but there is a relatively low probability that it can be generated or that it will take a very long period to occur. In that case, when using the comparison technique, there will be no need to assume a rezoning, but it will rather be enough to compare the plot to similar transactions in similar plots in the area, with similar zoning plans for use as an agricultural land. Such a technique indirectly expresses the zoning potential in the valuation, even if such potential is not supported, as aforementioned, by substantial evidence. On the other hand, in an area where no comparable transactions are carried out, the reporting entity will be required to make explicit assumptions regarding the change in the land's status (e.g., for the purpose of its cash flow forecast). In our view, in this case, the reporting entity will need to provide more substantial evidence regarding the rezoning of the land in order to be able to take this potential into account.

A practical question may also arise when pricing assets (or operations), the actual use of which does not correspond to their formal legal status or deviates from the permissible legal use. Where the assets in question are real estate properties, there is an entire range of such situations—minor breaches of building regulations, such as constructing nettings or awnings without first obtaining a building permit, performing parcellation in a property, using the basement floors or improper legal documentation of the construction documents, up to more significant breaches, such as nonconforming use (e.g., using the land for commercial purposes rather than for agricultural purposes), deviating from the building lines and even building without a permit or invading areas that are not part of the said property. In the case of operations, an operation may not meet all formal provisions of the law, such as employee rights or environmental laws. There is no dispute that when measuring the fair value of such assets, the deviation from the permissible legal status should also be taken into account. This means that, from a risk perspective, such assets will clearly be worth less than comparable assets with a similar use or similar economic characteristics that comply with all legal requirements. Indeed, the practical question is whether or not a reporting entity should completely ignore the potential impact of the current situation continuing for the purpose of measuring the fair value. Thus, it is clear that market participants would take into account at least the probability that a specific asset, whose formal intended use was for storage purposes and which has actually been used for commercial purposes for 20 years, will continue to be used in a nonconforming manner in the future, if such use significantly increases the income generated by the asset. In our view, the answer to this practical question depends on all relevant facts and circumstances. Thus, for example, when deciding what is the value that should be attributed to the nonconforming use, the following should also be taken into account: the extent of the deviation from the intended use and the implications of such deviation, the comparability to other assets (or cases), as well as factors such as the asset's history, legal or regulatory procedures, documentation of conversations or meetings held with relevant persons or entities and so forth. All of these should take place while adequately weighting the risk of this assumption and the costs involved, such as the legal costs, demolition costs, future payment of levies in respect of nonconforming use or betterment levies and fines.

Example—Highest and Best Use of a Plot of Land

Company A buys land as part of a business combination. The land is currently being developed for industrial use as a site for a manufacturing plant. According to the provisions of the Standards, the current use of the land (as a plant site) is presumed to be its highest and best use unless there is evidence suggesting otherwise. In this example, the assumption is that development for residential use as sites for high-rise apartment buildings has started in nearby plots. Based on the development activity and additional changes in the municipal master plans, the reporting entity determines that the plot could be developed as a site for residential use because market participants would take into account the potential to develop the land for residential use when determining the price of the land.

In this case, the highest and best use of the land would be determined by comparing both of the following alternatives:

a. The value of the land as currently developed for industrial use. This assumption will take into consideration the fact that the land would be used in combination with other assets, such as the plant, and with other liabilities.
b. The value of the land as a vacant site for residential use. This assumption would take into account the costs of demolishing the plant (if there is already one on the land) and other costs required to convert the asset to the alternative use and selling it as a vacant plot. It should be noted that if it is determined that the highest and best use is as a vacant site for residential purposes, and this use differs from the legally permissible use at the time of measurement, the appraisal will also need to take into account the uncertainty regarding the rezoning. Thus, for example, in our view, this issue can be taken into account by multiplying the value in a scenario where the intended use is changed by the probability that the change will actually take place (and weighting other scenarios), or by other means, such as by adjusting the discount rate used in the measurement, subject to all facts and circumstances (such as the inputs available for the measurement).

C. Financially Feasible Use

A use that is financially feasible is one that is required to generate adequate income or cash flow (taking into account the costs of converting the asset to that use) to produce a return on investment that market participants would require from an investment in that asset put to that use. In other words, when assessing whether or not a certain use is financially feasible, reporting entities need to assess the reasonableness of the return on investment in respect of the project and the overall feasibility of its execution. When making the assessment, in our view, reporting entities are required to take into consideration factors such as the reasonableness of the required investment (i.e., whether a market participant will be able to raise the funding required for the investment under current market conditions), the reasonableness of the return on investment (bearing in mind the level of risk) and the reasonableness of the timing of the various assumptions (e.g., whether the period until the asset is occupied, or until a building permit is obtained, is reasonable from the perspective of a market participant).

2.2. Defensive use of nonfinancial assets

At times, the reporting entity may decide not to use a nonfinancial asset at all, or alternatively, use it in a manner that is not its highest and best use. The reasons for such a decision may be competitive motives, such as acquiring a competing brand and preventing other market competitors from using that brand. The value obtained in such a situation is sometimes referred to as "defensive value." As in other situations, the fair value of the nonfinancial asset should be measured from the perspective of market participants rather than necessarily from the perspective of the reporting entity. It may very well be that (theoretically) the highest and best use from the perspective of market participants would have been to compete with the reporting entity itself, whereas the reporting entity actually uses the asset defensively.

Example—Highest and Best Use of an R&D Project

Company A acquires a research and development (R&D) project in a business combination. The company develops a technology that competes with the acquired project and therefore does not intend to complete the project but rather to use it defensively in order to prevent its competitors from continuing its development. Accordingly, the project will provide a defensive value by improving the prospects of the company's own competing technology.

In order to measure the fair value of the project at initial recognition as part of the allocation of the purchase price, the highest and best use of the project would be determined from the perspective of market participants. Following are examples of potential uses of the project:

a. The highest and best use of the R&D project would be to continue developing it—this will be the case if market participants would continue to develop the project, and that use would maximize the value they will generate from the combined use of the group of assets and liabilities. In other words, the valuation premise is that the project will be used in combination with complementary assets and liabilities in order to maximize its value. That might be the case if market participants do not have similar technology—either under development or commercialized—but do have the complementary assets and liabilities required in order to continue the development of the R&D project.
b. The highest and best use of the R&D project would be to cease development for competitive reasons—this will be the case if market participants have a technology that is at a more advanced stage of development or have a similar product that is already commercialized and wish to carry out a defensive acquisition in order to improve the prospects of their own technology. As in the previous alternative, the valuation premise in this alternative is that market participants have complementary assets and liabilities and that the R&D project will be used in combination with these assets and liabilities (in order to prevent the development of the project by competitors). It should be noted that it is not necessary that the defensive value from the perspective of other market participants will be identical to that of the company; under this alternative it is assumed that the company will continue competing with the project's acquirer. Thus, if the company has a relatively significant market share, it is possible that from the perspective of other market participants, the defensive use will generate a relatively lower defensive value than the one that will be generated to the company.
c. The highest and best use of the R&D project would be to cease development for economic reasons—unlike in the case described in Section b., the assumption here is that market participants would discontinue the development of the project, since the project is not expected to provide a market rate of return (if any) if completed, and there is no point in acquiring it for competitive reasons. The fair value of the project under this alternative is the price that would be received under the valuation premise that the project will be used on a standalone basis rather than in combination with other assets and liabilities, such that the price under this alternative might be zero.

3. Valuation Premise for Nonfinancial Assets

3.1. Guiding principle

A nonfinancial asset might provide maximum value to market participants through its use in combination with other assets as a group, in combination with other assets and associated liabilities (e.g., a business) or on a standalone basis, with no combination. According to the Standards, when measuring fair value, a reporting entity should determine the valuation premise regarding the manner of using the asset consistently with the highest and best use premise, which was determined as explained in Section 2.

The purpose of the valuation premise principle is to determine whether the highest and best use of the asset will be achieved if the asset is used on a standalone basis or with complementary assets or liabilities. To this end, a distinction should be made between the valuation premise and the unit of account: even when the unit of account relates to the asset on a standalone basis, the valuation premise may be that the highest and best use of the nonfinancial asset will be in combination with other assets and liabilities (for more information, see Chapter 3, Section 3, and Section 3.4 of this chapter).

3.2. A nonfinancial asset's highest and best use is in combination with other assets and/or liabilities

Under this assumption, the highest and best use of the asset is in combination with other assets as a group or in combination with other assets and liabilities (such as a business). In this scenario, the fair value of the asset is the price that would be received in a current transaction to sell the asset, assuming that the asset would be used in combination with other assets or with other assets and associated liabilities and that those assets and liabilities would be obtainable by market participants. The term "associated liabilities" includes both the liabilities associated with the measured asset and the liabilities associated with other complementary assets but does not include liabilities used to fund assets other than those within the asset group. One example of liabilities that can be normally included within the group's value are liabilities used to fund the business's working capital.

In practice, the value received under the said valuation premise may be described by asking the hypothetical question of what price would be received on the notional sale of the asset between market participants assuming that the buying market participant would have used the asset within the group of complementary assets and liabilities.

To achieve uniformity, the Standards emphasize that when the complementary assets and liabilities are held by the reporting entity, the assumption of the highest and best use of a nonfinancial asset should be consistent for all the assets of the measured group within which the asset would be used, even when the group is larger than the unit of account of the measured asset. This means that when the fair value of an asset is measured under the assumption that its highest and best use is within a group of assets and/or liabilities, this assumption regarding the highest and best use would be consistently applied to all other assets and liabilities included in that group.

In other words, if the optimal use for a certain group of assets held by the reporting entity is through their use as a group of assets, then it cannot be assumed that certain assets that belong to that group would be sold or used on a standalone basis, even if such a use is the highest and best use from the perspective of those specific assets but not from the perspective of the group of assets as a whole.

Let us assume, for example, that the reporting entity owns a plot of land with a profitable manufacturing plant. For the purpose of this example, let us assume that the land and plant components are separate units of account, which are measured according to the revaluation model under the provisions of International Accounting Standard (IAS) 16. To the extent that the highest and best use of the land is its development for residential use, the reporting entity will not be able to carry out valuations in which it will measure the value of the plant (without the land component) under the assumption that it will continue operating on the land and, on the other hand, measure the value of the land under the assumption that the plant will be dismantled and the land will be sold as vacant land for residential use. Moreover, in our view, in such cases, even if the fair value does not form the basis for measurement of some of the other assets within the group, the valuation premise may sometimes result in a carrying amount ceiling for the group as a whole.

A practical difficulty may arise when measuring the fair value of specialized nonfinancial assets that do not have significant value on a standalone basis but are treated as a separate unit of account. Examples of such assets may include machines that have been assembled as part of an assembly line, industrial refrigerators installed in a store and so forth. Once dismantled, such assets may only be melted or sold as scrap for another use, such that the adjustment costs, which brought the asset to its current condition, will not be reflected in its value (and the reporting entity might even be required to deduct the costs of dismantling the asset from the price expected to be received from its sale). IFRS 13's explanatory notes and the list of examples provided in the appendix to the Standards explain that even when the unit of account of a certain nonfinancial asset includes only the asset itself, but the fair value of the asset is measured under the assumption that its highest and best use will be in combination with complementary assets or liabilities, the reporting entity should also take into account the configuration, transport and installation costs of the asset when measuring its fair value. This is the case since the presumption is that the market participant buyer steps into the shoes of the reporting entity that holds the specialized asset. Thus, for example, let us assume that the reporting entity has an installed machine that is used as part of a plant. In this situation, it is possible that when measuring the fair value of the machine, the reporting entity will adjust the fair value (upward) to reflect the transport and installation costs of a similar machine (not installed or otherwise configured for use) so that the fair value measurement will reflect the current condition and location of the machine (installed and configured for use), provided that the valuation premise is that the highest and best use of the machine is being part of the production line to which it belongs. Similarly, if the asset is work in progress inventory that is unique and market participants would convert the inventory into finished goods, the fair value of the inventory would assume that market participants have acquired or would acquire any specialized machinery necessary to convert the inventory into finished goods.

In more limited situations, when a reporting entity uses an asset within a group of assets, for example, when the valuation involves land and leasehold improvements (which are separate assets)—bearing in mind that there is no practical way to transfer the assets separately—the reporting entity can allocate the overall fair value of the asset group to the individual assets of the group. However, the Standards do not provide details regarding such allocation. In our view, such allocation can be made on the basis of the relative fair values of a similar (but vacant) land plot and of the theoretical construction services required to construct comparable improvements (including an adequate allowance for risk and cost of capital).

Example—Highest and Best Use of an Asset Group

A company acquires assets and assumes liabilities in a business combination. One of the groups of assets acquired (a cash-generating unit) comprises assets A, B and C. Asset C is a billing software integral to the business developed by the acquired entity for its own use in combination with the other assets included in that group. The company measures the fair value of each of the assets individually, consistently with the specified unit of account for the assets. The company determines that the highest and best use of the assets is their current use since there is no evidence to suggest otherwise. As a valuation premise, the company determines that each asset would provide maximum value to market participants through its use in combination with other complementary assets and liabilities.

The company determines that the market in which the activity was acquired is identical to the principal (or most advantageous) market for the sale of the unit from the perspective of the company. The company determines that market participant buyers with whom it would enter into a transaction in that market belong to one of two principal groups: strategic buyers (such as competitors) and financial buyers (such as venture capital funds and private investors that do not own the complementary assets and liabilities).

To determine the fair value of each of the assets consistently with its unit of account and with the valuation premise, the manner in which each group of market participants will use each of the assets in the asset group (A, B and C) should be taken into account, as follows:

a. Strategic buyer group: The company determines that this group of buyers has complementary assets and liabilities that would allow the creation of synergies required to maximize the value of the asset group. These complementary assets also include an alternative asset for Asset C (the billing software), which would be used for only a limited test run period, after which it will be abandoned by the buyer. The assumption is that a strategic buyer has an alternative asset, and therefore, Asset C would not be used for its full remaining economic life. The company determines that the total price for the asset group—assuming that it is sold to a strategic buyer—is CU 650,000, reflecting values for Assets A, B and C of CU 360,000, CU 260,000 and CU 30,000, respectively. It should be noted that this example, which is based on a similar one in the Standards, does not specify how the company allocated the said value to the three assets.
b. Financial buyer group: The company determines that financial buyers do not have complementary assets and liabilities that would allow synergies to be formed so as to maximize the value of the asset group. Accordingly, Asset C (the billing software) will be used throughout its entire remaining economic life. The company determines that the total price for the asset group—assuming that it is sold to a financial buyer—is CU 600,000. The values allocated to Assets A, B and C within the asset group are CU 300,000, CU 200,000 and CU 100,000, respectively.

Based on the above analysis, the fair values of Assets A, B and C would be determined on the basis of the use of the assets as a group by the strategic buyer group. Although the use of the assets within the strategic buyer group does not maximize the fair value of each of the assets individually, it does maximize the total fair value of the assets as a group. In this situation, the fair value of Asset C will be only CU 30,000 and will be consistent with the valuation premise of the other assets, despite the fact that under the second valuation premise, the value of the asset would have been higher.

3.3. A nonfinancial asset's highest and best use is on a standalone basis

There may be situations where the highest and best use of a nonfinancial asset will not be in combination with complementary assets or liabilities but rather on a standalone basis. The fair value of the asset under this premise is the price that would be received in a current transaction to sell the asset to market participants that would use the asset on a standalone basis. As described above (for more information, see Section 3.2), if the optimal use for a certain group of assets held by a reporting entity is through their use as a group, then it cannot be assumed at the same time that the highest and best use of certain assets in that group would be to use them on a standalone basis.

It should be emphasized that even when the fair value of a nonfinancial asset is measured based on the assumption that it will be used on a standalone basis, the result of the measurement will depend on the nature of the measured asset and its unit of account. Thus, for example, it is definitely possible that the separate asset is an operation or a cash-generating unit defined as a single unit of account (for more information, see Section 3.4).

3.4. Valuation premise versus unit of account

When discussing the valuation premise, the difference between the valuation premise and the unit of account should also be discussed (for more information, see Chapter 3, Section 3). According to the Standards, the fair value measurement of a nonfinancial asset assumes that the asset is sold consistently with the unit of account (which may be defined as an individual asset). On the other hand, when the highest and best use of the asset is to use it in combination with other assets or with other assets and liabilities, the assumption is that the relevant market participants already hold the complementary assets and associated liabilities and therefore would not necessarily be willing to pay a higher price for the individual asset, only because the transaction included other assets or other assets and other liabilities as a group.

Thus, the Standards attempt to reconcile the unit of account principle with the valuation premise principle. However, in our view, under certain circumstances, it may still be difficult to reconcile the said principles. In particular, practical questions may arise with regard to situations where the unit of account is actually larger than the optimal unit under the valuation premise. For example, a real estate fund that holds a group of investment properties, whose overall value is lower than the aggregate value of each of its assets due to factors such as lack of focus or management quality. Another example is a closed mutual fund or a holding company that is traded at a discount compared to the aggregate value of each of their respective holdings due to factors such as liquidity, management quality and taxation issues. In such situations, in our view, it will be inappropriate to ignore characteristics included in the unit of account by dividing it into smaller units for the purpose of the valuation premise. A case in point is summing up the value of the holdings of each asset under the standalone use assumption in order to estimate the fair value of the entire unit of account, without taking into consideration other characteristics such as size, liquidity and shared costs, if such characteristics would have been taken into consideration by market participants when determining the price of the unit of account in its entirety.

Furthermore, the Standards establish a principle whereby the price that will be reflected in a transaction between market participants will take into account the potential use of the asset in ways available to market participants. Clearly, if the unit of account includes all assets that create the synergy (even if the synergy is unique), this synergy should be included in the fair value of the unit as a whole.

However, the question becomes more difficult when the reporting entity has a unique synergy, part of which is explained by assets or liabilities that are not included within the asset's unit of account. Here, practical questions as to the distinction between the unit of account and the valuation premise may arise. The Standards seem not to provide sufficient discussion on the distinction between complementary assets that are generally available to market participants and complementary assets that are available only to the reporting entity, such as the plant in which the machine was installed, the land that is located in close proximity to the measured plot of land, the software that is intended for a specific machine, the production line in which the work in progress inventory is manufactured, a related patent and so forth.

On the one hand, the Standards establish the principle whereby it is only the characteristics of the asset that will be taken into account in a fair value measurement rather than the characteristics of the reporting entity. On the other hand, the Standards expressly permit taking into consideration characteristics such as configuration and installation costs for assets that form an individual unit of account, assuming that the buyer "steps into the shoes" of the reporting entity with respect to the complementary assets and liabilities. Thus, for example, the costs of configuring and installing a machine in a production line have a value only under the assumption that the machine is part of the specific plant that is held by the reporting entity. This means that the unique characteristics of the reporting entity are also taken into account for the purpose of measuring the fair value of the asset. The Standards seem not to provide an adequate answer to the question of whether and to what extent other assets of the reporting entity, in addition to the production line, could also be taken into consideration for the purpose of measuring the fair value of the machine (both recognized and unrecognized assets); such assets include organized workforce, patents, franchises and licenses. However, the Standards do note that the fair value should not include a unique synergetic value that is unavailable to market participants.

In the above example, in our view, the price that would have been obtained by selling the plant in its entirety could potentially reflect a synergetic value that is not necessarily included in the unit of account of the individual machine. Therefore, in our view, in many cases, in order to avoid an over-attribution of synergetic value (assuming it is not included in the unit of account) to an asset that is measured under the valuation premise that it will be used in combination with other assets of the reporting entity, the fair value of the asset will be measured on the basis of the cost of obtaining a comparable standalone asset, plus the required configuration costs that are saved by the hypothetical buyer that holds all the other assets and liabilities, provided that such a purchase is worthwhile from the buyer's perspective. Conversely, in rarer cases, it would only be possible to allocate the selling price of the entire group between the asset and the complementary assets or liabilities on an arbitrary basis.

Chapter 10

MEASURING FAIR VALUE OF LIABILITIES AND EQUITY INSTRUMENTS

1. Guiding Principle

The Standards include a chapter dedicated to the manner in which a reporting entity should apply the fair value measurement to its liabilities and equity instruments. Generally speaking, it may be said that, in most cases that require a reporting entity to measure the fair value of its liabilities, the measured liabilities will be financial ones. For instance, under International Financial Reporting Standards (IFRS), in certain situations, IFRS 9 includes provisions that allow the reporting entity to designate financial liabilities as at fair value through profit or loss, and under certain circumstances (such as in the case of financial liabilities held for trading), it even requires the liability to be measured at fair value. In addition, the fair value of financial liabilities is also required to be measured at initial recognition, including when separating an embedded derivative that is not closely related to the host debt contract, or when separating a compound instrument into the debt component and the complementary equity component. Such measurement is also required when significant contractual changes are made to the terms of a financial liability.

It may be said that it is not often that IFRSs (or US Generally Accepted Accounting Principles (US GAAP) Standards, in this regard) require reporting entities to measure the fair value of their own equity instruments. This stems from the fact that IFRS 2—*Share-Based Payment* is excluded from the provisions of IFRS 13 (for more information, see Chapter 2, Section 2.2) as are Accounting Standards Codification (ASC) Topic 718—*Compensation—Stock Compensation* and ASC 505–50—*Equity—Equity-Based Payments to Non-Employees* with regard to ASC 820's scope.

Furthermore, normally, under IFRS when the reporting entity buys or issues its own equity instrument, International Accounting Standard (IAS) 32—*Financial Instruments: Presentation* requires to measure such a transaction at cost. Therefore, in our view, the most common cases in which a reporting entity may be required to measure the fair value of its equity instruments under the provisions of IFRS 13 are when the reporting entity pays consideration in a business combination (or acquires significant influence in an associate or joint control in a joint venture), by way of issuing or transferring its equity instruments. The same is true under ASC Topic 805—*Business Combinations.* Another potential situation may take place when the reporting entity settles financial liabilities by way of issuing its equity instruments, within the scope of International Financial Reporting Interpretations Committee's Interpretation 19 (IFRIC 19), or when the reporting entity is being paid with its own equity instruments as consideration in a transaction with customers.

In addition to the cases mentioned above, as a general rule, in a business combination, the acquired entity's financial and nonfinancial liabilities shall be measured at fair value, and the provisions of the Standards will also apply to this situation with regard to liabilities. For example, in a business combination, a reporting entity is required to measure the fair value of financial liabilities (such as bonds issued or loans taken) that, from the acquiree's perspective, are measured at amortized cost after initial recognition. Furthermore, at this point the acquirer is required to measure the fair value of the acquiree's nonfinancial liabilities such as in respect of decommissioning or restoring a site or provisions in respect of legal claims, which are normally not measured at fair value.

As a guiding principle, when measuring the fair value of a liability or an equity instrument of the reporting entity, the fair value is the price that will be paid in a theoretical transfer of the liability or equity instrument between market participants at the measurement date. This objective does not change regardless of whether or not the said liability or equity instrument has a quoted price in an active market. The market participant principle (for more information, see Chapter 5) applies to liabilities and equity instruments in a manner that is consistent with the manner in which it applies to assets. Thus, for example, if the reporting entity is a party to a commodity supply forward that is settled on a physical basis and that is measured at fair value as a derivative with a negative value, the fair value will be measured from the perspective of a market participant with a normal efficiency rather than from the perspective of the reporting entity, which may have higher or lower operational efficiency. In other words, the reporting entity's ability to settle the contract more or less efficiently than a market participant will be reflected in profit or loss only once the contract is settled rather than when its fair value is measured.

In substantially all cases, the fair value of the liability from the perspective of the debtor (such as issued bonds) or of the issuer of an equity instrument (such as an issued share) will be identical to the fair value of the "corresponding asset," which is a mirror image of the liability or the equity instrument from the perspective of the entity holding them (i.e., the entity that has invested in the bonds or shares). One of the reasons provided by the explanatory notes of IFRS 13 to the corresponding asset approach is that an ongoing difference between the consideration for assuming a liability and the cost of purchasing the corresponding asset is an opportunity to carry out arbitrage, through funding the acquisition of the asset by way of issuing an identical liability, or vice versa (for more details, see Section 3).

The Standards did not see fit to distinguish between the measurement principles that apply to a reporting entity's liabilities and those that apply to its equity instruments, since—among other things and as mentioned above—from the perspective of the corresponding asset's owner, there is no distinction between the two.

2. "Transfer" versus "Settlement"

The notional transfer of a liability or a reporting entity's own equity instrument assumes the following:

a. The liability would remain outstanding, and the market participant transferee would be required to fulfil the obligation. In other words, the liability would not be settled with the counterparty or otherwise extinguished on the measurement date.
b. Similarly, the assumption in a case of transfer is that a reporting entity's own equity instrument would remain outstanding, and the market participant transferee would take on the rights and responsibilities associated with the instrument. The instrument would not be canceled or otherwise extinguished on the measurement date.

Unlike in the case of immediate settlement, a transfer of a financial liability also embodies market participants' expectations as to the extent of liquidity, uncertainty and the other terms of the liability. Thus, for example, let us assume that the reporting entity issued a series of bonds for its par value of CU 100,000. On the measurement date, the bonds are actively traded on a stock exchange at a quoted price of CU 95,000 (for the entire series). Furthermore, under the terms of the bonds, the reporting entity may repay the bonds early at a price that approximates their amortized cost (say, CU 100,000 plus accrued interest). In that situation, to measure the liability's fair value, there is no need for the reporting entity to assume that the bonds will be settled immediately according to the terms of the liability (in this example, the par value plus accrued interest) but rather to determine what price would have been paid in a notional transfer—between market participants on the measurement date—of a liability with identical characteristics (taking into account both the contractual terms, such as the early repayment option, and the factors such as credit risk or level of liquidity). In the above example, the early repayment of the series of bonds according to their legal terms is not economically feasible, and therefore, it is not assumed that a market participant who would undertake or issue a similar liability would necessarily carry out the action. Similarly, in the case of equity call warrants, which were issued by the reporting entity, it is not necessary that their fair value will be identical to their intrinsic value at the measurement date. Rather, it is likely that their fair value will actually be higher than their intrinsic value because of the existence of time value in addition to the intrinsic value.

In practice, substantially all liabilities or equity instruments of the reporting entity will not be transferable due to contractual or other restrictions that prevent the transfer of such items by the reporting entity to other parties. It is thus clear that, under normal circumstances, a reporting entity that had issued bonds will not be free to transfer its obligation to another party (that will pay the bondholders in its stead and will release it from its primary obligation), since such a step causes a significant and undefined exposure to the bond holders, and it is reasonable to assume that without an explicit permission to do so, such a step will be forbidden by virtue of the terms of the bonds or even by virtue of the provisions of common law. A similar rationale will be all the more applicable to the transfer of shares by their issuer.

Indeed, the mere fact that the liability or equity instrument is in fact non-transferable does not mean that the objective of the fair value measurement changes. In such a situation, the fair value should still be measured from the perspective of the holder of the corresponding asset. In other words, there may be an observable market for the corresponding asset, and even if this is not the case, it may be that its fair value can be estimated. When the liability or the equity instrument is not held as an asset, the measurement will be carried out based on a hypothetical transfer transaction (for more information, see Section 4).

To meet the objective of fair value measurement for all cases and consistently with the measurement of assets, reporting entities should maximize the use of observable inputs and minimize the use of unobservable inputs (for more information, see Chapter 12, Section 8) even when measuring liabilities and equity instruments. Therefore, when a quoted price is available for the transfer of an identical or similar liability or the reporting entity's own equity instrument, such a quoted price should be used. Indeed, it is reasonable to assume that such situations will be rare. Therefore, in substantially all the cases, the reporting entity will be required to measure the fair value of the liability using other valuation techniques. For this purpose, the Standards distinguish between situations where the liability or the equity instrument is held by other parties as assets and other situations, as described below.

3. Liabilities and Equity Instruments Held by Other Parties as Assets

3.1. Measurement hierarchy

In many cases, there are no active markets in which a reporting entity can observe transactions for the transfer of its liabilities or equity instruments, since, among other things, legal or contractual restrictions were placed on such a transfer. Accordingly, the premise of the discussion is that such a quoted price is unavailable, and therefore, the measurement of fair value is to be carried out by using other assumptions.

Under this premise, the Standards distinguish between a situation where the measured liability or equity instruments are held as an asset by another party and other situations. When the measured item (a liability or equity instrument of the reporting entity) is held by another party as an asset, the fair value will be measured according to a certain hierarchy. This hierarchy was divided into levels according to the quality of the input. The highest priority is assigned to observable inputs (Level 1 inputs) and the lowest priority, to unobservable inputs (Level 3 inputs). In that respect, the hierarchy is similar to the general fair value hierarchy in the Standards (for more information, see Chapter 12, Section 8).

Set forth below is the hierarchy (in descending order) that the Standards set for the purpose of measuring the reporting entity's liabilities or equity instruments held by other parties as assets and for the transfer of which there is no quoted price in an active market (from the perspective of the issuer):

a. A quoted price in an active market for the identical item held by another party as an asset—for example, bonds or shares issued by the reporting entity and traded in an active market will generally be measured at their quoted price on the stock exchange (this price is based on the transactions between parties that hold those bonds or shares as assets).
b. If the quoted price in an active market is unavailable, reporting entities shall use other observable inputs, such as the quoted price in an inactive market for an identical item held by another party as an asset. These inputs may include quoted prices of recent transactions that are received from brokers or dealers who broker or trade in the reporting entity's bonds or shares (for more information, see Chapter 12, Section 8.2).

c. If the observable prices in a. and b. above are unavailable, the reporting entity shall use another valuation technique in relation to the corresponding asset, taking into consideration all facts and circumstances. This means that the reporting entity shall use the assumptions that are relevant to a market participant who trades in the corresponding asset. As to the use of valuation techniques, the Standards explicitly provide as examples the income approach (such as a present value technique that takes into account the future cash flows that a market participant would expect to receive from holding the liability or equity instrument as an asset) and the market approach (such as using quoted prices for similar liabilities or equity instruments held by other parties as assets). In any case, in our view, when applying those valuation techniques, reporting entities should maximize the use of objective and observable market inputs (for more information, see Chapter 12). Thus, for example, let us assume that a reporting entity whose stock is traded in an active market is required to measure the fair value of a warrant it had issued, for which there is no observable input regarding existing transactions. For that purpose, it shall be assumed that the reporting entity opts to use the Black-Scholes valuation technique, which is a generally accepted option pricing model. In such a situation, in our view, the reporting entity will have to use the quoted price of its stock as a parameter within the said pricing model.

Example—A Structured Note

On January 1, 2016, an investment bank with an AA credit rating issues a five-year structured note to a customer. The contractual principal amount to be paid by the bank at maturity is linked to a specific equity index. It should be assumed that no credit enhancements are issued in conjunction with or otherwise related to the contract (such as third-party guarantees or collaterals). The characteristic of linkage to the shares index is an embedded derivative that is not closely related to the host debt contract. Therefore, the bank opts to designate the entire financial liability as at fair value through profit or loss. The fair value of the note is measured using the present value technique.

At initial recognition of the financial liability, the bank assumes that the consideration received best reflects the fair value. By using the expected cash flow technique (which is not adjusted for the systematic risk) and taking into consideration the interest payable on government bonds and the general credit spread for AA corporate bonds, the bank extracts the required additional adjustment to the discount rate in respect of liquidity and other specific non-performance risks (for more information, see Chapter 12, Section 5).

As of the end of the first quarter, there is no observable change to the bank's relative credit risk, but the credit spread for AA corporate bonds grows, and the yield on government bonds increases. In such a situation, to measure the fair value by using the selected valuation technique, the bank adjusts the original discount rate to reflect the change in the risk spread for AA corporate bonds and also to reflect the change in the yield on government bonds.

As of the end of the second quarter, based on market-corroborated inputs—which are, in turn, based on other structured note issues as well as other qualitative information—the bank determines that there has been a change in the required additional adjustment to the discount rate in respect of liquidity and other specific non-performance risks and changes this component, as applicable (for more information, see Chapter 12, Section 8.6).

This example, which is based on a similar example provided in the Standards (with certain changes), clearly illustrates that even when there is no quoted price or transactions that include a corresponding asset of the measured liability, when measuring fair value, observable inputs and inputs that are corroborated by market inputs that are relevant to the corresponding asset should be relied upon as much as possible.

3.2. Adjustments to the quoted price of the corresponding asset

Using the quoted price of an item held as an asset by another party (instead of using the quoted price for the transfer of the liability or the equity instrument themselves, since such a price is unavailable) may require the reporting entity to make certain adjustments in respect of factors specific to the quoted asset, which—to use the Standards' own words—are not "applicable" to the fair value measurement of the liability or equity instrument of the reporting entity.

In that context, the Standards provide a list of several cases that may indicate the need for adjustments. The wording of the Standards implies that this is a nonexhaustive list:

a. The quoted price for the asset relates to a similar (but not identical) liability or equity instrument held by another party as an asset—for example, when the credit quality of the issuer (the reporting entity) is different from that reflected in the fair value of the similar liability or equity instrument held as an asset. In our view, such a difference may be explained by factors such as the passage of time from the date of the transaction on which the quote relies and the measurement date or a difference between the contractual terms of the similar instrument and those of the instrument under question—for example, series of bonds that have different maturity dates, different financial covenants or collaterals of different quality.

b. The unit of account of the asset is different than that of the liability or equity instrument. As noted above, the unit of account is the level at which the asset or liability is aggregated or disaggregated for recognition purposes (for more information, see Chapter 3, Section 3). For example, in some cases the quoted price for an asset reflects a "combined" price for a package comprising both the amounts due from the issuer and the effect of a third-party credit enhancement, such as a financial guarantee contract provided by the controlling shareholder of the reporting entity in respect of bonds it has issued. If the unit of account for the liability does not include the combined package, the reporting entity should adjust the quoted price of the asset and exclude the impact of the third party's credit enhancement from the asset's quoted price, in order to measure the fair value of the issuer's liability. In other words, the fair value of the liability that was issued with credit enhancements (which are accounted for separately) will take into account only the credit risk of the reporting entity itself. On the other hand, credit enhancements, which form an integral part of the liability (such as collaterals, financial covenants or priority in distribution upon insolvency), will be included in the fair value of the instrument. As to third-party credit enhancements (such as a financial guarantee contract, credit insurance or performance guarantee), the Standards appear to assume that the question of when those credit enhancements form an integral part of the (financial or nonfinancial) liability is answered by IFRS 9 (or by ASC Topic 825). However, this is not necessarily the case, especially under IFRS. ASC 825 defines a liability issued with an inseparable third-party credit enhancement as a liability that is issued with a credit enhancement obtained from a third party, such as debt that is issued with a financial guarantee from a third party that guarantees the issuer's payment obligation. Normally, when a credit event of the reporting entity occurs, the guarantor pays the debt amount to the creditor, but the reporting entity itself is not released from the debt but rather becomes the debtor toward the guarantor. IFRS 9 does not answer the question of when such a guarantee will be accounted for as an integral part of the related liability and when it will be accounted for as a separate asset, nor does IFRS 9 provide guidance on how to carry out the separation. Some claim under IFRS that even when the guarantee and the underlying liability have the same unit of account, the effect of the guarantee should be excluded in order to measure the fair value of the liability. This interpretation may stem from the fact that after an embedded third-party financial guarantee for a liability has been obtained, the reporting entity's financial position remains the same whether it is indebted toward the creditor, the guarantor or both. Hence, the fair value of the liability should remain the same from the reporting entity's perspective. One of the potential approaches that can be employed to make an adjustment in respect of a third-party guarantee is to adjust the discount rate used to discount the liability to the interest rate that would have been obtained without such a guarantee. Thus, for example, the independent credit rating of the reporting entity and the relevant credit rating of the combined liability could be assessed, and the additional interest spread (which corresponds to the rating difference) that would have been paid had the guarantee not been included in the asset could be added to the market yield of the corresponding asset. Another approach is to estimate the difference based on the cost of a corresponding credit insurance with and without the financial guarantee.

Example—Debt Instrument—Using a Quoted Price

On January 1, 2016, Company A issues BBB-rated five-year bonds bearing fixed annual interest rate of 10 percent, with a par value of CU 2 million. The Company designates this instrument as a financial liability at fair value through profit or loss according to the provisions of IFRS 9.

On December 31, 2016, the instrument trades as an asset in an active market at a quoted price of CU 929 per CU 1,000 par value after payment of accrued interest (as mentioned above, the Company is the issuing party and therefore has a liability rather than an asset).

The Company uses the quoted price of the asset in an active market as an input for the purpose of measuring the fair value of its liability. Since the Company issued CU 2 million par value, the total fair value of the obligation is CU 1,858,000 (= 929 / 1,000 × 2,000,000).

At the next stage, the Company is required to evaluate whether or not it should adjust the quoted price of the liability held by another party as an asset. As mentioned above, such adjustment is required when the quoted price of the asset reflects factors that are irrelevant to the liability, such as the impact of credit enhancements.

After assessing whether adjustment is needed, the Company determines that no adjustments are required to the quoted price of the asset. Accordingly, the fair value of the liability will be CU 1,858,000. Furthermore, the Company categorizes and discloses the fair value measurement of its debt instrument within Level 1 of the fair value hierarchy.

3.3. Restrictions placed on the transfer of the corresponding asset

As described above (for more information, see Section 3.2), the Standards provide several examples of situations where an adjustment to the quoted price of the corresponding asset may be required when measuring the fair value of a liability or equity instrument from the perspective of the reporting entity. In addition to those examples, the Standards originally stipulated that a reporting entity should ensure that the price of the asset "does not reflect the effect of a restriction preventing the sale of that asset." It should be noted that the Standards discuss quite extensively restrictions placed on a transfer both by the creditor (for more information, see Chapter 3, Section 2) and by the debtor (for more information, see Section 6) but did not explain the meaning of the additional provision quoted above.

In our view, under IFRS the above provision may be given a relatively broad interpretation or a more limited interpretation, as described below. However, it should be noted that codification improvements issued for US GAAP in July 2018 amended the paragraph to state the opposite: when the asset held by another party includes a characteristic restricting its sale, the fair value of the corresponding liability or equity instrument would also include the effect of the restriction. The explanation to this was that ASC 820's and IFRS 13's original wording, as mentioned above, did not reflect both Boards' discussions.

According to the broader interpretation of IFRS 13, it can be assumed that when the reporting entity issues restricted shares (e.g., shares that were issued in a private offering as part of the consideration paid by the reporting entity in a business combination transaction), or when the reporting entity issues bonds that are not listed for trading, the fair value of the consideration should be measured based on shares that are unrestricted or bonds that are listed for trading, as the case may be. This should be the case even if the restriction is clearly a characteristic of the corresponding asset and is transferred along with this asset. There is no doubt that in economic terms, the buyer will take into account the fact that the consideration includes restricted shares. Thus, in our view, this broad but simplistic approach will inflate the consideration paid in the business combination and as a result will also inflate the goodwill.

Indeed, in our view, the approach described above is not trivial at all. Clearly, when measuring the fair value of the corresponding asset, the level of liquidity or any transfer restrictions that form part of the asset's characteristics should be taken into account (for more information, see Chapter 3, Section 2). Therefore, the above approach results in a difference between the fair value of the corresponding asset and the fair value of the issued liability or equity instrument, even though their unit of account is identical. The notion of liquidity for liabilities suggests that the more illiquid liabilities are from the debtor's perspective (i.e., the more expectable the date and amount of future settlement), the greater the ability of the debtor to hold and manage illiquid investments in order to cover such liabilities as they become due. Since illiquid assets supposedly provide more return than liquid assets, illiquid liabilities that allow for more flexibility in investments should theoretically be valued at lesser amounts than more liquid liabilities (i.e., liabilities that carry more risk of early or unknown prepayment, such as on-demand bank balances or bonds with tight financial covenants). In other words, it may well be that while from the creditor's perspective two similar assets may have different levels of liquidity and hence different fair values (such as two series of bonds with significantly different trading volumes), these assets may actually correspond to liabilities with an identical liquidity profile for the debtor (same maturity date and financial covenants). Hence, it could be argued that the fair values of the liabilities should be the same even though there is a difference between the fair values of the corresponding assets. A similar argument can be made for issued equity instruments. However, the explanatory notes of IFRS 13 specifically note that illiquidity should not result in a difference between the fair value of liabilities or equity instruments and the fair value of the corresponding assets, and it is worthwhile noting here that a restriction on the transfer of an asset is a specific case of illiquidity. The explanatory notes also state that it is difficult to separate the effect of illiquidity on fair value from the effect of the general credit risk on fair value and that they should both be taken into consideration when measuring the fair value of the liability or equity instrument. Therefore, in our view, the approach described below will be more reasonable under IFRS, which means that illiquidity of equity instruments and liabilities is measured and treated from the perspective of the corresponding asset rather than from that of the reporting entity.

For the sake of argument, let us assume that the reporting entity has issued two series of bonds with identical characteristics, except for the fact that one series is listed for trading and is traded in an active market, whereas the other series is a private series with lower trading volumes. At least theoretically, there may be a price difference between the two series, since the first series has a higher level of liquidity from the perspective of the holder. In such a situation, in our view, the Standards will recognize that the fair value of the liabilities from the perspective of the reporting (issuing) entity will also be different because of the liquidity characteristic, particularly since there may be observable market inputs (such as prices of transactions involving the corresponding asset) to support this conclusion. Therefore, with respect to the above approach, the question is why the reporting entity should adjust the price of restricted instruments in order to exclude the effect of the restriction, but it is not required to carry out a theoretical adjustment to the quoted price of the second series in order to reflect its value under an assumption that it was listed for trading. Clearly, how to make such an adjustment requires reporting entities to exercise judgment, particularly in situations where the reporting entity does not have any tradable liabilities.

Under our approach, the effect of the restriction should be excluded from the price of the corresponding asset, only if the said restriction is not a characteristic of the asset itself (e.g., the restriction is not transferred with the asset) but did affect its price. With no clear guidance, in our view, this approach will be more consistent with the other provisions of the Standards. This means that according to this approach, if the reporting entity issues restricted shares, and the restriction is a characteristic of the shares, this matter will actually be taken into consideration not only when measuring the fair value of the shares from the perspective of those who invest in the shares but also when measuring their fair value from the perspective of the reporting entity. This conclusion is further reinforced by the recent amendments to ASC 820, as mentioned above.

4. The Measured Item Is Not Held by Other Parties as Assets

When the liability or equity instrument of the reporting entity, which are measured at fair value, is not held by another party as an asset (and there is no quoted price for the transfer of such liabilities), the Standards leave the reporting entity only with one alternative: using valuation techniques. In this case as well, the fact that the reporting entity may be unable to transfer the liability or the equity instrument to another party does not impact the objective of the measurement, and in such a situation, fair value should be measured based on a hypothetical transaction to transfer the liability or equity instrument.

It should be noted that both the Standards and professional literature give very few examples of situations where liabilities are not held by other parties as assets. Thus, the only practical example mentioned by the Standards is the one referring to decommissioning and restoration liabilities. Under IFRS, these are within the scope of IFRIC 1 and are measured at fair value in a business combination. It is possible that other relevant examples include provisions in respect of a restructuring. Taking into consideration the definition of financial liabilities, it is likely that this group of items will not include such liabilities. Furthermore, the Standards do not provide any illustrations of a situation where the reporting entity's equity instruments are not held by other parties as assets.

It should be noted that, unlike in the case of using valuation techniques where there is a party that holds the corresponding asset, in this case, the Standards instruct the reporting entity to use valuation techniques from the perspective of a market participant who owes the liability or has issued the equity instrument. As mentioned above, in the first situation, the valuation techniques were used from the perspective of a market participant who holds the corresponding asset.

Thus, for example, when applying a present value technique, a reporting entity might use either of the following:

a. The future cash outflows that a market participant would expect to incur in settling the obligation, including the compensation that a market participant would require for taking on the obligation. Such a compensation is required due to the fact that the market participant has undertaken the required activity (such as the decommissioning or restoration) by using its own resources, which it could have used for other activities. Furthermore, the compensation should include a component in respect of the risk associated with the liability, that is, a risk premium that reflects the risk that the actual cash outflows might differ from the expected cash outflows; or
b. The amount that a market participant would receive to enter into or issue an identical liability or equity instrument, using the assumptions that market participants would use when pricing the identical item (e.g., having the same credit characteristics) in the principal (or most advantageous) market for issuing a liability or an equity instrument with the same expected terms.

It is reasonable to assume that liabilities that are not held by other parties as assets will be unique, and therefore, it will be difficult to apply valuation techniques that aim to assess the amount that a market participant would receive to issue an identical liability or equity instrument. It, therefore, appears that of the two methods mentioned above, the more common valuation method will be the first one.

When applying this method, the various components of return and risk may be indistinguishable from one another in view of the fact that nonfinancial liabilities do not contain a contractual rate of return, and there is no observable market yield for them. In some cases, if the reporting entity can estimate the price a third-party contractor would charge on a fixed fee basis (i.e., the contractor bears the risks), this price reflects both the costs of fulfilling the obligation and the compensation required in respect of the uncertainty component. In other cases, for example, when the reporting entity can only use in its estimation the price a third-party contractor would charge on a cost-plus basis, it is required to add to the expected profit of the contractor, the compensation in respect of the remaining risk arising from the variability of the cost estimates. Adding this compensation involves the exercise of judgment, especially when the liabilities in question are settled after a significant period of time, which may increase the amount of the compensation payable due to the uncertainty component. In our view, one of the possible ways to estimate the compensation is to estimate the difference between quotes for jobs of similar scope and nature issued by contractors working on a cost-plus basis versus quotes issued by contractors working on a fixed fee basis.

It should be noted that, due to factors such as risk aversion and the wish to avoid losses, the impact of uncertainty on assets will sometimes be different than its impact on liabilities. Where assets are concerned, uncertainty normally impairs the fair value of the assets compared to the value that would have been received from discounting the expected cash flows by a risk-free discount rate (usually, excluding products such as insurance and lottery cards and excluding diversifiable uncertainty). In other words, market participants would have rather received a cash flow that is slightly lower than the expected cash flows of the asset, provided that they would have the certainty that they will, indeed, receive such cash flow.

Where liabilities are concerned, and especially if the liabilities embody scenarios of significant losses or risks, risk aversion may lead to an increase in the fair value of the liability due to uncertainty. This means that market participants would be willing to pay a cash flow that is slightly higher than the expected cash flows of the liability, provided they have certainty regarding this cash flow. This is usually true for a party assuming a transferred liability as well.

A reporting entity is required to ensure that it does not double-count or omit adjustments for risk. For example, if the estimated cash flows are increased to take into account the compensation for assuming the risk associated with the obligation, the discount rate should not be adjusted again to reflect that risk.

It should be noted that when measuring the fair value, the aforesaid reference may cause a difference between, on the one hand, liabilities or equity instruments held by other parties as assets, in respect of which uncertainty generally reduces the fair value of the assets and therefore also reduces the fair value of the reporting entity's equity instrument or liability, and, on the other hand, liabilities and equity instruments that are not held by other parties as assets. As to the latter, uncertainty generally increases their fair value. This issue also increases the importance of distinguishing between types of liabilities and equity instruments. Thus, for example, the question arises of whether liabilities in respect of legal claims are considered liabilities held by other parties as assets. After all, the impact of the uncertainty inherent in such liabilities, that is, whether to increase or decrease the fair value of the liability due to such expected uncertainty, depends, among other things, on the said question of classification.

Example—Measurement of Fair Value of a Decommissioning and Restoration Liability

On January 1, 2016, Company A assumes a decommissioning and restoration liability as part of a business combination. The Company is legally required to dismantle an offshore oil platform at the end of its useful life, which is estimated to be 10 years. The Company uses the present value technique to measure the fair value of the obligation. The Company concludes that had it been contractually allowed to transfer the obligation to a market participant at the measurement date, the market participant would have taken into consideration the following inputs, probability-weighted as appropriate, when estimating the transaction price it would expect to receive:

a. Labor costs: Labor cost estimates depend on current marketplace wages for employees relevant to fulfill the obligation, adjusted for expectations of future wage increases until the work has been completed (which are uncertain). Set forth below are the scenarios that were estimated by the Company on the basis of its experience with fulfilling obligations of this type and its knowledge of the relevant market (in real terms):

Scenario	**Probability (%)**	**Cash flow estimate in real terms (in CU)**
Low	25	100,000
Medium	50	125,000
High	25	175,000

Thus, the expected cash flow (in real terms) in respect of labor costs is CU 131,250 (= 25% × 175,000 + 50% × 125,000 + 25% × 100,000).

b. Overheads and equipment costs: The Company estimates those costs at 80 percent of labor costs (for each scenario). This is consistent with the cost structure of market participants.

c. Compensation that includes a profit margin in respect of labor and overheads, which the Company estimates at 20 percent, according to the profit that contractors in the market generally earn to dismantle offshore oil platforms. Further compensation is required in respect of the risk that the actual cash flows will differ from the expected cash flows; this compensation is estimated at 5 percent of the whole amount, including the profit margin normally earned as above, noting that the 20 percent margin refers to situations in which work is carried out immediately rather than many years after the measurement date.
d. The expected inflation, which is estimated by the Company at 4 percent per year on the basis of available market information (such as inflationary expectations, which are embodied in bond prices). It is assumed that the Company expects the payroll costs to increase at the general rate of inflation.
e. The time value of money, represented by the risk-free (unlinked) interest rate for a period of 10 years. This cost amounts to 5 percent per year.
f. Non-performance risk, including credit risk, assuming that the market participant will have a non-performance risk that is identical to that of the Company (for more information, see Section 5). The Company adjusts the risk-free interest by 3.5 percent in respect of the non-performance risk, including the credit risk.
g. According to the provisions of the Standards (for more information, see Section 6), the Company concludes that it is not required to adjust the fair value for the existence of a restriction preventing it from transferring the obligation.

Following is the calculation of the fair value of the obligation as of January 1, 2016, subject to the assumptions listed above:

	In CU	**Further details**
Expected labor costs	131,250	In real terms
Overhead and equipment costs	105,000	= 0.8 × 131,250
Profit margin	47,250	= (105,000 + 131,250) × 0.2
Subtotal	283,500	
Additional risk premium	14,175	= 0.05 × 283,500
Total in real terms	297,675	
Total in future value terms	440,631	= 297,675 × 1.04 ^ 10
Total, fair value at the measurement date (present value)	194,884	= 440,631 / 1.085 ^ 10

5. Non-Performance Risk

5.1. Overview

In order to unify the mixed accounting treatment that was previously applied to this issue, the Standards stipulate explicitly that the fair value measurement of a liability (regardless of whether it is financial or nonfinancial) should reflect the effect of non-performance risk (of the reporting entity itself). Non-performance risk is defined in the Standards as the risk that the reporting entity will not fulfil an obligation. It includes, but may not be limited to, a reporting entity's own credit risk. Under IFRS, credit risk is defined in IFRS 7—*Financial Instruments: Disclosures*, as the risk that one party to a financial instrument will cause a financial loss for the other party by failing to discharge an obligation.

The impact of non-performance risk on the fair value of a liability may vary in accordance with the nature of the liability, that is, a financial liability or a nonfinancial liability, such as an obligation to deliver goods or services, and in accordance with credit enhancements related to the liability, if any (for more information, see Section 3.2).

The higher the non-performance risk of the reporting entity, the lower the fair value of its liabilities. When the liabilities in question are financial, generally the main (and in practical terms, sometimes the only) non-performance risk that is taken into consideration is the credit risk. Nevertheless, in our view, in some cases there may also be operational risks associated with the payment, clearing or transfer of the amounts. Thus, when the credit quality of the reporting entity itself deteriorates—for instance, when the reporting entity has liquidity difficulties and, as a result, its credit rating is lowered—there will be a corresponding decrease in the fair value of its financial liabilities (such as bonds it had issued). In order to prevent (or reduce) the occurrence of nonintuitive situations, in which a reporting entity recognizes profits when its non-performance risk (usually its credit risk) increases, and vice versa, IFRS 9 stipulates that in the case of financial liabilities designated as at fair value through profit or loss, the effect of changes in fair value attributed to the credit risk of the liability will be presented in other comprehensive income.

Although the reporting entity is not released from the obligation as a result of the deterioration of its position and the increase of its non-performance risk, the conclusion that the fair value of the liabilities decreases in such a situation is consistent with the concept of the corresponding asset, whose fair value also decreases accordingly. For example, it is reasonable to assume that the quoted price of bonds in the stock exchange will decrease when the issuer's credit risk increases. Indeed, the result whereby the fair value of the liabilities decreases along with the increase of the non-performance risk is also relevant to the fair value of nonfinancial liabilities, such as liabilities for decommissioning and restoration of a site (for more information, see Section 4) or liabilities in respect of legal claims. In our view, in the case of nonfinancial liabilities, non-performance risk may also be reflected by full or partial failure to transfer the consideration—for example, when delivering (physical) goods at a quantity that is lower than the contractual quantity, at a quality that does not correspond to the specification or after the contractual supply date. Therefore, the principle set in the Standards, whereby sometimes a reporting entity will need to exclude the effect of third-party credit enhancements, will apply here as well (for more information, see Section 3.2). Credit enhancements whose impact may be relevant in this context may also include third-party performance guarantees provided to the customers of the reporting entity.

5.2. The underlying assumption—the non-performance risk is identical before and after the transfer

Bear in mind that the Standards adopt the conceptual approach whereby the measured liability is transferred between market participants on the date of fair value measurement. With regard to the non-performance risk, the underlying assumption is that it will remain the same before and after the notional transfer. This is also the reason why the non-performance risk of the reporting entity itself is taken into consideration when measuring the fair value of a liability. This assumption has been the subject of controversy in the past, but the explanatory notes of IFRS 13 explain that, although it is unlikely that this assumption will be fulfilled in a particular transaction—since it is unreasonable that the credit rating of the transferor reporting entity and of the market participant assuming the liability will be identical—there are several arguments that tip the scale in favor of the assumption:

a. A market participant who enters into a transaction for the transfer of a liability, changing the non-performance risk of the liability during the transfer, will expect this change to be reflected in the transaction price. In other words, the lender will not allow the borrower to transfer the liability to a borrower with a lower credit quality without demanding further compensation or change of terms (such as an increase in the interest rate). Similarly, the borrower will find it difficult to transfer the liability to another borrower with a higher credit quality without further compensation or change in terms (such as a decrease in the interest rate).
b. Fair value measurement aims to obtain uniformity. Without making this assumption as to the credit strength of the entity that assumes the liability, different reporting entities will have different assumptions as to the credit

standing of the party that assumes the liability, which will lead to non-uniform measurement of liabilities.

c. Taking the non-performance risk of the reporting entity into account is consistent with the manner in which the holders of the corresponding asset will take the said risk into consideration. This means that if the non-performance risk was not taken into account, there would be a difference between the fair value of the liability and the fair value of the corresponding asset.

5.3. Practical considerations in adjusting fair value in respect of a reporting entity's own non-performance risk

Generally, the Standards do not discuss the different practical implications of adjustments to the fair value of liabilities in respect of the reporting entity's own non-performance risk. In certain situations, such as when there is a quoted price for the corresponding asset, this quoted price embodies the non-performance risk of the liability, and therefore, no adjustments are required.

When a quoted price is unavailable for the corresponding asset, the technique and the model being used to determine the fair value of the liability should be analyzed in order to determine whether or not further adjustments are required in respect of the reporting entity's own non-performance risk (and particularly, the credit risk). Thus, for example, if the liabilities in question are simple and "unilateral" liabilities, such as assumed loans, whose fair value is estimated using a present value technique, a reporting entity will have to verify that the discount rate includes the appropriate credit spread of the reporting entity or, alternatively, that the cash flow used in the measurement was adjusted to reflect the certainty equivalent, that is, the cash flow was calculated net of the expected credit losses and includes an additional decrease in respect of uncertainty (for more information, see Chapter 12, Section 3.4).

When the items in question are more complex, such as derivative financial liabilities, or even financial instruments, which may, over different periods of their contractual life, become assets or liabilities and then revert into their original status, such as an interest-rate swap (IRS), whose fair value depends on factors such as the prevailing market interest rate, the reporting entity will need to exercise judgment in order to determine the type of adjustment needed in respect of the reporting entity's own credit risk. Common option pricing models, such as the Black-Scholes model or the binomial model, usually do not take into consideration the credit risk of the option writer. In other words, the option's price according to the model is calculated under the assumption that, in case it expires in the money, the counterparty will fulfil their part of the contract if the option is exercised. Therefore, when such a model is used to measure the fair value of an option written by the reporting entity, the price determined according to the model should be adjusted (i.e., reduced) in respect of the reporting entity's own credit risk. The adjustment can sometimes be carried out within the model itself, such as by calculating the binomial tree differently. This reduction in value is sometimes called the Debit Valuation Adjustment (DVA); its execution depends largely on the type of item, on the model and on questions such as whether or not there are various correlations between the probability of default of the reporting entity and the factors that determine the intrinsic value of the instrument for each scenario. It may be said that the holder of the corresponding asset is also required to make a corresponding adjustment, if and when this holder uses a basic pricing model that does not take into account the credit risk of the reporting entity to measure the instrument's fair value. The adjustment to the model-derived price of the corresponding asset is sometimes called Credit Valuation Adjustment (CVA). In practice, it can be said that there is a symmetry between the DVA from the perspective of the reporting entity and the CVA from the perspective of the counterparty.

When the items in question are "bilateral derivatives" (e.g., a forward contract), a reporting entity needs to take into consideration the effect of both the credit risk of the reporting entity and the counterparty's credit risk in order to determine the fair value of the instrument. Thus, the DVA will take into account (e.g., by using a stochastic simulation or a tree) the effect of the reporting entity's credit risk in those scenarios where the derivatives are in a liability position (negative cash flows). In other words, the purpose of the calculation of DVA is to estimate the extent (on a probability-weighted basis) to which the cash flows generated by the counterparty from the derivative be impaired, as a result of the probability that the reporting entity will be unable to fully meet its obligations. On the other hand, the CVA will take into account the effect of the counterparty's credit risk, which will be reflected in the scenarios in which the derivative is projected to be in an asset position (positive cash flows) from the perspective of the reporting entity. It may be said that such adjustments take into account factors such as the potential credit exposure at the insolvency point, the probability of insolvency and the expected rate of loss in case of insolvency.

By nature, the non-performance risk of the financial liability may be impacted by other specific characteristics of the liability, such as the existence of credit enhancements that are not provided by third parties—for instance, collaterals or liens placed on the reporting entity's assets by virtue of the instrument, priority given to holders of the instrument over other liabilities of the reporting entity on insolvency, or the existence of financial covenants. In such a situation, the fair value of the liability will be affected not only by the general non-performance risk of the reporting entity but also by those additional credit enhancements.

Another practical issue relating to the non-performance risk is the issue of the effect of netting agreements, such as a master netting agreement, on the measurement of the risk and its impact on the fair value of the liability. Generally speaking, netting agreements determine that, in the event of default of one of the parties to the agreement, all open positions between the parties are netted into a single net position. In some jurisdictions, the law itself stipulates that netting will take place on default. To illustrate this point, let us assume that the reporting entity and one of its customers have a netting agreement in place. Let us also assume that the customer is also a creditor of the reporting entity and holds loans granted to the reporting entity. According to the provisions of the netting agreement, in the event of default by the reporting entity or the customer, all mutual balances will be automatically netted. Thus, for example, if the amount of the loans when the default of the reporting entity occurs is CU 1 million, and the trade receivable balance as of that date is CU 1.5 million, the customer will not absorb a loss in respect of the loan, since its amount will be automatically netted against the trade receivable balance (which will be CU 0.5 million after netting). Thus, the customer will not find itself in a position where it will have to pay the full amount of the trade receivable balance to the reporting entity, the liquidators or creditors of the reporting entity and at the same time absorb a loss in respect of the loan amount owed to it by the reporting entity. Such netting agreements can, therefore, reduce the credit risk (and the non-performance risk), from the perspective of both the reporting entity and the other parties. Indeed, this begs the question whether or not a netting agreement should be taken into account when measuring the impact of a reporting entity's non-performance risk. As a rule, a netting agreement, which is separate from the instrument to which it relates (such as a master netting agreement), is not a characteristic of the measured item but rather of the reporting entity; therefore, its effect will not be reflected in the measurement of the non-performance risk of the financial liability or asset. Notwithstanding the aforesaid, one potential way by which the impact of netting agreements on the fair value of the instruments to which they apply can be taken into consideration is to apply the exception set by the Standards regarding financial assets and financial liabilities with netting positions (for more information, see Chapter 11).

6. Restriction on the Transfer of a Liability or Equity Instrument

When a reporting entity measures the fair value of a liability or equity instrument, it shall not include a separate input (or an adjustment to other inputs) for restrictions that prevent the transfer of a liability or an equity instrument of the reporting entity to a market participant. It should be noted that this provision dates back to an amendment of ASC 820 issued in 2009 that dealt with the fair value measurement of liabilities. One of the reasons mentioned in the explanatory notes of the aforementioned amendment was that it was not clear how to measure the fair value in a hypothetical transaction when a restriction prevents such a transfer.

According to IFRS 13's explanatory notes, the reasoning behind this is that the effect of the restriction is taken into account when determining the price of the transaction by the parties to it either explicitly or implicitly in other fair value measurement inputs. For example, at the transaction date, both the lender and the borrower accept the transaction price for the liability with full knowledge that the obligation includes a restriction that prevents its transfer. Consequently, the transaction price already reflects the effect of the restriction. This applies both to the measurement at initial recognition and to subsequent measurements, since the assumption is that the parties are aware of the restriction and take it into account in the transaction price, and therefore, no additional adjustments are needed after the initial recognition date.

Practically speaking, almost all liabilities and equity instruments will include a condition that prohibits their transfer to another party, since such a transfer may adversely affect the credit risk of the corresponding asset and cause uncertainty from the perspective of the holder. Indeed, according to the IFRS 13's explanatory notes, if the reporting entity is aware of the fact that the restriction on the transfer of the liability is not reflected in the inputs used for fair value measurement, adjustments should be made to reflect that restriction. In our view, such circumstances will be quite rare. Below is an example of a situation where such an adjustment may be in order.

Example—Restriction on the Transfer of a Liability

Bank A issues two series of private bonds with similar characteristics except as detailed below. With regard to the first series, the bank may unconditionally transfer the obligation to repay the bonds to another bank (by virtue of the contractual terms), without making any changes to the interest rates or repayment dates, and provided that the credit rating of the other bank will not be lower than A. With regard to the second series, Bank A has no such transfer option. After a certain period, the credit rating of Bank A increases to AAA, whereas the credit rating of the other bank remains unchanged (A). It is reasonable to assume that the fact that Bank A can transfer the liability in respect of the first series to another bank with a lower credit rating will increase the level of market yields on that series (and reduce its market price) compared with the second. In such a situation, the use of quoted market prices for each series (the so-called corresponding assets) would have incorporated the option of transfer or nontransfer of each series into their price, and therefore, no adjustment should be made to such a quoted price when measuring the fair value of the liabilities. However, from a theoretical point of view and with no available transactions involving the second series of bonds or other available inputs, if the bank were to choose to use the quoted price of the first series as an input for fair value measurement of the second series, in our view, it would have to be adjusted in order to reflect the said transfer restriction, hence increasing the relative fair value of the second series compared with the first one.

7. Financial Liability with a Demand Feature (IFRS Only)

7.1. Overview

A demand feature of a financial liability is a feature that confers upon the counterparty the right to demand the unconditional settlement of the financial liability prior to the agreed-upon settlement date. The demand feature may require immediate settlement (i.e., the counterparty can demand the repayment of the liability at any given time); it may be conferred at certain points in time (e.g., on optional settlement dates) or may be conditional upon the occurrence of an event (such as a breach of financial covenants).

According to IFRS 13 (but not ASC 820; for more information, see Chapter 1, Section 4), the fair value of a financial liability with a demand feature is not lower than the amount payable on demand, discounted from the first date on which the payment of the amount could be demanded. In other words, under certain circumstances the fair value may, indeed, be higher but not lower; an example of where the fair value would typically be higher than the current settlement value is when the interest accrued on a liability is higher than the market interest rate for a similar liability, and therefore, it is not worthwhile from the perspective of the holder to demand early withdrawal of their balance.

The so-called minimal fair value restriction (or "deposit floor") set in IFRS 13 is particularly relevant to the accounting treatment (from the perspective of banks) applied to current accounts, deposits or savings plans at initial recognition under IFRS.

Furthermore, the question arises whether or not this provision also applies to security deposits received by the reporting entity from customers in exchange for physical items (such as gas containers), and those deposits are refundable when the engagement is discontinued. In our view, the aforesaid restriction will apply only when the liability is a financial one, which happens when the asset, which is given to the customer in exchange for the security deposit, is not derecognized from the reporting entity's financial statements. When such an asset is derecognized, the refund of the deposit in exchange for returning the asset is a transaction for the exchange of cash for a nonfinancial consideration (the container), and therefore, the liability is not a financial one. For instance, assisted living companies sometimes receive deposits from tenants when they enter the assisted living housing facility. When the tenant leaves, the deposit is refunded (net of a certain contractual discount) to them or (God forbid) to their heirs. As a rule, the receipt of the deposits is not followed by the derecognition of the units that are used by the tenants from the companies' statements of financial position. Therefore, in our view, and according to the current practice, those liabilities should be considered financial; hence, IFRS 13's minimal fair value restriction should also apply to them, on the date of measuring them at fair value or on the basis of fair value (normally, at initial recognition). This will be the case even though the business model of the assisted living companies is based on an actuary assumption whereby it is not expected that all tenants will actually withdraw the deposits immediately after the reporting date.

When there are several optional demand dates (such as an interest-bearing bank deposit with several optional maturity dates available to the depositor), in our view, the minimal fair value restriction will only apply to the first potential maturity date. In other words, in our view, for the purpose of applying the requirement, the reporting entity will need to calculate the fair value of the liability from the perspective of a market participant that assumes the liability (which will take into account all available options) and thereafter verify that this value is not lower than the minimal value set according to the provisions of IFRS 13.

The minimal fair value restriction in respect of the existence of a demand feature was already included in IAS 39, and before that in IAS 32, and was replicated in IFRS 13. The underlying concept of the restriction is that, in many cases, the price of a transaction between the customer and the entity receiving the deposit already reflects the demand feature. Furthermore, the explanatory notes of IFRS 13 clarify that recognizing a financial liability at less than the demand amount may create an immediate and "inappropriate" gain at initial recognition due to the difference between the deposit received and the liability. It should be noted that IFRS 9 restricts anyway the number of cases where immediate gain arises at the recognition date.

As described above, the restriction applies only to financial liabilities. Normally, financial liabilities are measured at fair value (or at fair value less transaction costs) only at initial recognition. Therefore, this restriction is particularly important at initial recognition and may sometimes impact the effective interest rate set for an instrument (causing it, for example, to be zero). Thus, even if past experience indicates that there is a considerable probability that the depositor is not expected to immediately exercise their demand right, this right will still be taken into account when determining the fair value of the liability for purposes of the minimal fair value restriction. Another case where the restriction may be relevant is when a reporting entity measures the fair value of financial liabilities as part of a purchase price allocation in a business combination.

For a discussion regarding potential exceptions in connection with the restriction under IFRS, see Section 7.2.

Example—Financial Liability with a Demand Feature (IFRS Only)

On January 1, 2017, a customer deposits a lump sum of CU 10,000 in a savings plan with Bank A. According to the terms of the plan, the customer has several opportunities to withdraw the funds from the plan, as described below:

Withdrawal date	Withdrawal amount (in CU)	Annual interest calculated from the deposit date (%)
December 31, 2017	10,400	4
December 31, 2018	11,025	5
December 31, 2019 (expiry date, unless the amount has already been withdrawn)	11,910	6

It shall be assumed that the instrument was classified by the Bank into the amortized cost group. On the date of deposit and initial recognition of the liability, the terms of the savings plan reflect market conditions, and therefore, it was determined that the fair value of the deposit as of that date is CU 10,000. Given the stepped interest mechanism and the forward interest rate prevailing in the market, the Bank assumed, in order to calculate the effective interest rate, that the amount will be withdrawn on December 31, 2019, and therefore, an effective interest rate of 6 percent was set for the instrument.

On December 31, 2017, before the customer decides whether to withdraw on that date, Bank B obtains control over Bank A in a business combination. As part of the purchase price allocation, it needs to measure the fair value of the said financial liability. For the sake of this example, let us assume that the relevant interest rate in the market for one-year deposits is 7 percent, and the relevant forward interest rate for the year 2019 is 9 percent (in annual terms).

Therefore, under an early withdrawal assumption and under the assumption that early withdrawal will not take place, the fair value at different dates will be as follows (in CU):

Under the assumption of withdrawal at the end of 2017:	10,400
Under the assumption of withdrawal at the end of 2018:	10,304 = 11,025 / 1.07
Under the assumption of withdrawal at the end of 2019:	10,212= 11,910 / 1.07 / 1.09

In this case, in view of the minimal fair value restriction and with no other considerations or inputs, the fair value will amount to CU 10,400. It should be noted that this fair value would not have changed even if past experience would have indicated that there is significant probability that the customer will withdraw the deposit only at the end of 2018 or at the end of 2019.

On the other hand, if, for the sake of the example, the assumption is that the relevant interest rate in the market for one-year deposits is 5 percent, and the relevant forward interest rate for the year 2019 is 9 percent (in annual terms), the fair value under an early withdrawal assumption and under the assumption that early withdrawal will not take place at different dates will be as follows (in CU):

Under the assumption of withdrawal at the end of 2017:	10,400
Under the assumption of withdrawal at the end of 2018:	10,500 = 11,025 / 1.05
Under the assumption of withdrawal at the end of 2019:	10,406 = 11,910 / 1.05 / 1.09

In this scenario, the amount to be withdrawn, discounted from the earliest withdrawal date, is CU 10,400. However, it can be seen that the fair value will be higher, since the economic incentive of the counterparty is not to withdraw the funds at the end of 2017. In this situation, the minimal fair value restriction will be ineffective since the normal economic scenario provides a higher value.

It should be noted that there may be a difference between the fair value of such liabilities and their amortized cost in Bank A's books. As a rule, financial instruments measured at amortized cost are not subject to the aforesaid minimal fair value restriction at subsequent measurement dates. Furthermore, when estimating the cash flows generated by those financial instruments, it is, indeed, required to take into consideration (probability-wise or according to the most likely scenario) the expected cash flows (including for purposes of early repayment), but the effective interest rate remains at its original level.

7.2. Potential exceptions in connection with the minimal fair value restriction under IFRS

One of the most significant difficulties arising from the minimal fair value restriction when measuring financial liabilities with a demand feature (for more information, see Section 7.1) is the fact that this restriction ignores the non-performance risk (and in particular, the credit risk) of the reporting entity when the potential demand is immediate and the discount period is zero.

Thus, for example, let us assume that a reporting entity is required to measure the fair value—as of a certain date—of bonds it previously issued and which were designated as at fair value through profit or loss. As of the measurement date, the bonds' par value plus interest accrued amounts to CU 100,000. As of the said date, the reporting entity is in financial difficulties and in breach of the financial covenants set for the bonds. This gives the bond holders the right to demand the immediate repayment of the bonds at par value. The bonds are actively traded on a stock exchange at a quoted price of CU 45,000 for the entire series, which reflects a debt settlement arrangement that includes a projected "haircut" of 55 percent compared to the par value.

In this case, applying the minimal fair value restriction and measuring the fair value of the bonds at CU 100,000 may lead to an absurd situation, due to, among other things, the discrepancy between the fair value and the Level 1 quoted price of the corresponding asset, that is, the quoted price of the bonds on the stock exchange. Applying the minimal fair value requirement may also create difficulties in connection with the manner of applying the requirement to present in other comprehensive income the effect of the own credit risk of financial liabilities designated as at fair value through profit or loss. Furthermore, in this case, the rationale behind the restriction, that is, to prevent reporting entities from recognizing inappropriate gains at initial recognition, does not necessarily apply.

It should be noted that, according to IFRIC 19—*Extinguishing Financial Liabilities with Equity Instruments*, if the fair value of the equity instruments issued in such a transaction cannot be reliably measured, then the equity instruments will be measured based on the fair value of the financial liability being extinguished. According to IFRIC 19, the minimum restriction should not be applied in measuring the fair value of an extinguished financial liability that includes a demand feature. The explanatory notes to IFRIC 19 explain the said exception by the fact that in case of an arrangement entered into while breaching the terms of a financial liability, such that it can immediately be made payable, the demand feature is no longer substantive. Therefore, it may be possible to apply a similar rationale to similar situations in which the demand feature is clearly no longer substantive, such as in the case of the bonds referred to above.

Another interesting exception to the minimal fair value restriction is included in the transition provisions of IFRS 17—*Insurance Contracts.* Generally speaking, IFRS 17 allows under some circumstances for a fair value-based transition method, where insurance contracts are measured at their fair values as at the transition date. While IFRS 17 refers to IFRS 13 for fair value measurement, it explicitly excludes IFRS 13's deposit floor restriction, that is, insurance liabilities may actually have a lower fair value than their policyholder's current withdrawal amount. IFRS 17's explanatory notes state that utilizing deposit floors for fair value measurement of insurance contracts would contradict the principle that an entity should incorporate in the measurement of an insurance contract the future cash flows on a probability-weighted basis.

Chapter 11

APPLICATION TO FINANCIAL INSTRUMENTS WITH NETTING POSITIONS

1. Overview

Sometimes, financial institutions and other similar reporting entities manage a group of financial assets and financial liabilities (a portfolio) on the basis of the net exposure to market risks or to credit risk (of a particular counterparty). This means a portfolio that includes financial assets and financial liabilities with risks that offset one another, which is done intentionally (rather than arbitrarily or incidentally).

As a rule, fair value is measured at the level of the relevant unit of account. Normally the unit of account of financial instruments is an individual instrument (for more details, see Chapter 3, Section 3). The offset (netting) of mutual exposures within the portfolio (e.g., offsetting a mutual credit risk) is an entity-specific characteristic rather than a separate characteristic of each of the portfolio's instruments. Therefore, it cannot be taken into account in the measurement of fair value in an ordinary situation. This means that if a portfolio has a shared characteristic that causes a certain risk to be mitigated or diversified, such as a master netting agreement (for more information, see Chapter 10, Section 5.3), this characteristic will generally not be taken into consideration in a fair value measurement of its components. Furthermore, even if from the perspective of a market participant it made sense to transfer the financial assets along with the financial liabilities, the Standards reject the joint valuation premise when it comes to financial instruments (for more information, see Chapter 9, Section 3), and therefore, such an assumption should not be made.

In other words, according to the ordinary principles established by the Standards, each of the exposures within the portfolio should be estimated separately (on a gross basis). Indeed, this accounting treatment may be different from the reporting entity's internal risk management and may even require the reporting entity to maintain a dual system: one for risk management purposes (based on net exposures) and another to estimate the risk for financial statement purposes.

As a result, the Standards include an exception to the measurement principles, whereby a reporting entity that holds a group of financial assets and financial liabilities and that is exposed to market risks and to the credit risk of counterparties may measure the fair value of the group on the basis of the price that would be received to sell a net long position (an asset) for a particular risk exposure or paid to transfer a net short position (a liability) for a particular risk exposure in an orderly transaction between market participants at the measurement date under current market conditions. It should be noted that this exception is not mandatory and that the reporting entity is entitled to choose not to apply it. In our view, in essence, this exception extends the unit of account from the individual financial instrument level to the level of exposure to net risk with respect to its fair value measurement. Therefore, some believe that when measuring the fair value of a net position, reporting entities should also take into consideration other characteristics of the position (in addition to its offsetting of credit risk or market risk), such as the extent of the position (in terms of liquidity or nontradability), even if in practice, the position comprises several separate and highly liquid financial instruments.

Nevertheless, it should be noted that even when the exception is applied, the unit of account is still separate for other purposes (other than fair value management), and therefore, the adjustment arising from taking the portfolio's characteristics into account should be allocated to the individual assets and liabilities that make up the portfolio (for more information, see Section 7).

2. Relevant Definitions

As described above, the exception is relevant to exposures to market risks and counterparties' credit risks. Set forth below are several definitions that are relevant for that purpose, as defined in International Financial Reporting Standard (IFRS) 7:

a. Market risk—the risk that the fair value or future cash flows of a financial instrument will fluctuate because of changes in market prices. Market risk comprises three types of risk: currency risk, interest rate risk and other price risk (a similar definition is included in the US Generally Accepted Accounting Principles (US GAAP) Master Glossary).
b. Currency risk—the risk that the fair value or future cash flows of a financial instrument will fluctuate because of changes in foreign exchange rates (a similar definition is included in the US GAAP Master Glossary).

c. Interest rate risk—the risk that the fair value or future cash flows of a financial instrument will fluctuate because of changes in market interest rates (under the US GAAP Master Glossary, this risk is currently defined as the risk of changes in a hedged item's fair value or cash flows attributable to changes in the designated benchmark interest rate).
d. Other price risk—the risk that the fair value or future cash flows of a financial instrument will fluctuate because of changes in market prices (other than those arising from interest rate risk or currency risk), whether those changes are caused by factors specific to the individual financial instrument or its issuer or by factors affecting all similar financial instruments traded in the market (e.g., a price risk of a share or a price of a commodity) (a similar definition is included in the US GAAP Master Glossary).
e. Credit risk—the risk that one party to a financial instrument will cause a financial loss for the other party by failing to meet an obligation. For more information, see Chapter 10, Section 5.3.

In addition to the said definitions, the Standards use the term "net long position," which describes a situation where the reporting entity has more long positions than short positions within the relevant portfolio, that is, the reporting entity will generate a profit from an increase in the value in relation to a particular market risk or credit risk. Similarly, the term "net short position" describes a situation where the reporting entity has more short positions than long positions (net), that is, the reporting entity will generate a profit from a decrease in the value of those instruments in relation to a particular market risk or credit risk.

3. Scope of the Exception

As noted above, the application of the exception is not mandatory. The exception not only applies to financial assets and financial liabilities but may also be applied to other contracts treated as if they were financial instruments. In this respect, "other contracts" may include, for instance, derivatives that are embedded in nonfinancial contracts and that were bifurcated from the host contract, as well as contracts for the sale or purchase of nonfinancial items for which the provisions of IFRS 9 are mandatory or such contracts that were voluntarily designated to be measured as derivatives.

Using the exception (subject to meeting the conditions set out below) is defined as making an accounting policy choice. As in the case of the policy regarding the allocation of the overall adjustment to the specific instruments in the portfolio, this policy should be applied consistently for a particular portfolio (but in our view, this is not necessarily the case for other portfolios). A reporting entity need not maintain a static portfolio to use the measurement exception; it may continue applying the accounting policy even if the composition of the portfolio changes over time. Furthermore, the explanatory notes of IFRS 13 clarify that the accounting policy (regarding accounting for the portfolio's exposures on a net basis) may change if the reporting entity's risk exposure preferences change.

According to the Standards, a reporting entity may apply the exception regarding measurement on a net exposure basis only to a portfolio for which all the following conditions are met on a cumulative basis:

a. The existence of a documented risk management or investment strategy—the reporting entity manages the group of financial assets and financial liabilities on the basis of a net exposure to a particular market risk (or risks) or to the credit risk of a particular counterparty, in accordance with a documented risk management or investment strategy. This means that the process is a documented business process that is based on a methodology rather than merely an incidental matter or an arbitrary accounting decision.
b. Reporting to key management personnel—the reporting entity provides information about the portfolio on the basis of the net exposure to its key management personnel. Key management personnel are those persons having authority and responsibility for planning, directing and controlling the activities of the reporting entity, directly or indirectly, including any director (whether executive or otherwise) of that reporting entity.
c. Fair value measurement—the reporting entity is required or has elected to measure those financial assets and financial liabilities at fair value in the statement of financial position at the end of each reporting period. It should be noted that the implication of this condition is that a reporting entity that measures the fair value of financial assets or financial liabilities only for specific cases (e.g., measurement at recognition of fair value of an obligation to a creditor who is also a customer of the reporting entity, when a master netting agreement is in place) shall not apply the exception to the measurement provision.

The explanatory notes of IFRS 13 clarify that there may be situations in which, for the purpose of exposure to a particular net market risk, portfolios will be defined differently than (or partially similar to) portfolios for purposes of exposure to the counterparty's credit risk. Thus, for example, there may be a situation where a particular instrument is included in a portfolio that features a net position to a particular market risk, such as exposure to currency risk. That same instrument may also be included in another portfolio with respect to exposure to net credit risk with a particular counterparty.

4. Qualifying Offsetting in Respect of Market Risk Exposure

As described above, market risks include interest rate risk, currency risk or other price risk (for more information, see Section 2). When applying the exception for a group of financial instruments in respect of a net exposure to a particular market risk of that group, the reporting entity shall select the price within the bid-ask spread that is most representative of the reporting entity's net exposure to those market risks (for more information, see Chapter 12, Section 8.3).

Before offsetting a particular market risk, a reporting entity shall ensure that the market risk (or risks) to which the reporting entity is exposed within that group of financial assets and financial liabilities is substantially the same. This means that reporting entities shall not combine and offset different market risks that do not mitigate their exposure. For example, a reporting entity would not combine the interest rate risk associated with a financial asset with the commodity price risk associated with a financial liability, because doing so would not mitigate the reporting entity's exposure to interest rate risk or commodity price risk, and they are not substantially the same. Clearly, when measuring the fair value of financial assets and financial liabilities within the group, risks that are not offset shall be taken into account.

Similarly, the duration of the reporting entity's exposure to a particular market risk is another component that impacts the offsetting and reporting entities should ensure that it is substantially the same.

5. Qualifying Offsetting in Respect of the Credit Risk of the Reporting Entity and the Counterparty

One of the relevant applications of the portfolio exception concerns the offsetting counterparty credit risk. A reporting entity that holds a group of financial assets and financial liabilities with a particular counterparty may agree on arrangements that mitigate the exposure to the credit risk of the group of financial instruments. Examples of such arrangements include:

a. A master netting agreement with the counterparty that determines that, upon the occurrence of events such as bankruptcy of one of the parties, assets and liabilities are settled on a net basis (for more information, see Chapter 10, Section 5.3); and

b. An agreement that requires the exchange of collateral on the basis of each party's net exposure to the credit risk of the other party.

Where there is an arrangement in place that mitigates the exposure to the counterparty's credit risk, the reporting entity may (subject to the conditions for the applicability of the exception; for more information, see Section 3) apply the measurement exception and include the effect of the reporting entity's net exposure to the counterparty's credit risk or the counterparty's net exposure to the credit risk of the reporting entity in the fair value measurement. Such an arrangement may be taken into consideration only to the extent that market participants would take into account such an arrangement as one that mitigates credit risk exposure in the event of default. This relates, among other things, to market participants' expectations regarding the probability that such an arrangement would be legally enforceable in the event of default.

6. The Relationship between the Measurement of the Fair Value of a Net Position and Its Presentation in the Statement of Financial Position

A reporting entity's accounting policy choice whereby a group of financial assets and financial liabilities is measured based on the net exposure to a particular market risk or credit risk of the counterparty does not affect the presentation of the assets and liabilities in the statement of financial position. Under IFRS, International Accounting Standard (IAS) 32 discusses the offsetting of financial instruments for purposes of presentation in the statement of financial position. Other rules exist under US GAAP, where offsetting is optional (according to Accounting Standards Codification (ASC) Topic 210 and ASC Topic 815).

7. Allocation of the Portfolio-Level Adjustments to Individual Instruments

When a reporting entity measures the fair value of a group of financial assets and financial liabilities based on its net exposure to a particular market risk or credit risk of the counterparty, the reporting entity needs to allocate the resulting portfolio-level adjustments (i.e., allocate the offsetting impact for the portfolio's effect relative to the total of its components on a gross basis) to the individual assets and liabilities that make up the group. A reporting entity shall perform such allocations on a reasonable and consistent basis using a methodology appropriate under the circumstances. It should be noted that the manner of performing the allocation of the adjustments to individual instruments is defined by the Standards as an accounting policy and, therefore, should be consistent from period to period for a particular portfolio.

It should be clarified that there are many reasons why a reporting entity may be required to allocate the adjustments arising from offsetting risk positions. Among other things, a reporting entity may be required to allocate the adjustments for purposes of presentation in the statement of financial position, where specific instruments are presented by groups rather than necessarily at the level of the portfolio in which offsetting was performed (e.g., for the purpose of separating between assets and liabilities, or different information items in the statement of financial position or in the notes to the financial statements); for purposes of disclosure in the notes to the financial statements; for offsetting purposes, separating between profit or loss components and other comprehensive income (if some of the instruments are measured at fair value through other comprehensive income); and even for purposes of assessing the effectiveness of hedge accounting.

The Standards do not determine the appropriate allocation method, but the explanatory notes of IFRS 13 recognize the fact that any allocation may be arbitrary. Thus, in our view, the Standards allow allocations that are based solely on quantitative measures, provided that they are reasonable and performed consistently. Among other things, the professional literature mentions methods of allocating portfolio-level adjustments to the individual instruments based on the relative fair value of each instrument on a gross basis (i.e., on a standalone basis, not taking the offsetting into account).

Chapter 12

VALUATION TECHNIQUES

1. Overview

The Standards require fair value to be measured by way of some calculation. In some cases, this calculation can be quite simple. For example, when the fair value is estimated based on a quoted price in an active market of an identical asset or liability, such as an investment in listed shares held by the reporting entity. In such cases, the reporting entity shall multiply the quoted price in the active market by the number of instruments (e.g., shares) it holds. This calculation is sometimes called P × Q (for more information, see Section 2.2).

Another example of a relatively simple calculation is when the fair value of a certain item (such as an investment property) is estimated based on the price paid in an orderly and recent transaction involving that specific asset. For instance, when the reporting entity holds, as of the measurement date, a nonspecific half of a particular building and measures the fair value of that half according to the price in an orderly and current transaction in which the other nonspecific half of the building was recently sold.

Sometimes, however, the calculation will be much more complex, and performing it or selecting the inputs to be used will require the reporting entity to exercise more significant judgment. Thus, for example, it is possible that the market inputs being used in the measurement or the valuation technique itself may need to be adjusted due to unique characteristics of the measured item or due to other factors. Sometimes, reporting entities will need to use various forecasts or relatively complex mathematical methods and formulae and so forth.

The calculation used to measure the fair value (regardless of whether it is a simple or a complex calculation) is called in the Standards a "valuation technique." The Standards provide provisions and guidelines regarding various aspects of valuation techniques, such as:

a. Considerations in selecting a valuation technique (for more information, see Section 2);

b. Principal approaches of valuation techniques (for more information, see Section 3);
c. Using multiple valuation techniques (for more information, see Section 4);
d. Calibration of valuation techniques (for more information, see Section 5);
e. Changing the valuation techniques (for more information, see Section 6);
f. Adjusting inputs used in the valuation or adjusting the valuation techniques themselves (for more information, see Section 7); and
g. Selecting the inputs used in the valuation technique and the fair value hierarchy (for more information, see Section 8).

A discussion of the aforementioned aspects is provided below.

2. Considerations in Selecting a Valuation Technique

2.1. Guiding principle

Selecting one valuation technique over another does not change the objective of the measurement or the definition of fair value. In other words, the objective of using a valuation technique is to estimate the price at which an orderly transaction to sell the asset or transfer the liability would take place between market participants at the measurement date under current market conditions.

The Standards list three widely used valuation approaches: the market approach, the cost approach and the income approach. It may be said that each of the abovementioned approaches may be applied using more than one valuation technique. A reporting entity should use specific valuation techniques consistent with one or more of those approaches to measure fair value (for more information, see Section 3).

In principle, a reporting entity should select and use valuation techniques that are appropriate under the circumstances and for which sufficient inputs are available to measure fair value, maximizing the use of relevant observable inputs and minimizing the use of unobservable ones (for more information, see Section 8.2).

Selecting a valuation technique normally requires the exercise of judgment. The Standards do not include a hierarchy of valuation techniques or a hierarchy of valuation approaches, since under certain circumstances, it may be preferable to use particular approaches over other ones, whereas under other circumstances, the conclusion may be different. Furthermore, under certain circumstances, reporting entities should consider using multiple valuation techniques. In our view, the following factors may impact the selection of the appropriate valuation technique:

a. To what extent does the technique take into account all the characteristics of the measured item, noting its unit of account (for more information, see Chapter 3, Section 3)?
b. What are the adjustments, if any, that the reporting entity needs to make to the technique in order to accurately represent the measured item (for more information, see Section 7)?
c. What are the inputs needed to apply the technique, and to what extent does the use of the technique require observable inputs compared to more subjective, unobservable ones (for more information, see Section 8.2)?
d. Within which level of the fair value hierarchy will the entire measurement be categorized (for more information, see Section 8.2)?
e. To what extent are the results of the valuation technique sensitive to subjective inputs, and is the resulting range of values reasonable?
f. Are there other reliable techniques that make a more extensive use of observable inputs without neglecting material characteristics of the measured item, which market participants would have taken into account?
g. How acceptable is the use of the valuation technique under the circumstances? For example, certain techniques may be more acceptable than others for particular types of items; this may also depend on factors such as the industry, the life-cycle stage of the measured item and so forth.
h. Does past experience show that the results of using the valuation technique correspond to observable market inputs (when such market inputs are available, for example, when transactions are performed), or is the reporting entity required to significantly calibrate the results of the measurement (for more information, see Section 5)?

It may be said that a policy whereby all items included in a certain category will always be measured using the same technique—with no consideration given to the circumstances or the specific characteristics of the measured item—will not necessarily meet the requirements of the Standards. Thus, for example, it is not acceptable to automatically price all financial investments in all shares of investees held by the reporting entity, by using a uniform price to earnings multiple ratio technique (for more information, see Section 3.2), while ignoring questions such as the relevance of this ratio to each investment, the existence of other fair value indications (such as actual transactions that involved the shares or quoted prices) and so forth.

Thus, for example, when measuring the fair value of a noncontrolling financial investment in shares, if there are sufficiently comparable companies, and observable background or information is available regarding transactions involving the shares of such comparable companies, this may increase the use of valuation techniques that are based on the market approach, such as the multiples method. On the other hand, if sufficiently comparable companies are unavailable (e.g., since the growth stage of the investee is more advanced than that of the comparable companies), or if no observable information about transactions involving their shares is available, it may be more appropriate to use other techniques—such as those based on the income approach (for more information, see Section 3). It should be emphasized that the Standards do not explicitly require reporting entities to use multiple valuation techniques, but under certain circumstances, the selection of an appropriate valuation technique may require the reporting entity to weigh several alternatives and even compare their results in order to analyze the nature of the differences.

Furthermore, it is important to note that the Standards restrict the reporting entity's ability to exercise judgment when selecting valuation techniques in cases where a quoted price in an active market is available for the measured asset or liability. If this is the case, the reporting entity must use the quoted price to measure the fair value (for more information, see Section 2.2).

2.2. The quoted price restriction when there is an active market for an identical asset or liability

The Standards restrict the reporting entity's ability to exercise judgment when selecting valuation techniques in cases where a quoted price in an active market is available for the measured asset or liability, or in cases where there are available quoted prices for the individual assets or liabilities that make up the reporting entity's position. If that is the case, the reporting entity should use the quoted price in order to measure the fair value of the entire position, and no adjustments should be applied, except for a limited list of adjustments—mainly technical in nature—that are permitted (for more information, see Section 8.5). Thus, for example, if the reporting entity holds 50,000 ordinary shares of a particular company (which do not confer control, significant influence or joint control over the investee), and those shares are traded on a stock exchange that meets the definition of an active market for these shares, then the reporting entity must use the quoted share price in order to measure the fair value of the entire position.

With regard to this provision, it is first important to note that the provision should be examined while bearing in mind the relevant unit of account. In other words, if the unit of account of the reporting entity's holdings does not correspond to the unit for which there is a quoted price, this restriction is irrelevant. Similarly, this restriction will not apply when the item for which there is an active market is similar, but not identical, to the item that makes up the reporting entity's position. In such a situation, the reporting entity should select a valuation technique after considering all the facts and circumstances.

Furthermore, when there is a quoted price in a market that does not meet the definition of an active market, it is reasonable to assume that the valuation technique used will take the quoted price into account, but—to the extent needed—it will also make adjustments, such as in respect of control premiums, illiquidity discount, weighting of other valuation techniques and so forth. For more information, see Chapter 3, Section 3 and this chapter's Section 7.

The quoted price restriction increases the importance of determining whether or not there is an active market for the asset or liability that makes up the reporting entity's position. If it is determined that there is an active market for an asset or a liability, the reporting entity must use the quoted price in this market in its fair value measurement. If, on the other hand, it is determined that the market is not an active one, the reporting entity may consider other valuation techniques and inputs, bearing in mind all the relevant facts and circumstances. When the market for a particular instrument does not meet the definition of an active market, in our view, the question of the weight that should be placed on the observable inputs of that market (such as the quoted price on a stock exchange or a current transaction, compared to other valuation techniques) is in essence similar to the weight placed on quoted prices when the volume of trade for an asset or a liability has significantly declined (for more information, see Chapter 7, Section 3).

The term "active market" is defined in the Standards as a market in which transactions for the asset or liability take place with sufficient frequency and volume to provide pricing information on an ongoing basis. According to current practice, it is insufficient for a certain asset or liability to be listed for trade on the stock exchange to determine that the stock exchange is necessarily an active market for that asset or liability. Furthermore, it is possible that a market that was active will no longer meet the definition of an active market due to significant decline in its trade volumes, or vice versa. This means that in order to determine whether or not a stock exchange is an active market at the measurement date, a reporting entity should also examine the volume of trade on the stock exchange for the specific instrument as well as other factors. As to the uncertainty in the current practice regarding the criteria for the existence of an active market, in our view, the characteristics that could impact the determination of whether there is an active market for a certain share include factors such as the absolute amounts of the daily trading volume close to the measurement date, the percentage of active trading days out of the total number of trading days, the rate of the trade turnover out of the capitalization of the company or series (as the case may be), significant differences between the bid price and the ask price (when no trading takes place) and the inclusion of the security in the stock exchange's preservation list or list of illiquid securities. It is interesting to note that the interpretation of the term "active market" may not necessarily be the same in practice under US Generally Accepted Accounting Principles (US GAAP) and International Financial Reporting Standards (IFRS). The US GAAP Master Glossary defines Readily Determinable Fair Value (RDFV) for an equity security as, inter alia, situations where the security is traded in a registered US stock exchange or has price quotations for over-the-counter (OTC) trading, provided that the quotations are publicly reported by NASDAQ systems or by OTC Markets Group. RDFV is also said to exist if the security is traded in a non-US market, provided that the market is of a breadth and scope comparable to one of the US markets mentioned above. RDFV is used in US GAAP, inter alia, to limit the practical expedients in Accounting Standards Codification (ASC) 820 that relate to the usage of reported net asset value (NAV) instead of actual fair value (for more information, see Chapter 1, Section 4) and is also used to determine if an investment in an equity instrument must be measured at fair value. While RDFV and active market definitions are different, it is unclear whether the requirement for market breadth and scope comparable to that of US capital markets should also be applied to the active market definition under US GAAP.

3. Principal Approaches of Valuation Techniques

3.1. Overview

As described in Section 2.1, the Standards list the three "master groups" of valuation approaches. Each of the said approaches may be applied by using more than one valuation technique. In order to measure fair value, reporting entities should use specific valuation techniques that are consistent with one or more of the following valuation approaches:

a. Market approach: The Standards define the market approach as a valuation technique that uses prices and other relevant information generated by market transactions involving identical or comparable (i.e., similar) items (for more information, see Section 3.2).
b. Cost approach: The Standards define the cost approach as a valuation technique that reflects the amount that would be required currently to replace the service capacity of an asset (often referred to as current replacement cost) (for more information, see Section 3.3).
c. Income approach: The Standards define the income approach as a group of valuation techniques that convert future amounts (e.g., cash flows or income and expenses) to a single current (i.e., discounted) amount. The fair value measurement is determined on the basis of the value indicated

by current market expectations regarding these future amounts (for more information, see Section 3.4).

Below is a description of the nature of the approaches as well as examples for the application of several specific techniques that are derived from such approaches. For information about the various considerations to be taken into account when selecting a valuation technique, see Section 2.

3.2. The market approach

A. The nature of the approach

The market approach uses prices and other relevant information generated by market transactions involving assets, liabilities or a group of assets and liabilities that are identical or comparable (i.e., similar) to the item being measured. Obviously, in order to use such an approach, a reporting entity needs access to a particular market's data, such as multiples in merger and acquisition transactions of comparable companies or inputs about the level of multiples in the capital market. As a rule, it may be said that the greater the number of (and the more current) available market inputs about items that are identical or significantly comparable to the item being measured, and the less adjustments required in respect of those inputs or the technique itself, the more reliable the results these market approach techniques will provide for the fair value.

The market approach can be reflected in a variety of valuation techniques, from simple valuation techniques to relatively complex ones. The simplest example for the application of the market approach is the case where a reporting entity has current market inputs about the measured item (originating from ordinary transactions). Thus, for example, if the reporting entity holds shares of a company as a financial investment and the said shares are traded in an active market (such as a stock exchange with sufficient trading volumes), the application of the market approach will simply entail multiplying the quoted share price by the number of shares held by the reporting entity. It should be noted that in such a case, the use of this technique is mandatory (for more information, see Section 2.2).

Other typical situations in which the application of the market approach is simple are when there are orderly (for more information, see Chapter 7) and current transactions involving the specific asset or liability being measured, which should usually reflect the fair value of the asset or liability, even if there is no active market as aforementioned—for example, estimating the fair value of a nonspecific half of a particular building according to the price in an orderly and current transaction in which the other nonspecific half of the building was sold or estimating the fair value of a financial investment in a private company's shares based on the price paid by the reporting entity or by another party in a recent investment round involving identical shares of the private company.

It should be noted that in cases where no significant adjustments are required to be applied to market inputs in order to determine the fair value, the result of the application of the market approach may be categorized within Level 2 of the fair value hierarchy, which may give this method a certain priority over other methods that typically use unobservable inputs (for more details, see Section 8.4). Thus, for example, an investment round involving the shares of an investee close to the measurement date normally makes it possible to achieve a relatively reliable measurement of the fair value of other shares of the same class, and under such circumstances, in our view, the application of the market approach (according to the share price in the investment round) will be preferable to the application of other approaches or techniques requiring the use of more subjective inputs. In our view, the weight that should be placed on the share price in the last investment round when measuring the fair value of the shares of an investee with no quoted share price depends on the specific facts and circumstances, such as the following:

a. Was the round carried out pro rata to existing investors, such that there is a relative indifference to the share price?
b. How much time has elapsed since the investment round?
c. Have material changes taken place in the investee or in its business environment since the investment round?
d. Is the investment round not an orderly transaction?
e. Is the scope of the investment round negligible?
f. Are there more recent investment rounds?

One issue related to the use of transaction prices for the purpose of estimating the fair value of the investment, which is discussed in IFRS 9, is the circumstances under which the historical cost of an investment in an equity instrument of another entity (i.e., the cost paid when acquired) may be used as a (practical) approximation of the fair value of the instrument in subsequent dates and the circumstances in which it is possible to make such a practical approximation.

In certain situations, the use of the market approach may require various adjustments. Such adjustments may stem from factors such as timing differences between the transaction date and the measurement date; a different unit of account (such as excluding or adding a control premium); differences between the items being measured and the items for which there are market inputs, such as the calculation of the fair value of preferred shares of a startup company based on the price of ordinary shares or taking into consideration a restriction feature; and so forth.

It should be noted that the Standards allow the use of a valuation technique (which is consistent with the market approach) referred to as "matrix pricing." Matrix pricing is a mathematical technique used principally to value financial instruments (mainly debt instruments) without relying exclusively on quoted prices for the specific securities but rather on the securities' relationship with other benchmark quoted securities (for more information, see Section 8.5).

B. The market multiples technique

One of the most widely used valuation techniques within the market approach is the market multiples technique, which uses market multiples derived from a set of comparable transactions. Multiples might be in ranges, so the selection of the appropriate multiple within the range requires exercising judgment (both in terms of the type of multiple and in terms of the position within the range), taking into consideration qualitative and quantitative factors specific to the measurement.

The application of the market multiples technique to measurement of the fair value of real estate properties is sometimes referred to as the "sales comparison approach." Basically, the multiples approach (regardless of whether it is applied to measure the value of an enterprise or the value of an asset, such as an investment property) involves several stages, which are summarized below:

a. Identifying several comparable companies or assets for which data are available. Thus, for example, factors such as the industry, size, risks, location or relevant market shall be taken into account.
b. Selecting a shared characteristic(s) for comparison between the measured enterprise or asset and the companies or assets included in the sample (the "multiple"). When the measurement in question is that of enterprise value (EV), the selection of the type of multiple depends on factors such as the prevailing practice in the relevant industry, the maturity level of the enterprise, the level of variability in the different types of multiples and so forth. Furthermore, it is important to emphasize that some of the multiples used take into account only operational aspects (EV multiples),

while others also take into account leveraging aspects (equity value multiples).

Set forth below are several examples of relatively common types of multiples used to measure the value of enterprises or companies:

Multiple type	**Calculation**	**Details**
Earnings before Interest, Tax, Depreciation and Amortization (EBITDA) multiple	EV / EBITDA	The ratio between the enterprise value of the companies in the sample (i.e., the value of their equity + net financial debt) and their EBITDA
EBIT multiple	EV / EBIT	The ratio between the enterprise value of the companies in the sample (i.e., the value of the equity + net financial debt) and their operating profit
EBITA multiple	EV / EBITA	The ratio between the enterprise value of the companies in the sample (i.e., the value of the equity + net financial debt) and their operating profit + the amortization of intangible assets only
Profit multiple	P / E	The ratio between the share price of the companies in the sample and their earnings per share
Funds from Operations (FFO) multiple	P / FFO	The ratio between the share price of the companies in the sample and their FFO per share
Equity multiple	P / B	The ratio between the market capitalization of the companies in the sample and their book equity, excluding noncontrolling interest
Revenue multiple	EV / Revenue	The ratio between the enterprise value of the companies in the sample (i.e., the value of the equity + net financial debt) and their revenue

In addition to the aforementioned multiples, in certain situations and certain industries, it is also customary to use multiples based on operating data, such as a multiple based on the number of customers or active users, multiples based on managed portfolios, multiples based on the number of employees and so forth. The most common multiple in real estate appraisals when using the sales comparison approach is the multiple of the price per unit of area, such as price per square meter or per square feet.

c. Analysis and adjustments: When measuring the value of companies or enterprises, it is customary to make various adjustments, such as excluding nonrecurring effects in the results of the sample companies (e.g., excluding a one-off profit of the sample companies prior to calculating the multiples); excluding the effect of nonoperational items, such as cash (when calculating the ratios); excluding nonrecurring results; giving a different weight to each specific multiple due to differences (or similarities) between the assessed enterprise and each of the sample companies for various aspects that may affect the multiple (such as size, growth potential, financial position and market positioning); and even making adjustments in respect of different accounting policies. Once the adjustments and the analysis have been carried out, the reporting entity should select the most relevant multiple within the range. In the case of real estate appraisals, the most common adjustments to the price per square meter are in respect of characteristics such as location, size, occupancy level or risk, physical condition, rent in excess/below the market rates and additional building rights.

d. Applying the selected multiple to the characteristics of the measured enterprise or asset: A specific figure, such as the EBITDA, revenues or equity of the valued enterprise or company (or the area of a building in square meters, as relevant), should be multiplied by the selected multiple in order to calculate the EV or the net value of the measured enterprise or asset (according to the type of multiple). In this case as well, the selection of the specific figure may require the reporting entity to exercise considerable judgment. Furthermore, it should be verified that the specific figure is also adjusted where needed (e.g., in order to exclude the effect of nonrecurring items in the revenues of the measured enterprise).
e. Making additional adjustments: Such adjustments may be required due to the fact that the multiple used is an operational multiple, whereas the fair value measurement relates to the net value, in which case the net financial debt should be excluded from the value resulting from using the multiple. Furthermore, adjustments may be needed due to the fact that there are other nonoperational assets that were not valued as part of the multiple. Furthermore, adjustments may include control premiums' exclusion, in cases where the sample was formed on the basis of transactions that included transfer of control, but the reporting entity does not control the valued company; another example of a potential adjustment may be to apply an illiquidity or nonmarketability discount in cases where the sample was formed on the basis of prices in active markets, but the reporting entity has nontradable shares or shares that are restricted from trading.

It should be noted that the use of the market multiples technique for the purpose of valuing companies or enterprises may be prone to some form of error; listed below are some potential reasons for such error:

a. The selected sample of comparable companies is inadequate;
b. Using a sample based on transactions carried out over a long period, during which the market conditions have changed significantly;
c. Using the average of multiples where there is a broad range of multiples, without analyzing the reasonableness or the effect on the valued enterprise;
d. Combining multiples used to estimate operational items with multiples used to value items on a net equity basis, such as calculating a multiple on the basis of the ratio between the market capitalization and EBITDA;
e. Failing to adjust or normalize irregular results of the sample companies when calculating the multiples;
f. Combining multiples calculated on the basis of historical data (such as the previous year's profit) with a figure for the valued enterprise calculated on the basis of forward-looking information, such as projected EBITDA of the valued company after three years;
g. Combining post-tax multiples with pre-tax performance measures; and
h. Failure to make adjustments in respect of the characteristics of the valued enterprise, such as discount in respect of nonmarketability.

Set forth below is an example of the application of the market multiples technique to a financial investment in nontradable shares.

Example of the Application of the Market Multiples Technique

Company A holds 5 percent of the share capital of private Company B. Company B's normalized EBITDA (after adjustments in respect of nonrecurring items) is $100 million. In addition to the operational liabilities (such as trade payables or deferred income), Company B also has net financial liabilities (such as loans or bonds) whose fair value amounts to $350 million.

It should be assumed that there are no current transactions involving Company B's shares and that after considering the nature of Company B's activities, the nature of the activities of the comparable companies and scope of observable inputs relating to the comparable companies, Company A opted to use the market multiples technique as the most relevant valuation technique.

In order to measure the value of the holding in Company B as of the end of 2017, Company A selects a sample of six public companies, which operate in the same industry and geographic area as Company B. The multiple selected for the purpose of carrying out the valuation is EV / EBITDA, bearing in mind, among other things, the differences among the sample

Compa-rable company 1	Compa-rable company 2	Compa-rable company 3	Compa-rable company 4	Compa-rable company 5	Compa-rable company 6	Range	Median	Average
× 4.5	× 8.0	× 8.5	× 15.0	× 9.0	× 8.5	× 4.5–× 15.0	× 8.5	× 8.9

companies themselves and the differences between the sample companies and Company B in terms of the leverage level and depreciation policy. During the calculation of the comparable companies' multiples, it was determined that no special adjustments were needed, such as adjustments in respect of non-operating assets of the sample companies or exclusion of nonrecurring items.

Set forth below are the calculated multiples:

After further analysis, Company A removed comparable companies 1 and 4 from the sample, based on considerations such as growth and ability to generate cash flows as compared to Company B. After removing the said companies, Company A used the average multiple of the remaining sample companies, which is × 8.5. The average multiple was selected bearing in mind the characteristics of the remaining sample companies. As a result, the EV of Company B's activity is \$850 million (= 100 × 8.5). Company A deducts the fair value of the net financial liabilities amounting to \$350 million from the said value, such that the value of Company B's shares (before other adjustments) is \$500 million (= 850 − 350). Now Company A needs to assess whether it should apply further adjustments. The Company concludes that, since the multiples in the sample were estimated on the basis of quoted prices, which do not reflect control premiums, the value should not be discounted in respect of the fact that its shares represent noncontrolling interests. However, in view of the fact that the shares held by Company A are those of a private company, whereas the multiples were calculated in relation to listed public companies, discount for lack of marketability (DLOM) should be applied. In this case, the discount was set at 30 percent of the equity value (which includes marketability), based on several studies that were performed in connection with the relevant geographic region and industry, as well as the specific facts and circumstances. Therefore, the fair value of Company B's shares after adjustments is \$350 million (= 500 × 0.7), and the fair value of the shares held by Company A is \$17.5 million (= 350 × 0.05).

3.3. The cost approach

A. The nature of the approach

The valuation techniques included in this approach attempt to estimate the amount that would be required to replace the service capacity of an asset on the measurement date (this technique may be referred to as "current replacement cost," not to be confused with "current cost" basis mentioned in the IFRS Conceptual Framework for Financial Reporting 2018, which may also include transaction costs). The rationale behind this method is that a market participant would not pay more for an asset than the amount for which it could replace the service capacity of that asset.

In this case, the term "cost" does not refer to historical cost but rather to the current cost that a market participant will incur in order to buy or construct a replacement asset of comparable utility, adjusted for obsolescence. Under this approach, obsolescence includes physical deterioration, functional obsolescence (technological obsolescence, such as when there are other assets in the market with preferable technology) or economic obsolescence (external, i.e., change in market preferences or economic conditions). The adjustments are generally broader than depreciation for financial reporting purposes or tax purposes.

In many cases, the cost approach is used to measure the fair value of tangible assets used in combination with other assets or with other assets and liabilities. Sometimes, the cost approach is used in combination with other approaches, such as the market approach. Thus, for example, let us assume that the reporting entity has a standard used machine that was customized to suit its specific needs (such as by way of installation or programming). Let us also assume that, although the installation or programming processes are specific, they are not unique since they can be replicated by a market participant. If the valuation premise of the machine takes into consideration that the highest and best use of the machine will be in combination with a group of other assets and liabilities, the reporting entity will need to take into account the customization costs of the machine when measuring its fair value (for more information, see Chapter 9, Section 3). Therefore, one of the ways to measure the fair value of the machine will be to base its fair value (prior to the installation or programming) on current market prices of similar used or new machines while adjusting for the machine's condition in respect of factors such as obsolescence or depreciation. Furthermore, in order to reflect the added value arising from the said customization, the reporting entity may take into account an added value, which will be estimated using the cost approach, based on the total costs that a market participant who holds the complementary assets and liabilities would incur in order to make the customization—for example, estimated current transport costs, costs for labor and materials used to customize the machine, a certain margin in respect of unexpected costs or even a developer's margin, if needed. This is the case since the assumption is that a market participant buyer who would "step into the shoes" of the reporting entity would be spared these costs.

B. Limitations of the cost approach

In our view, the most significant limitations of the cost approach are actually referred to directly in the examples provided by the Standards. It may be said that the two most significant limitations are those listed below:

a. Economically infeasible projects: In certain cases, and specifically where the project in question is one whose theoretical construction or reconstruction was economically infeasible as of the cut-off date, the value arising from the approach might exceed the economic benefits that a market participant would derive from using the asset. In order to illustrate this limitation (using an extreme example), let us assume that the reporting entity needs to estimate the fair value of a failed investment in an amusement park in a remote location. Applying the cost method to calculate the fair value of the investment would involve estimating the fair value of a comparable plot of land, with the addition of the various costs incurred in the construction of the park (including finance costs, unexpected costs, etc.). However, it may be that, from the perspective of a market participant, the future cash flows from the park would not have justified such an investment as of the measurement date. This means that the costs incurred in the construction of the park are sunk costs, and a market participant would not necessarily make those investments as of the measurement date; it is also possible that the sale price at the reporting date would have been significantly lower. In such a situation, it is clear that the use of the cost approach may produce an erroneous estimate.
b. Unique assets: Sometimes, the theoretical cost that would have been incurred in order to replicate a particular asset is irrelevant to the measurement of its fair value, due to the asset's uniqueness or to its unique position in the market. Thus, for example, let us assume that a reporting entity needs to measure the fair value of a market-leading software that benefits from economies of scale. In this case, it is possible that developing a similar or competing software costs a certain amount of money (which is estimated while taking into account costs of labor, time, etc.), but it is clear that even if the said amount is invested, a market participant would not necessarily be able to replicate the measured software's leading position in the market or its economies of scale. In such cases, using the cost approach may lead to underestimating the fair value. Similarly, using the cost approach may be irrelevant where there is no clear way of replicating the asset, such as in the case of a real estate property situated in a unique location (where there is no comparable

vacant plots that could have been used to build a similar property) or a software using a unique technology.

The abovementioned disadvantages, as well as other disadvantages, are the reason why this approach is normally not used to value enterprises or companies. The cost approach may particularly be appropriate when the valued asset is a generic one, which can be replicated in a simple manner by a market participant, provided that the construction of the asset would have been economically feasible as of the measurement date.

3.4. The income approach

A. The nature of the approach

The income approach converts future amounts (e.g., cash flows or income and expenses) to a single current (i.e., discounted) amount. When the income approach is used, the fair value measurement reflects current market expectations about those future amounts.

It may be said that the "income approach" is a master group of many valuation techniques based on discounting, or whose model directly or indirectly relies on discounting. The Standards list the following valuation techniques in a nonexhaustive list of techniques that are part of the income approach:

a. Present value techniques: Present value is a tool used to link future amounts (e.g., a series of future cash flows) to a present amount using a discount rate. For more information, see below.
b. Option pricing models: Those models, such as the Black-Scholes-Merton (B&S) formula or a binomial model (i.e., lattice model), incorporate present value techniques and reflect both the time value and the intrinsic value of an option. Furthermore, in our view, techniques that rely on performing multiple simulations under scenarios or statistical distributions and discounting the results obtained from running those simulations (such as the Monte Carlo simulation) could also be classified into the income approach.
c. The multi-period excess earnings (MPEE) method: This method is used to measure the fair value of assets (normally intangible assets, such as customer relationships), which generate revenue in combination with other assets. Putting it simply, this method calculates the expected cash flow of a group of assets, and then, in order to isolate the value of the intangible asset, the reporting entity deducts contributory charges related to the use of the other assets in the group, such as charges in respect of using brands

or property, plant and equipment. The remaining excess is discounted, and after other adjustments are applied (such as in respect of the tax effect and tax shield on depreciation), it is attributed to the asset.

In our view, other accepted techniques that can be included under the income approach and may also be used to measure the value of intangible assets (such as brand names) are the relief from royalties technique, whereby the costs a company will save in the future due to the fact that it will not be required to pay for the right to use the brand are discounted and the "with or without" technique, which may be applied to items such as noncompete agreements; in this technique, the expected cash flow is discounted while taking into account two scenarios: one in which the measured agreement exists, and one that is hypothetical, in which it does not exist.

B. Consistency between the cash flow and the discount rate

As described above, present value is a tool used to link future amounts to a present amount using a discount rate. A fair value measurement of an asset or a liability using a present value technique captures all the following elements from the perspective of market participants at the measurement date:

a. An estimate of future cash flows for the asset or liability being measured;
b. Expectations about possible variations in the amount and timing of the cash flows representing the uncertainty inherent in the cash flows;
c. The time value of money, represented by the rate on risk-free monetary assets that have maturity dates or durations that coincide with the period covered by the cash flows. The time value of money poses neither uncertainty in timing nor risk of default to the holder (i.e., a risk-free interest rate);
d. The price for bearing the uncertainty inherent in the cash flows (i.e., a risk premium);
e. Other factors that market participants would take into account under the circumstances; and
f. For a liability, the non-performance risk relating to that liability, including the reporting entity's (i.e., the borrower's) own credit risk. For more information, see Chapter 10, Section 5.

Often, a fair value measurement using present value techniques is made under conditions of uncertainty because the cash flows used are estimates rather than known amounts. In many cases, both the amount and the timing of the cash flows are uncertain. Even contractually fixed amounts, such as the payments on a fixed interest rate loan, are uncertain, because there is a default risk on the part of the borrower.

To put it simply, present value techniques discount a future amount to a present one. On the mathematical level, the calculation generally includes a numerator (the cash flow) and a denominator (the discount or interest rate). Thus, there may be several ways to reach the same present value, since certain risks of the item (and even other characteristics, such as the liquidity level) may be compensated for by changing the cash flow or by changing the discount rate. The required compensation is estimated from the perspective of a market participant. The selection of a technique depends on the facts and circumstances, but the complexity level of compensation in respect of the risk is not a sufficient reason for excluding a risk premium from the measurement.

One of the most important points when performing such risk adjustments is to take into account all the relevant factors that market participants would take into account and, on the other hand, to avoid double-counting by reflecting those factors both in the numerator and in the denominator. Therefore, the question of which risk factors should be included in the denominator depends on the question of which risk factors were reflected in the numerator, and vice versa. Thus, for example, if the cash flow used in the calculation is based on a nominal forecast (i.e., a forecast that includes price increases due to the effect of inflation), then the discount rate will also be nominal and will be based as a starting point on yields of unlinked bonds. On the other hand, if the forecast was calculated in real terms (i.e., without taking into account the effect of inflation), the discount rate should also be based on real yields. The above is also applicable to the issue of the consistency between the currency in which the projected cash flow is denominated and the currency used to estimate the discount rate. Similarly, pre-tax projected cash flows should be discounted at a rate consistent with those cash flows (i.e., pre-tax discount rate), and vice versa.

The Standards discuss several specific present value techniques, which result in a different allocation of the risk between the projected cash flow and the discount rate (for more information, see Sections C and D below).

Example—Applying the Present Value Technique to an Office Building

Company A holds an occupied office building that is classified as investment property and measured at fair value. The annual net operating income (NOI) from the office building, comprising rent plus management fees and incidental revenues (such as revenues from billboards or stalls located on the ground floor), net of current operating costs of the building (such as cleaning, security, municipal taxes and electricity for shared spaces, maintenance and repairs and overheads in respect of general expenses), is CU 25 million before tax. It shall be assumed that the said income is steady in the sense that it is not expected to materially change in the future. For example, no material lessees are expected to terminate their leases, and none of the lessees pay rent that is different from the current market rent. In order to measure the fair value of the office building, the Company samples the capitalization rates in comparable transactions involving office buildings that took place close to the measurement date. For this purpose, the capitalization rate is the ratio between the known or estimated annual NOI of the comparable assets and the price paid for those assets in the reported transactions. The capitalization rates in such transactions range between 6.75 percent and 9 percent. After removing unsuitable transactions and taking into account other indications (such as market surveys), the Company reaches the conclusion that taking into account the risk and prospect characteristics of the asset (such as location, occupancy, risk level and physical condition), the appropriate capitalization rate for the asset is 8 percent. As a result, the estimated fair value of the asset (in millions of CU) is 312.5 (= 25 / 0.08). To estimate the fair value, the Company used a discounting formula of a perpetual cash flow. When the current NOI level of the building is no longer considered to be representative of its long-term expected performance, a more detailed cash flow forecast may be required, in which different years may be represented differently. Alternatively, in such cases, the Company may estimate the fair value based on a perpetuity formula taking into account long-term (rather than current) performance and adjust the result for any expected differences in the transition period from the current to the expected level of performance.

The importance of consistency between the discount rate and the nature of the cash flow can be illustrated through the above example. As described in the example, it is not customary to use cash flows that include financing or tax effects in real estate appraisals. In other words, the above amount of NOI does not take into account the interest incurred on the loan (if any) and the income tax payable by the Company or market participant. Nevertheless, the fact that the capitalization rates in the sample were calculated consistently with the calculation of the NOI compensates for the exclusion of interest and income tax. If the capitalization rates in the sample were calculated differently (e.g., on the basis of the weighted average cost of capital (WACC) of companies in the industry, or on the basis of return on equity, which takes into account certain leveraging, as well as tax effect), but the NOI in the numerator remained the same, there would have been inconsistency between the cash flow and the discount rate used to discount it, and the result of such calculation might not have represented the fair value.

C. Discount rate adjustment technique

The first present value technique described in the Standards is called the "discount rate adjustment technique." This technique uses a risk-adjusted discount rate and contractual, promised or most likely (but not necessarily expected) cash flows. This technique is typically used, for example, to price debt instruments, especially those not characterized by very high default probability. On the other hand, debt instruments characterized by very high default probability are commonly priced using other methods, which also take into account the expected "haircut." Since the discount rate adjustment technique uses contractual, promised or most likely cash flows and durations, the discount rate is consistently derived from the rates of return reflected in observed prices in respect of contractual, promised or most likely cash flows from the comparable assets. When using this technique, the most important thing is to establish the comparability of the comparable assets, by considering the amounts, credit standing (e.g., credit ratings), collaterals, period to maturity, financial covenants, liquidity and currency or mechanism for determining the interest rate. This technique is most commonly applied when using yield curves (e.g., according to credit ratings) to price loans and bonds. The yield curves reflect the relationship between the level of risk (e.g., the credit ratings) and the period to maturity, on the one hand, and the internal rate of return (IRR, in relation to the contractual debt payments), on the other; they are normally determined by taking into account various observable inputs. Alternatively, these curves may reflect the required credit spread by different risk levels and different periods to maturity.

Example—Discount Rate Adjustment Technique

As of December 31, 2016, Company A holds 10 percent of the Series 1 bonds of Company B. The investment in the bonds was classified into fair value through profit or loss measurement category. The par value of the whole Series 1 bonds is CU 100,000, and the bonds bear contractual annual interest rate of 5 percent, payable at the end of each year (starting on December 31, 2017). The principal of the bonds is payable in a single installment on December 31, 2018.

It is assumed that the said bonds are not traded. As of the end of 2016, Company B has two other series of bonds that have a level of seniority, collaterals and financial covenants similar to those of Series 1; however, the other two series of bonds are traded, as follows:

a. Series 2—a zero-coupon series, which matures on December 31, 2017. The yield rate of the series—as reflected in the quoted market price, which was calculated by dividing its price by its contractual cash flows—is 6 percent.
b. Series 3—a zero-coupon series, which matures on December 31 2018. The yield rate of the series—as reflected in the quoted market price, which was calculated using an IRR that takes into account the quoted price of the bond and its contractual cash flows—is 7 percent.

Since the Series 1 bonds are not traded, Company A concludes that the yield rate should be further adjusted by 0.2 percent in order to reflect the illiquidity effect, based on studies in this field. Therefore, the fair value of the Series 1 bonds is estimated at

CU 96,077 (= 5,000 / 1.062 + 105,000 / 1.072 ^ 2), and the fair value of Company A's investment is CU 9,608 (= 0.1 × 96,077).

The discount rate used in this example reflects, among other things, the compensation in respect of the credit risk (in relation to the contractual amount) and in respect of the liquidity risks.

D. Expected present value technique

According to the Standards, there are two possible approaches called "expected present value techniques":

a. As part of the first technique, which will be referred to below as the "certainty-equivalent cash flow technique," all existing risks (volatility), as well as the compensation in respect of the risks, are reflected in the expected cash flow, which is therefore discounted using a risk-free discount rate.
b. In the second technique, which will be referred to below as the "expected cash flow technique," the cash flow is an expected cash flow that reflects all existing risks and volatility but does not reflect the compensation in respect of its volatility, and this compensation is reflected in the discount rate.

Both techniques use as a starting point a set of cash flows that represents the probability- and distribution-weighted average of all possible future cash flows (i.e., the expected cash flows). Since the expected cash flow is probability weighted, it is not conditional upon the occurrence of specified events, in contrast to the discount-rate adjustment technique mentioned above (in which the cash flow is conditional upon the occurrence of events, such as repayment of bonds with no default by the debtor). It is important to note that the expected cash flow does, indeed, reflect volatility, but it does not include the compensation in respect of that volatility. The generally accepted assumption in the finance industry is that market participants are risk averse. This means that they will generally prefer to receive a slightly lower certainty-equivalent amount than an uncertain amount with identical expected value (that may actually be higher or lower). The generally accepted approach is that the compensation in respect of risk is only relevant when the investor cannot diversify the risk (systematic risk) through a diversified portfolio. Theoretically, compensation is not required for a risk that is not systematic (and can be diversified), since the assumption is that the investors themselves will diversify this risk and will not seek to be compensated for that risk in a sufficiently efficient market.

According to the certainty-equivalent cash flow technique, the compensation for the systematic risk is achieved by reducing the expected cash flow. On the other hand, according to the expected cash flow technique, the compensation for the systematic risk is achieved by using a discount rate that is higher than the risk-free interest rate, based on models that take into account the extent of the correlation (which embodies the systematic risk) between the item and the market (such as the Capital Asset Pricing Model (CAPM)). The choice of technique depends to a great extent on the type of the item being valued, the observable inputs and the circumstances of the case. Generally speaking, it may be said that the second technique (in which the compensation for systematic volatility is reflected in the discount rate) is mainly used in corporate valuations.

Example—Discount Rate Adjustment Technique versus the Expected Present Value Technique

Company A holds bonds of Company B, which mature within one year; the par value of the holding is \$100,000 (interest should be ignored); the bonds are not risk free (it is assumed they are rated B) and are not tradable. It is assumed that the probability of default (PD) for Company B is 3.76 percent for one year. The loss given default (LGD) in this scenario is expected to be 60 percent, based on statistical data and individual analysis. In this case, while the contractual cash flow of the bonds in a year's time is \$100,000, their expected cash flow (i.e., weighted average) in a year's time is $97,744 (= 100.000 × 96.24% + 100,000 × 0.4 × 3.76%).

It is assumed that the IRR in the market (in relation to the total contractual cash flow) for bonds with a similar risk level and similar investment period is 8 percent, and the risk-free interest rate for a one-year period is 3 percent. It is also assumed that the risk premium (payable in cash within one year) a market participant would agree to receive in exchange for holding the bonds instead of holding risk-free bonds of $97,744 par value to be paid within one year is $2,373 (this amount is explained by a market participant's risk aversion). Another assumption is that the excess return (risk premium, compared to the risk-free return) a market participant would expect to receive for investment in the bonds is 2.563 percent.

Below is the estimate of the fair value of the bonds according to each of the techniques:

a. When using the discount rate adjustment technique, the fair value of the bonds will be: $92,593 (= 100,000 / 1.08).
b. When using the certainty-equivalent cash flow technique, the fair value of the bonds will be: $92,593 = (97,744 − 2,373) / 1.03.
c. When using the expected cash flow technique, the fair value of the bonds will be: $92,593 = 97,744 / (0.02563 + 1.03).

It is important to note that although the IRR on the bonds is supposedly 8 percent, market participants evidently know that this return is higher than the expected return, since it ignores the PD. The expected return market participants expect to receive for their investment is 5.563 percent per year, which embodies a volatility risk compensation of $2,373 (in terms of future value). Market participants would be unwilling to buy the bonds for $94,897 (= 97,744 / 1.03), since in such a scenario, they would rather pay an identical amount for risk-free bonds with identical expected cash flow (par value of $97,744) that mature within one year.

E. Valuation of an enterprise using the discounted cash flow technique

One of the most common uses of the discounted cash flow (DCF) technique is to estimate the value of companies or enterprises. There are some relatively simple techniques, such as the Gordon growth model, in which the expected dividend inflow from the holding (assuming a fixed annual growth rate) is discounted by the required rate of return. However, in our view, of all the said techniques for pricing enterprises or companies, the most popular model is the DCF/EV model. The advantage this model has over others (such as the multiples technique; for more information, see Section 3.2) is that it enables to express in detail aspects or expectations, which are specific to the measured enterprise or company. Therefore, using this model may be appropriate in circumstances where it is difficult to find companies that are sufficiently comparable, in terms of profitability, size, markets, risks, growth, life cycle, type of products and so forth. However, to a large extent, the model's advantage is also its disadvantage, since in order to apply the technique, it is required to form and use numerous projections and assumptions, some of which are subjective. Therefore, it is reasonable to assume that the fair value resulting from using this model will almost always be categorized within Level 3 of the Standards' fair value hierarchy (for more information, see Section 8.4). Another disadvantage of this technique is the level of technical complexity, which its application involves.

In sum, the application of the model separates between pricing the operating part of the valued operation or company and the value of the company's equity or shares. Normally, the application of the technique involves the following stages:

a. Separating between the operating part and the excess assets (such as surplus cash, land or other assets, which are not necessary for the operation of the company), the excess liabilities and the financial liabilities (such as loans from banks or bonds) of the measured company.
b. Preparing a detailed free cash flow to firm (FCFF) forecast in respect of only the operating part of the measured company for the defined forecast period. The free cash flow is the cash flow that a company's activity is expected to generate during and after the detailed forecast period. Such cash flow should take into consideration, among other things, the investments required to support the operations (capital expenditures such as buying machines and property, plant and equipment), changes in the operating working capital (such as changes in the trade receivable, inventory and trade payable line items) and other factors. The cash flow should be net of income tax or corporate tax. In other words, it is assumed that tax will be paid in respect of the operation profits, but such tax forecast is theoretical and does not take into account the deduction of interest expenses in respect of the company's financial liabilities, since interest expenses are not taken into consideration when measuring the operating part. Often, free cash flow forecast is carried out by projecting the operating profit, projecting the notional related income tax payment and adjusting the operating profit in order to calculate the free cash flow. The principal adjustments include the exclusion of noncash expenses included in the forecast, such as depreciation or amortization, making adjustments in respect of expected changes

in operating working capital line items and deducting the amounts of required capital investments (taking into consideration the forecasts' assumptions). The preparation of a cash flow forecast may require a reporting entity to exercise considerable judgment (and it may therefore also be required to make various reasonableness assessments from the perspective of a market participant) relating to factors such as growth, profitability, scope of the fixed assets and scope of the working capital that were assumed when preparing the forecast. Other elements of the model, such as the detailed forecast period or weighted future tax rates, require the reporting entity to exercise judgment and should be determined after taking into consideration all relevant facts and circumstances.

c. The free cash flow is discounted by the WACC. The said discount rate weighs the required rate of return on equity against the required rate of return on financial debt, including the tax shield's effect on the debt. The tax shield taken into account within the weighted discount rate reduces the WACC, thereby compensating for the theoretical tax payments that were included in the forecast and that do not take into account interest expenses in respect of the financial debt. The WACC is usually determined according to the following formula :

$$WACC = \frac{D}{D+E} \times Kd\left(1-t\right) + \frac{E}{D+E} \times Ke$$

Listed below are the meanings of the different parameters used in the formula:

$D =$ fair value of the company's financial debt;
$E =$ fair value of the company's equity;
$Kd =$ required rate of return on the financial debt;
$t =$ the tax rate; and
$Ke =$ the required rate of return on equity. This rate is mostly estimated by using finance models such as the CAPM.

Estimating the weighted discount rate and each of its components also involves exercise of judgment, including in connection with aspects such as the currencies relevant to the calculation, the markets relevant to the calculation of the adjustments, the methods employed to calculate the adjustments, taking into account special premiums, relying on the company's inputs or on market inputs and so forth. Sometimes, WACC is calculated under an assumption that the company is currently not financed in an optimal or representative manner; hence, the leverage is assumed to be at a different level, such as a level that is typical to the relevant industry.

d. Once the present value of operations is calculated, the components that were not included therein should be added or deducted, as the case may be, and in particular, the excess nonfinancial assets, excess nonfinancial liabilities and the net financial debt of the valued company. Depending on the assumptions and technique used, the value of any existing tax loss carryforward is sometimes taken into account at this stage if it was not included within the projected tax expenses.
e. When needed, further adjustments should be made at the last stage, such as due to lack of marketability or lack of control (assuming that the weighted average discount rate used reflects control or liquidity), reasonableness checks based on indications from other valuation techniques or splitting the equity into its components (where the equity is composed of several types of instruments, such as preferred shares, warrants or ordinary shares).

As in the case of other valuation techniques, the application of the DFC technique may be prone to error. Some of the potential reasons for such an error are listed below:

a. Inconsistency between different assumptions made as part of the forecast, such as inconsistency between the scope of investment in operating working capital and the scope of revenue growth;
b. When preparing the forecasts, failure to take into account other scenarios that embody uncertainty, such as reliance solely on management's forecasts or on an optimistic scenario alone;
c. Using an inappropriately high permanent growth rate in the long term;
d. Errors or inconsistencies in calculating the WACC, such as estimating it on the basis of the interest rate in respect of a currency that does not correspond to the currency in which the cash flow forecast is denominated or using wrong weights of debt and equity, which are based on their carrying amounts rather than on their proportionate weight in the value;
e. Failing to make further needed adjustments, such as adjustments in respect of illiquidity or lack of control; and
f. Assuming that the cash flow in the representative year is permanent, when the valued enterprise is a limited-life enterprise, such as a project with a

defined period or a project that requires renewal, about which there is no certainty.

Example—Application of the DCF Technique to an Enterprise

As of December 31, 2017, Company A holds 5 percent of the share capital of Company B. It is assumed that there are no current transactions involving the shares of Company B and that after considering the nature of Company B's activities, the nature of the activities of comparable companies and the quantity of observable inputs relating to the comparable companies, Company A opted to use DCF as the most appropriate valuation technique to estimate the fair value of the investment. Below is a description of the projections and the additional inputs relevant to the valuation. It is assumed that the projections were formed after taking into consideration all relevant facts and circumstances from the perspective of a market participant, such as Company B's growth rate in the past, the markets in which it operates, its market share, the scope of competition, regulation, market price levels, barriers to entry and exit, Company B's profitability and the profitability of its competitors and so forth (financial data are denominated in CU):

a. According to the projections, Company B's revenues are expected to amount to CU 100,000 in 2018 (a 10 percent increase compared to 2017). A further 10 percent increase in revenues is expected in 2019, and thereafter, the growth rate is expected to decline to 3 percent per year.
b. In 2018, Company B's annual rate of EBITDA is expected to be 25 percent. This rate is expected to decrease by 1 percent per year, until stabilizing at 22 percent from 2021 and thereafter.
c. The annual depreciation and amortization are expected to form 10 percent of revenues.
d. In the forecast years, Company B's annual investment in property, plant and equipment and in intangible assets is expected to be CU 5,000. As from 2022 and thereafter, the investment amount is expected to equal the depreciation and amortization expenses.
e. Company B's operating working capital as of December 31, 2017, which is composed of inventory, trade receivables and trade payable, is CU 40,000 (debit, i.e., a net asset). The assumption is that the rate of change in operating working capital in the forecast period will correspond to the rate of change in revenues.

f. During the forecast period, the corporate tax rate applicable to Company B is 25 percent. Company B does not have any operations that are subject to tax rates other than the regular corporate tax rate, and it does not have carryforward losses for tax purposes or other material deferred tax differences.
g. Company B has no further excess assets that do not form part of its operation.
h. Company B has net financial debt (i.e., a debt such as bonds and loans net of liquid assets such as investments, deposits or cash and cash equivalents) at a fair value of CU 30,000.
i. The appropriate WACC in respect of Company B's operations is estimated by Company A at 11 percent.
j. Company B's equity does not include noncontrolling interest, warrants, preferred shares or other instruments other than ordinary shares.
k. Company A estimates that a 15 percent deduction (from the equity value before the deduction) is required due to the fact that Company B is a private company, since the WACC was calculated while relying on liquid investments, with no adjustments. It should be noted that there may be other methods to calculate to said deduction.
l. On average, Company B's cash flow is obtained in the middle of each year.

Set forth below is a calculation of Company B's fair value according to the said assumptions used in the DCF technique:

Forecast for:	**In CU**				
	2018	**2019**	**2020**	**2021**	**2022 (representative)**
Revenue	100,000	110,000	113,300	116,699	120,200
EBITDA	25,000	26,400	26,059	25,674	26,444
Depreciation and amortization	(10,000)	(11,000)	(11,330)	(11,670)	(12,020)
Operating profit	15,000	15,400	14,729	14,004	14,424
Operating tax	(3,750)	(3,850)	(3,682)	(3,501)	(3,606)
Profit after taxes	11,250	11,550	11,047	10,503	10,818
Adjustments from post-tax profit to cash flow					
Exclusion of depreciation and amortization	10,000	11,000	11,330	11,670	12,020
Investment in assets	(5,000)	(5,000)	(5,000)	(5,000)	(12,020)

Forecast for:	In CU				
	2018	2019	2020	2021	2022 (representative)
Investment in working capital, net	(4,000)	(4,400)	(1,452)	(1,496)	(1,540)
Free cash flow	12,250	13,150	15,925	15,677	9,278

The discount of the free cash flow projections in 2018–2021—according to the WACC rate, assuming that on average the cash flow is obtained in the middle of each year—is CU 46,019. The present value of the cash flows as from 2022 and thereafter should be added to this amount. Since that cash flow is stabilized and is expected to grow at a fixed rate of 3 percent, the perpetual cash flow formula can be used: CU 115,975 (= 9,278 / (11% − 3%)). This amount should now be discounted as of valuation date: CU 80,489 (= 115,975 / 1.11 ^ 3.5). Note that the use of the perpetual cash flow formula has already brought the cash flow one year back. Therefore, the overall EV is CU 126,508 (= 80,489 + 46,019). The value of the net financial debt (CU 30,000) should now be deducted from the EV so that the resulting equity value (before adjustments) is CU 96,508. A 15 percent liquidity premium should be deducted from the said value, such that the equity value (after adjustments) is CU 82,031. Therefore, the fair value of Company A's holdings in Company B is CU 4,102 (= 82,031 × 5%).

4. Using Multiple Valuation Techniques

In some cases, using a single valuation technique for estimating fair value will be appropriate (e.g., when valuing an asset or liability using quoted prices in an active market for identical assets or liabilities). In other cases, multiple valuation techniques will be possible or appropriate (e.g., when valuing a cash-generating unit as defined in International Accounting Standard (IAS) 36), after taking into consideration all facts and circumstances. Formally, even if the reporting entity estimated the fair value using several valuation techniques and selected only one of them, this will be considered using more than one valuation technique.

Thus, for example, if appropriate, a reporting entity can weigh the result obtained from using the multiples technique against the result obtained from using the DCF technique or weigh the results obtained under the multiples technique from several types of relevant multiples (for more information, see Section 3). In these cases, the reasonableness of the range of values within each indication shall be evaluated, and the point within the range that is most representative of fair value in the circumstances shall be selected. Sometimes, reporting entities may need to analyze the nature of the differences between the results of the various valuation techniques. In other words, reporting entities may need to understand the factors that may cause the differences and decide how market participants would have taken those factors into account. The weighting of valuation techniques shall be applied consistently, unless a change in a valuation technique's weighting will result in an equally or more representative measurement of fair value under the circumstances. Thus, for example, if there is a current and an observable transaction in a comparable company, it might be appropriate to place a higher weight on the multiples approach when estimating the fair value, compared to the weighting used in previous valuations.

Below are two examples dealing with the considerations that should be taken into account when weighting the valuation techniques. The examples are based on similar examples provided by the Standards:

Example A—Using Multiple Valuation Techniques to Measure the Fair Value of a Machine

Company A obtains control over Company B in a business combination. As part of the allocation of the cost of acquisition, Company A is required to estimate the fair value of a machine used by the acquired enterprise. Company B had originally bought the machine from an external supplier. The machine was customized (to a certain extent) for use by Company B, and the customization included, among other things, installation of the machine. Although the machine is a separate unit of account, the valuation premise is that the highest and best use of the machine will be in combination with other assets and liabilities; therefore, Company A has also taken into account the theoretical value of the machine's customization from the perspective of a market participant who holds the other assets and liabilities (for more information, see Chapter 9, Section 3).

Since the machine does not generate separate and identifiable cash flows, and since there is no information about the rent for machines of this type for the relevant period, Company A believes that the income approach is inappropriate for measuring the machine's fair value. Company A decided that the cost approach (i.e., the cost of obtaining a customized machine of comparable utility) will be the appropriate method to measure the fair value. Furthermore, since the customization of the machine was not extensive, the market approach may also be appropriate under the circumstances.

Below is a description of the results of the application of the two valuation approaches:

a. When applying the market approach, the Company uses quoted prices of similar machines (in our view, in that case, the Standards refer to price lists or to prices of transactions involving secondhand machines); the Company then adjusts those prices in respect of the differences between the purchased machine and similar machines, including its current condition (used machine) and location (installed and customized for use). The resulting fair value ranges between CU 40,000 and CU 48,000.
b. When applying the cost approach, the Company estimates the cost that would have been incurred to construct (to use the Standards' term) a substitute customized machine of comparable utility while making adjustments to account for the machine's condition as a used machine, including physical wear and tear and obsolescence, improvements in technology, external conditions (economic depreciation, such as reduced demand for machines of the said type) and installation costs. The fair value obtained under this approach ranges between CU 40,000 and CU 52,000.

The Company believes that the fair value at the high end of the range under the market approach best represents the fair value of the machine. The reasons for this are the inputs used for making an estimate according to this approach were fewer and less subjective than those used in the other valuation approach; additionally, the range indicated by the market approach was narrower than the range indicated by the cost approach; furthermore, there were no additional known and unexplained differences between the measured machine and the comparable machines. Accordingly, the Company determines that the fair value of the machine is CU 48,000.

It should be noted that there may be circumstances in which the market approach would have been given less weight. Thus, for example, if the scope of customization of the machine was significant and the market transactions involved only machines sold for scrap, this approach might have resulted in an irrelevant estimate, and the Company would have only used the cost approach.

Example B—Using Multiple Valuation Techniques to Measure the Fair Value of Software

Company A purchases a group of assets (that does not meet the definition of a business). The asset group includes an internally developed software and other complementary assets, such as a database used by the software. The asset group generates income from selling software licenses to customers. To allocate the cost of the acquisition to the individual assets acquired, Company A is required to measure their relative fair value. As part of this process, Company A also measures the fair value of the software asset. Company A's valuation premise is that the software will be used in combination with the complementary assets (such as the database). Company A concludes that under the circumstances, it can use the income approach and that there are also sufficient inputs that will allow it to apply the cost approach. However, the market approach cannot be applied in this case, since there is no available information about market transactions for comparable assets.

The Company applies the income approach and the cost approach as follows:

a. The income approach is applied using a present value technique. The cash flows used in that technique reflect the income expected to result from the software asset (license fees from customers) over its economic life, net of contributory costs and charges in respect of the use of other assets. The fair value indicated by that approach is CU 15 million.
b. The cost approach is applied by estimating the amount that would be required to construct a substitute software asset of comparable utility while taking into account functional and economic obsolescence. For instance, the Company can estimate the cost of hours invested by employees, the additional overheads as well as the unexpected costs relating to the development of a similar software. The fair value indicated by that approach is CU 10 million.

Once the Company obtains the results from the application of both valuation techniques and after further analysis, it decides that market participants would not be able to construct or develop a substitute software asset of comparable utility, since some of the characteristics of the software are unique, having been developed using intellectual property that is unavailable to market participants and cannot be readily replicated. Accordingly, the Company determines that the fair value of the software is CU 15 million, as indicated by the income approach.

5. Calibration of Valuation Techniques

As explained in the section dealing with measurement of fair value at initial recognition (for more information, see Chapter 8, Section 1), reporting entities should assess whether or not the transaction price reflects the fair value. When the reporting entity concludes that the transaction price does, indeed, reflect the fair value of the asset or liability at initial recognition, and in subsequent periods the reporting entity will use a valuation technique that uses unobservable inputs, it is important to calibrate the valuation technique according to the transaction price, that is, use the transaction price to obtain the appropriate assumptions and inputs that generate this result. It is important to note that calibration may be required even if the item was not measured at fair value at initial recognition and is measured at fair value only in subsequent periods. Another relevant example is when market inputs become unavailable at a subsequent measurement date and the reporting entity needs to resort to using a valuation technique. Here as well, calibration ensures that the valuation reflects current market conditions and will also help a reporting entity to determine whether any adjustments to the valuation technique are necessary. Calibration may be explained by the fact that there might be a characteristic of the valued item that is not captured (on not sufficiently captured) by the valuation technique used or by the inputs otherwise used in it. If a reporting entity measures fair value after initial recognition using a valuation technique (or techniques) that uses unobservable inputs, it must ensure that the valuation technique(s) also reflects observable market inputs (e.g., the price for a similar asset or liability) at the measurement date.

The following example illustrates a calibration of a valuation technique.

Example—Calibration

On January 1, 2017, Company A acquires 5 percent of the share capital of private Company B for CU 5,000. After considering the circumstances of the transaction, Company A concludes that it is an orderly transaction and that the transaction's consideration best reflects Company B's fair value, that is, Company B's fair value as of the transaction date is CU 100,000 (= 5,000 / 5%). It is assumed that after taking into account the characteristics of Company B, the comparable companies and the observable inputs that are available for the comparable companies, Company A plans to use the multiples technique to measure the fair value of the investment in Company B in subsequent periods (for more information, see Section 3.2). The relevant multiple selected for the purpose of measuring the fair value of Company B is the EV/EBITDA multiple. Company A also concludes that adjustments (deductions) should be made due to lack of marketability as well as lack of control. As of acquisition date, Company B's representative EBITDA is CU 12,500, and it has a net financial debt of CU 5,000.

Below is a description of the model that will be used by Company A, calibrated as of the acquisition date (in CU):

Enterprise value of Company B (multiple of 10)	:	125,000	=	12,500 × 10
Less, net financial debt	:	120,000	=	125,000 − 5,000
Discount due to lack of marketability (at 5% of the value)	:	(6,000)	=	120,000 × 5%
Discount due to lack of control (at 11.67% of the value)	:	(14,000)	=	120,000 × 11.67%
Equity value	:	100,000		
Value of Company A's holding (5%)	:	5,000		

It is possible to see, then, that as part of the calibration, Company A adjusted the model or the assumptions (particularly the appropriate multiple and the required deductions), such that its result equals the result of the transaction as of the transaction date. In subsequent periods, Company A will need to take into consideration all observable market inputs in order to estimate the changes to be made in each of the model's assumptions or in the model itself. Calibration is important because it takes into account the existing information regarding the transaction itself as part of the model's assumptions. Thus, for example, if in subsequent periods the average level of multiples in the industry will increase from 12 (as of the transaction date) to 15 and no other changes will occur, Company A will need to consider how to reflect this change in the model. It is possible that, in view of the fact that under the calibration as at the transaction date, the selected EV/EBITDA multiple for Company B (10) was lower than the market average (12), Company A will use a multiple of, for example, 13 rather than 15, in order to reflect the difference between Company B's multiple and the average (unless there are other inputs that indicate that this difference has changed). Something else that is evident from this example is that the method of calibration is subject to judgment, since Company A could have calibrated the model in the example by adjusting multiples, deductions due to lack of control or marketability (or a combination of both). In more complex models, calibration can be achieved by changing multiple parameters. When deciding on calibration, reporting entities need to take into consideration all facts and circumstances. The effect of calibration will usually be reflected in adjustments to unobservable inputs, which are characterized by the highest level of subjectivity.

6. Changing the Valuation Techniques

Generally, a valuation technique shall be selected and applied consistently in subsequent measurements, as long as the circumstances did not change in a way that justifies changing the technique applied or the way it is applied (e.g., a change in its weighting when multiple valuation techniques are used). A change in a valuation technique or in the way it is applied is appropriate only if the change results in a measurement that is equally or more representative of fair value under the same circumstances.

The Standards provide a nonexhaustive list of circumstances in which a reporting entity may be required to change a valuation technique or its application:

a. New markets develop.
b. New information becomes available.
c. Previously used information is no longer available.
d. Valuation techniques improve.
e. Market conditions change.

It can be concluded from the aforementioned provision that the valuation technique should not be changed merely in order to avoid the need to recognize an impairment loss and without an evident change in the circumstances (including improvement in valuation techniques). Despite the requirement that valuation techniques be applied consistently, revisions resulting from a change in the valuation technique or its application will be accounted for as a change in accounting estimate in accordance with IAS 8—*Accounting Policies, Changes in Accounting Estimates and Errors* (under IFRS) or ASC Topic 250—*Accounting Changes and Error Corrections* rather than as a change in accounting policy. This means that the value obtained from the application of the new technique should be applied prospectively. It should be noted that according to IAS 8 and ASC Topic 250, when an accounting estimate is changed, the reporting entity should usually disclose (among other things) the effect of the change on the current reporting period. Under normal conditions, this would require the reporting entity to estimate the fair value by applying simultaneously the previous valuation technique and the new technique, as of the end of the reporting period, and may require the reporting entity to obtain inputs that are unavailable. Therefore, due to cost-benefit considerations, the Standards as well as ASC Topic 250 and IAS 8 exempt the reporting entity from the usual disclosure requirements regarding a change in accounting estimates. Despite the aforesaid, it should be emphasized that a change in a valuation technique as a result of prior period errors, such as when a wrong valuation technique is selected, or when specific characteristics of the measured item or existing market inputs are ignored, would be accounted for as a prior period error rather than as a change in an accounting estimate.

7. Adjusting Inputs Used in the Valuation or Adjusting the Valuation Techniques Themselves

7.1. Overview

Another issue that is referred to in the Standards and related literature has to do with various considerations that should be taken into account when making valuation adjustments to valuation techniques or to inputs used in the application of the valuation technique.

The need for adjustments stems from the fact that sometimes the technique used (before the adjustment) or the inputs used in the valuation do not fully reflect the assumptions that market participants would have taken into account when pricing the item relevant to the measurement, including with regard to risk.

The Standards list examples of situations where reporting entities might need to adjust the model's result, structure or the inputs used in the application of the model:

a. An adjustment to a valuation technique in order to take into account a characteristic of the asset or the liability that is not captured by the valuation technique. It should be noted that the need for such an adjustment is typically identified during calibration (for more information, see Section 5). Examples of such adjustments may include adjustment for restriction or illiquidity, such as when the model relies on data obtained from liquid markets or on prices of tradable shares, whereas the measured item is illiquid or restricted; adjustment for lack of control, or alternatively an adjustment to reflect a control premium, such as when the model relies on transactions that include a control premium, whereas the measured item does not include a control component, or vice versa; adjustment due to size, such as when there are size differences between the transactions, the prices of which were used as inputs in the valuation and the relevant characteristic of the measured item; adjustment due to other restrictions, such as restrictions placed on the use of the measured item, which do not exist in respect of the inputs used in the valuation; and adjustment for an additional risk, which is not reflected in the inputs or the technique but is relevant to the measured item or the valuation model.
b. An adjustment to identify the point within the bid-ask spread that is most representative of fair value under the circumstances (for more information, see Section 8.3).
c. An adjustment to reflect non-performance risk, which was not taken into account in the model (for more information, see Chapter 10, Section 5);

for example, when a reporting entity uses an option pricing model that assumes that the settlement of an option does not embody a credit or other non-performance risk, even though such a risk does actually exist.

d. An adjustment to reflect measurement uncertainty, such as when there has been a significant decrease in the volume or level of activity as compared with normal market activity for the asset or liability, and the reporting entity has determined that market transaction prices do not represent fair value (for more information, see Chapter 7, Section 3).

The need to make adjustments depends on all relevant facts and circumstances. However, any adjustments should be consistent with the unit of account of the measured item (for more information, see Section 7.2). Premiums or discounts that reflect a characteristic of the reporting entity, rather than a characteristic of the measured item, shall not be taken into consideration in a fair value measurement.

7.2. The connection between making adjustments and the unit of account

The key principle established by the Standards regarding the application of adjustments (including premiums or discounts) is that such application will only take place if the premiums or discounts relate to a characteristic that is part of the measured item's unit of account (for more information, see Chapter 3, Section 3). In other words, if a particular characteristic is not a characteristic included in the unit of account, but rather an entity-specific characteristic, the reporting entity should not make an adjustment in respect of that characteristic. Thus, for example, if the reporting entity has restricted shares, the question of whether to apply a discount (in relation to the quoted market price of otherwise identical unrestricted shares) depends on whether the restriction is part of the restricted shares' unit of account (for more information, see Chapter 3, Section 2). For example, does the restriction result from a lien placed on the shares, or will it be transferred to a buyer of the shares in a theoretical sale? Similarly, if the reporting entity has 100 apartments that are rented, the question of whether to apply a volume (size) discount (in relation to the price obtained from the total value of each of the apartments) depends largely (in addition to the characteristics of the market) on the question of whether the apartments are defined as a single unit of account.

The relevant unit of account of financial instruments is usually the individual financial instrument. Therefore, when the reporting entity holds a position that is made up of many financial instruments, the fair value of the position will be the sum of the value of each individual financial instrument, without taking into account size adjustments due to the size of the position. One of the specific provisions of the Standard, which deals with volume discounts and which is consistent with the rationale noted above, is that a reporting entity shall not take into account a blockage factor, which adjusts the quoted price of an asset or a liability, because the market's normal daily trading volume is not sufficient to absorb the quantity held by the reporting entity (see example below). The logic behind this provision can be that holding a large block of shares is actually an entity-specific characteristic, rather than a characteristic of the shares, and the decision of how to sell the shares, which affects the amount of the potential loss, is made by the reporting entity and is not related to the asset. In that respect, the loss that might be incurred on disposal is similar in nature to transaction costs. It should also be noted that the underlying principle of the valuation premise (for more information, see Chapter 9, Section 3) does not apply to financial instruments, and therefore, it should not be assumed that a market participant will sell an entire position. For an exception regarding a portfolio of financial instruments that includes offsetting positions, see Chapter 11.

In order to illustrate the aforementioned provisions, let us assume that the reporting entity holds 50,000 (tradable) shares of a particular public company (for which there is an active market), which do not confer upon the reporting entity control, significant influence or joint control over the investee. However, the number of shares held by the reporting entity is large, and selling all the shares in a single transaction may cause the quoted price to plummet (due to excess supply). Another way to sell the shares is to use distribution services in an off-floor transaction. However, the reporting entity will incur high costs in such a transaction (or will obtain a price that is lower than the quoted price). In this case, even though it is clear that the value of the entire position is lower than the quoted price multiplied by the number of shares held by the reporting entity, the adjustment in respect of the size of the position should not be taken into account, since each share (financial instrument) is a separate unit of account, and therefore, the fair value of each of the shares held by the reporting entity will be derived solely from the quoted price.

At this point, it should be clarified that if volume is a characteristic of the unit of account of the individual financial instrument, and will be taken into consideration by market participants, it should be taken into account when measuring the fair value. Thus, for example, let us assume now that the reporting entity holds a single, nontradable call warrant, upon the exercise of which the public company will issue to the reporting entity the aforementioned 50,000 shares. In this situation, since the financial instrument in question is an individual unit of account, the discount applied to the fair value (of the underlying asset) should be taken into account when measuring the value of the warrant, if a market participant would have taken this discount into account when determining the price of the warrant.

It is important to note that the rule whereby application of premiums or discounts (such as a discount in respect of a blockage factor) is required only when such premiums or discounts refer to a factor that is part of the unit of account (and which was not taken into account in the valuation technique and inputs) is applicable to all levels of the fair value hierarchy. In other words, the decision as to whether a particular characteristic will be taken into account is not derived from the level of the valuation or inputs of the fair value hierarchy (Level 1, Level 2 or Level 3). Thus, for example, the rationale applicable to a size discount is relevant even when the components of the position in question do not have a quoted price in an active market (for more information, see Section 8.4). If the reporting entity holds a portfolio comprising 1,000 separate debt instruments, with a par value of CU 10 million each, then the question of whether a volume discount should be taken into account and what the rate of such a discount will be is derived from the separate value of each of the instruments rather than from the size of the entire portfolio. The answer to this question remains the same regardless of whether the debt instruments have a quoted price in an active market (Level 1) or if the said instruments are nontradable, and therefore, their valuations were categorized within Level 2 or Level 3 of the fair value hierarchy. However, had the reporting entity held a single loan of CU 10 billion, the need to apply a volume discount would have been taken into account based on this value, so long as such a discount would have been taken into account by a market participant.

8. Selecting the Inputs Used in the Valuation Technique and the Fair Value Hierarchy

8.1. Overview

Application of every valuation technique requires the use of inputs. The term "input" is defined in the Standards as the assumptions that market participants would use when pricing the asset or liability, including assumptions about risk, such as the risk inherent in a particular valuation technique used to measure fair value (model risk) or the risk inherent in the inputs to the valuation technique (input risk). In other words, the compensation for using a particular model or input that carries the risk that they would not fully account for the characteristics of the item or the market conditions is an input in itself.

The most commonly used inputs required for the application of valuation techniques are discount or interest rates (including all components used to estimate them), cash flow forecasts, multiples, standard deviations, different transaction prices, maturity periods, various premiums or discounts and so forth (for more information, see Section 3).

The Standards divide the inputs required for fair value measurement into observable inputs and unobservable inputs (for more information, see Section 8.2). As a guiding principle, valuation techniques used to measure fair value should maximize the use of relevant observable inputs and minimize the use of unobservable ones. Obviously, the mere fact that an input is observable does not automatically make it significant to the measurement; the inputs also need to be relevant to the fair value of the measured item. Furthermore, the mere fact that a relevant observable input is available does not necessarily mean that the reporting entity will not need to adjust this input to account for other characteristics of the asset or liability (for more information, see Section 7).

8.2. Observable versus unobservable inputs

As mentioned above, the Standards divide the inputs required for fair value measurement into observable and unobservable inputs and state that valuation techniques used to measure fair value will maximize the use of observable inputs and minimize the use of unobservable ones.

Observable inputs are defined as inputs that are developed using market inputs, such as publicly available information about actual events or transactions, and which reflect the assumptions that market participants would use when pricing the asset or liability. Unobservable inputs, on the other hand, are defined as inputs for which market data are not available and that are developed using the best information available about the assumptions that market participants would use when pricing the asset or liability.

The Standards provide several examples of markets where inputs might be observable for some assets and liabilities (such as financial instruments); these markets include the following:

a. Exchange markets: In an exchange market, closing prices are both readily available and generally representative of fair value. The London Stock Exchange (LSE) is an example of such a market mentioned in IFRS 13, while ACS 820—somewhat amusingly—chooses to mention the New York Stock Exchange. In our view, the mere fact that a particular security is listed for trading on a stock exchange does not necessarily mean that it is traded in an active market. For more information, see Section 2.2.
b. Dealer markets: In a dealer market, dealers stand ready to trade (either buy or sell for their own account), thereby providing liquidity by using their capital to hold inventory of the items for which they make a market.

Typically bid and ask prices (representing the price at which the dealer is willing to buy and the price at which the dealer is willing to sell, respectively) are more readily available than closing prices. OTC markets (for which prices are publicly reported) are dealer markets. Dealer markets also exist for some other assets and liabilities, including some financial instruments, commodities and physical assets (e.g., used equipment). ASC 820 clarifies that OTC markets (for which prices are publicly reported by the National Association of Securities Dealers Automated Quotations systems or by OTC Markets Group Inc.) are dealer markets. For more information, see Section 8.3.

c. Brokered markets: In a brokered market, brokers attempt to match buyers with sellers but do not stand ready to trade for their own account. In other words, brokers do not use their own capital to hold inventory of the items for which they make a market. The broker knows the bid and ask prices proposed by the respective parties, but each party is not necessarily aware of the other party's price requirements. Prices of completed transactions are sometimes available. Brokered markets include electronic communication networks, in which buy and sell orders are matched, as well as commercial and residential real estate markets. Thus, for example, in countries that do not have a governmental database of real estate transactions, firms providing estate agent services may sometimes supply or maintain detailed information on comparable transactions in which they were involved.
d. Principal-to-principal markets: In a principal-to-principal market, transactions—both originations and resales—are negotiated independently with no intermediary. Little information about those transactions may be made available publicly. Thus, for example, there could be a governmental database of real estate transactions, but detailed information about the characteristics of the sold assets (such as physical condition and occupancy rates) is not always available. There are many markets where reporting the transaction price is not obligatory, or where transactions are typically carried out by transferring other rights, such as transfer of shares of single-asset entities.

It is important to note that the mere fact that a certain input or price was received from a third-party pricing service does not necessarily mean that this input is an observable one. After all, according to the Standards' definition, observable inputs are ones that reflect the assumptions that market participants would use when pricing the asset or liability. In our view, then, a price quotation provided to the reporting entity by a third party, which was developed according to a methodology in which the third party used the DCF technique to measure the fair value of a company's shares, is not an observable input, since the third party also used unobservable inputs when developing the price. Therefore, in order to determine whether particular inputs or prices (such as price quotations received from asset pricing companies or services) are observable inputs, the method used to develop such inputs should actually be assessed.

Furthermore, the mere fact that a certain input is an observable one does not necessarily mean that the valuation that made use of the observable input will be categorized within Level 1 or Level 2 of the fair value hierarchy (for more information, see Section 8.4). Often, reporting entities need to adjust observable inputs, either due to the obsolescence of the inputs (e.g., due to the period of time that had elapsed since the date of the comparable transaction) or due to specific characteristics of the measured asset or liability. In such situations, the overall categorization of the valuation in the fair value hierarchy will be affected by the method employed to make the adjustment (i.e., whether the adjustment was made purely on the basis of observable inputs) and by the materiality of the adjustment.

8.3. Inputs based on bid and ask prices

Sometimes, markets that use intermediaries, such as dealer or brokered markets (for more information, see Section 8.2), lack transparency (e.g., quoted prices) regarding the prices of actual recent transactions. However, for such markets there may be inputs based on bid prices (the price at which the dealer or another party is offering to buy the item) or ask prices (the price at which the dealer or another party is offering to sell the item) for the asset or liability being measured at fair value. If a certain item measured at fair value has a bid price and an ask price, the fair value of the item shall be measured only within the bid-ask spread. In this case, the price within the bid-ask spread that is most representative of fair value under the circumstances shall be used to measure fair value regardless of the category within which the input is categorized in the fair value hierarchy (i.e., Level 1, 2 or 3; for more information, see Section 8.4). The rationale behind this provision is clear—the said prices are the "boundaries" within which negotiations on the actual price are conducted (and even more so if these prices bind the party offering them).

As noted above, reporting entities are required to select the point within the bid-ask spread that best represents the fair value under the circumstances. Under IFRS, IAS 39, which was superseded by IFRS 9, established (at the time) relatively conservative and uniform accounting treatment for the measurement of financial instruments using bid and ask prices. According to this method, assets (or asset positions) were measured at the bid price, and liabilities (or liability positions) were measured at the ask price of the corresponding asset. Under US GAAP, Accounting Series Release (ASR)118 originally allowed for a more diverse practice for investment companies and dealer-brokers. Statement of Financial Accounting Standard (SFAS) 157, as originally issued, did not intend to change the then-existing practice under US GAAP and, hence, only set the boundaries and principles for bid-ask pricing while retaining the flexibility. It may be said that this flexibility was carried forward to ASC 820 and IFRS 13, as they note that the use of bid prices for asset positions and ask prices for liability positions is permitted but not required.

The Standards also note that it does not preclude the use of mid-market pricing (i.e., the average of the bid and ask prices) or other pricing conventions used by market participants as a practical expedient for fair value measurements within a bid-ask spread. In our view, using the said practical expedients is not meant to contradict the main principles of the Standards. Therefore, in situations where there are significant differences between the bid price and the ask price (a relatively broad bid-ask spread), and where using simplistic conventions as aforementioned may generate results that are not achievable, it would be best to carry out further analysis before using the said practical expedients. Thus, when the bid-ask spread is very broad, it is possible that selecting the appropriate point within the bid-ask spread would require the application of another valuation technique to the measured item (such as the DCF technique). In our view, a similar principle should also apply when there are only bid prices or only ask prices or when the offered prices do not bind the parties offering them.

The explanatory notes of IFRS 13 state that for the purpose of selecting the point within the bid-ask spread, the spread itself should be analyzed and explained. One of the potential explanations for the differences between bid and ask prices is the existence of transaction costs that create such differences. In other words, some of the differences may be bridged by analyzing the transaction costs applicable to the parties. On the other hand, according to IFRS 13's explanatory notes, the bid-ask spread may not be used to compensate for offsetting positions of counterparty credit risk, and such offsetting positions can only be accounted for by applying the exception set by IFRS 13 for that purpose (for more information, see Chapter 11).

Bid or ask prices can also be relevant in other situations, such as when there are no sufficiently recent transactions on stock exchanges that involve the measured asset or liability, but the orders book includes buy and sell orders that did not match (due to price differences) but are observable. It should be noted that the explanatory notes of IFRS 13 clarify that pricing according to the bid-ask spread is only relevant in markets where an intermediary such as a broker is necessary and only for financial instruments. SFAS 157's original Basis for

Conclusions mentioned a dealer market as an example. In our view, by limiting the use of bid-ask spread as aforementioned, IFRS 13's Basis for Conclusions allegedly restricts reporting entities' ability to use the above practical expedients in other scenarios. However, in our view, the basic rationale, whereby recent bid and ask offers typically determine the fair value range (especially if they are binding or involve significant volume), may also be relevant to other items, even if the aforementioned practical expedients are inapplicable to these items.

8.4. The fair value hierarchy

A. Overview

To increase consistency and comparability in fair value measurements, the Standards establish a fair value hierarchy that categorizes into three levels the inputs to valuation techniques used to measure fair value. It is important to emphasize that the fair value hierarchy prioritizes the inputs to the selected valuation technique rather than the different valuation techniques. Indeed, the extent of the use of observable inputs within a particular valuation technique may certainly be one of the considerations for selecting such a valuation technique (for more information, see Section 2). In addition to the hierarchy regarding the inputs used in a valuation, the Standards also include a similar hierarchy in respect of the result obtained from the fair value measurement in its entirety (see Section b. below).

The fair value hierarchy is important for two reasons: firstly, in situations where a particular input can be estimated in more than one method (and this input is required for the application of the valuation technique), the hierarchy assigns the highest priority to observable inputs; secondly, and as described below, the Standards use the fair value hierarchy as an indication of the level of reliability of the valuation in its entirety. Thus, when a reporting entity uses unobservable inputs that are more subjective and whose impact on the result is significant, it will be required to provide more extensive disclosures about the valuation in the notes to the financial statements than in a situation where no unobservable inputs were used (for more information, see Chapter 13).

In order to illustrate the Standards' hierarchy provisions, let us assume that the reporting entity holds nontradable call warrants that are exercisable (on a gross basis) into one ordinary share of a public company, whose shares are listed for trading on a stock exchange and which have an active market. It is also assumed that, under the circumstances, the reporting entity opts to measure the fair value of the warrants by using a generally accepted pricing model, such as B&S. One of the inputs required for the application of the model is the fair value of the underlying asset, that is, the fair value of the public company's share. In such a situation, in our view, the reporting entity could only use as a valuation technique the quoted price of the share in order to measure its fair value. Thus, for example, in our view, the reporting entity will not be able to use the multiples technique or the DCF technique in order to calculate the value of the share, since an observable input is available for the share (a quoted price in an active market). Similarly, let us assume that the reporting entity holds restricted shares of a public company; those shares, which are restricted as to their tradability on the stock exchange, have characteristics that are identical to those of other shares that have a quoted price in an active market (except for the restriction characteristic). The reporting entity estimates the fair value of its investment by applying a technique that uses the following inputs: (a) the value of an unrestricted share and (b) the effect of the restriction characteristic. In this situation, in our view, the reporting entity will have to use the quoted share price as the first input (before making the adjustment in respect of the restriction). However, in the latter example, it is possible that the valuation technique selected by the reporting entity might not have used the quoted price of an unrestricted share as of the measurement date, and in such a case, the reporting entity was not required to use this input either. Thus, for example, under special circumstances, it is possible that for the purpose of measuring the restricted share, the reporting entity would have used the price of a current transaction involving identical restricted shares, which took place exactly at the end of the measurement date (and therefore, the reporting entity would not have been required to make any adjustments to the said price).

The fair value hierarchy divides the inputs into three levels, as follows:

a. Level 1 inputs—are defined as quoted prices (unadjusted) in active markets for identical assets or liabilities that the reporting entity can access at the measurement date.
b. Level 2 inputs—are defined as inputs other than quoted prices included within Level 1 that are observable for the asset or liability, either directly or indirectly.
c. Level 3 inputs—are defined as unobservable inputs for the asset or liability.

The fair value hierarchy gives the highest priority to Level 1 inputs and the lowest priority to Level 3 inputs. As a rule, the lower the use of observable inputs and the higher the subjectivity level of the assumptions, the lower the fair value hierarchy level within which the inputs will be categorized. The Standards provide specific rules for categorization of inputs within each level and guidelines as to the permitted adjustments and the implications of these adjustments (for more information, see Sections 8.5–8.7).

B. Categorizing the entire measurement level

As described above, the Standards use the fair value hierarchy not only for the purpose of prioritizing inputs that are used in the application of valuation techniques but also for disclosure purposes. To this end, the valuation in its entirety should be categorized within Level 1, 2 or 3 of the fair value hierarchy. For this purpose, the Standards set a rule that may be referred to as "the weakest link rule," that is, when inputs that are used to measure the fair value of an asset or a liability are categorized within different levels of the fair value hierarchy, the entire fair value measurement is categorized within the same level of the fair value hierarchy as the lowest level input that is significant to the entire measurement.

Thus, for example, a fair value measurement that uses Level 2 inputs (observable inputs) and Level 3 inputs (unobservable inputs), which are significant to the measurement in its entirety, will be categorized in its entirety within Level 3 of the fair value measurement. Assessing the significance of a particular input to the entire measurement requires judgment and taking into account factors specific to the asset or liability.

Consistently with the aforementioned rationale, when an observable input is adjusted by an unobservable input and the effect of this adjustment is significant to the valuation, the resulting measurement will be categorized within Level 3. Thus, for example, let us assume that the reporting entity holds a restricted share. To measure its value, the reporting entity uses the observable share price (a Level 1 or 2 input, as the case may be) as a starting point and adjusts the observable price in order to reflect the effect of the restriction that is specific to the held share; the adjustment is an unobservable input (i.e., Level 3). In such a situation, if the required adjustment is significant to the measurement in its entirety, the measurement will be categorized in its entirety within Level 3 of the fair value hierarchy for purposes of the Standards' disclosure provisions.

As an exception, adjustments to fair value that are required for fair value–based measurements (such as deducting costs to sell when measuring fair value less costs to sell according to IFRS 5 or IAS 36 under IFRS) will not be taken into account when determining the level of the fair value hierarchy within which a fair value measurement is categorized in its entirety. This is the case even if such adjustments are unobservable and significant to the result.

Sections 8.5 through 8.7 below provide additional details regarding the types of inputs categorized within each level, the permitted adjustments to those inputs and their effect on the categorization of a fair value measurement in its entirety.

8.5. Level 1 inputs

A. Inputs categorized within Level 1

Level 1 inputs are defined as quoted prices (unadjusted) in active markets for identical assets or liabilities that the reporting entity can access at the measurement date. A quoted price in an active market provides the most reliable evidence of fair value and should be used without adjustment to measure fair value whenever available, except for the defined situations in which adjustments are required, as described in Section b. below. In that respect, Level 1 inputs are inputs at their "rawest" level. When the Standards permit the application of certain adjustments to such inputs, this will result in a categorization within a lower level of the fair value hierarchy. For an input to be categorized within Level 1, the item to which the input relates must be identical to the item that is being measured.

The importance of Level 1 inputs in the fair value hierarchy stems from the fact that, according to the Standards, it is mandatory to estimate the fair value of the holding by using a quoted price, and no exercise of judgment is permitted in that respect (for more information, see Section 2.2).

The definition of Level 1 inputs uses the term "active market." Therefore, when there is a market in which a particular asset or liability is traded, but this market does not meet the definition of an active market, the prices quoted in that market will not be defined as Level 1 inputs. Although the most prominent example for a situation where there is an active market is when a financial instrument is listed for trading in a stock exchange and there is a sufficient level of trading involving this instrument to meet this definition, not every share or other financial instrument listed for trading is necessarily being traded in an active market. On the other hand, the Standards do not necessarily require an instrument to be listed for trading on a stock exchange in order for it to qualify as having an active market. Thus, in our view, instruments that have significant trading volumes in OTC markets or through intermediaries can also be considered as having an active market, and therefore, their prices can also be Level 1 inputs.

Another element in the definition of Level 1 inputs is the fact that it is mandatory that the price be quoted. However, the Standards do not clarify the meaning of the word "quoted." Different stock exchanges may present quoted prices or quoted closing prices by using different calculation methods. Thus, for example, the price may reflect recent transactions carried out within an immediate period only if the volume of the transactions exceeds a particular minimum; if this is not the case, the prices of previous transactions will also be taken into account. However, in the Standards' own words, closing prices in a stock exchange are "generally representative" of fair value, and in our view, the Standards' starting point (as well as the current practice's starting point) is that when there is an active market, quoted prices based on recent transactions will be sufficiently representative of fair value, using generally accepted weighting methods applied to closing rates in stock exchanges. Clearly, when a market is defined as an active one, reporting entities cannot rely on a price quotation based on an average price over a period of time which is not immediate (such as the average share price over 30 days).

Another question that arises in connection with the word "quoted" is whether or not bid and ask prices may meet the definition of quoted prices (for more information, see Section 8.3). As described above, assets or liabilities may have active markets even when they are not listed for trading on a stock exchange but rather traded by dealers or even brokers. Therefore, in our view, quotations of binding bid or ask prices in such markets (rather than only quotations of prices in recent transactions) may meet the definition of quoted prices and, as a result, may be considered Level 1 inputs, provided that the market is considered an active one. On the other hand, in our view, third-party price quotations, which are not binding and do not rely on the prices of recent transactions, may not be considered Level 1 inputs. Similarly, in our view, binding bid and ask prices in a stock exchange's orders book (i.e., orders that have not yet been matched with a counter order) may be used as a quoted price, where there is no sufficiently recent quoted price of an actual transaction and may even be considered as a Level 1 input, provided that the item to which the quotation relates is traded in an active market. If the prices used are binding bid and ask prices within a limited bid-ask spread, some believe that even after weighting and selecting the point within the bid-ask spread that is most representative of fair value, the fair value in its entirety will still meet the definition of a Level 1 input.

Sometimes, quoted prices can be obtained from multiple sources—for example, when a financial instrument is traded in multiple markets (such as the shares of a dual-listed company traded in more than one stock exchange). In those cases, the Standards stipulate that the source of the quoted price should be selected on the basis of the following two parameters:

a. The market in which the transaction will take place—which is the principal market for the asset or liability or, in the absence of one, which is the most advantageous market for the asset or liability; and
b. The ability to enter into a transaction—the reporting entity shall determine whether it can enter into a transaction for the asset or liability at the

price in that market at the measurement date (for more information, see Chapter 4).

B. Adjustments to Level 1 inputs

As a rule, the Standards do not allow adjustments to Level 1 inputs, except for a detailed list of cases, which appears to be exhaustive. The result of such adjustments will cause the measurement in its entirety to be categorized within a lower level of the fair value hierarchy, according to the level of inputs used to make the adjustment.

Adjustments to a Level 1 input are permitted only in the following circumstances:

a. Using an alternative pricing method as a practical expedient. The Standards provide a practical expedient (as an exception to the general principles) to reporting entities holding a large number of similar (but not identical) assets or liabilities that are measured at fair value, and a quoted price in an active market is available but not readily accessible for each of those assets or liabilities individually. Under this exception, a reporting entity may measure fair value using an alternative pricing method that does not rely exclusively on quoted prices (e.g., matrix pricing). In our view, even when a reporting entity uses the matrix pricing method, it should ensure that the estimated fair value still appropriately reflects the assumptions that would have been taken into consideration by market participants.
b. When a quoted price in an active market does not represent fair value at the measurement date. This scenario refers to circumstances where the quoted price does not reflect other significant transactions or events that have taken place after the close of a market and the determination of the quoted closing price but before the measurement date. As an example of such a scenario, the Standards refer to a change in the price reflected in transactions in a principal-to-principal market or in a brokered market during after-hours trading or announcements of significant events (such as a significant business combination). In our view, another technical example of such a scenario is the adjustment to the closing price in respect of dividends, the entitlement to which was established after trading hours but before the measurement date. Reporting entities are required to establish and consistently apply a policy for identifying those transactions and events that might affect fair value measurements. Thus, for example, let us assume that the reporting entity normally adjusts the

quoted price in the relevant market to reflect changes in the asset's price, or changes in the prices of the assets that are relevant to the asset's pricing in transactions carried out after trading is closed (e.g., the effect of changes in the price of an underlying asset of a future contract that is held by the reporting entity) or changes in the price that are reflected in trade on other stock exchanges. In such a case, in our view, a reporting entity should determine the threshold of the change for making such adjustments, the type of events in respect of which prices should be adjusted and the adjustment method and then apply this policy consistently. Furthermore, it is important to note that the adjustment method should be consistent with the principles of the Standards and that the use of observable inputs should be maximized. In our view, even if the adjustment to closing prices is based on quoted prices of the asset or the liability in other markets (such as other exchanges), the adjustment will result in the fair value measurement being categorized within a level that is lower than Level 1 of the fair value hierarchy. Clearly, quoted prices should not be adjusted to reflect events that have taken place after the measurement date, since adjustments relate only to events that have taken place between the quotation date and the measurement date.

c. Measuring the fair value of a liability or a reporting entity's own equity instrument. Typically, there is no quoted price for the transfer of a reporting entity's liability or equity instrument, but there may be a quoted price for an identical item held as an asset by another party (for more information, see Chapter 10, Section 3). In such cases, reporting entities may sometimes need to adjust the quoted price to reflect characteristics that are irrelevant to the measurement of the liability or equity instrument (such as third-party credit enhancements). If there is no need to adjust the quoted price of the asset held by another party, the result is a fair value measurement categorized within Level 1 of the fair value hierarchy. However, any such adjustment to the quoted price of the asset results in a fair value measurement categorized within a lower level of the fair value hierarchy.

8.6. Level 2 inputs

A. Inputs categorized within Level 2

Level 2 inputs are defined as inputs other than quoted prices included within Level 1 that are observable for the asset or liability, either directly or indirectly. Level 2 inputs are more subjective than Level 1 inputs. As described below, the calculation or extraction of Level 2 inputs from market inputs may require the use of mathematical or statistical tools.

Level 2 inputs include the following:

a. Quoted prices for similar assets or liabilities in active markets—clearly, if it were an identical item, it would be a Level 1 input.
b. Quoted prices for identical or similar assets or liabilities in inactive markets—in this case as well, the price in question is a quoted price of an identical or a similar item, but the relevant market is not active; therefore, the input will not be categorized within Level 1.
c. Inputs—other than quoted prices—that are observable for the asset or liability, for example:
   (1) Interest rates and yield curves observable at commonly quoted intervals;
   (2) Implied volatilities; and
   (3) Credit spreads.
d. Market-corroborated inputs—for more information, see below.

According to the fair value hierarchy, if a particular asset or liability is not traded in an active market, their fair value measurement will not be categorized within Level 1. Indeed, there may be other observable inputs that will enable the categorization of the measurement within Level 2. The most basic example of Level 2 inputs is observable prices in transactions involving assets or liabilities that are not traded in an active market (such as shares, bonds or real estate assets). It is interesting to note that the basis for conclusions of a recent amendment (finalized in 2018) to ASC 820's disclosure rules states that the Financial Accounting Standards Board (FASB) notes the lack of a clear distinction between less active Level 1 fair value measurements and Level 2 fair value measurements based on prices of instruments trading in an active market.

Other examples provided by the Standards in this context include the royalty rate set in a licensing contract that was negotiated at inception with an unrelated party and the price of inventory for customers in a retail market or its price for retailers in a wholesale market. However, it is important to note that the mere fact that an input is observable (as presented in the above examples) does not automatically lead to categorization of the valuation that relies on that input within Level 2 of the fair value hierarchy. This is the case, since one of the main questions arising from the use of Level 2 inputs is whether such inputs should be adjusted and what impact will such adjustment have. Thus, for example, let us assume that the reporting entity uses an observable price in a relatively recent transaction involving an asset or a liability in an inactive market (a Level 2 input). The reporting entity decides that no price adjustments are required, since the transaction involves an identical asset (such as an inventory item or a share), and the transaction is an orderly and recent transaction. In such a case, the valuation only uses Level 2 inputs and will therefore be categorized in its entirety within Level 2 of the fair value hierarchy. Indeed, in many cases, Level 2 inputs will require adjustments to reflect the characteristics of the item from the perspective of a market participant. This is particularly true when the inputs in question relate to transactions that are not recent, and those inputs should be adjusted to reflect changes that have taken place, or when the inputs in question relate to transactions involving assets or liabilities that are not identical to the measured item. In such a situation, the nature of the said adjustments (i.e., whether they are observable), as well as the extent to which they are significant to the measurement, will determine the categorization of the valuation in its entirety at Level 2 or 3.

Adjustments to Level 2 inputs may be required depending on factors specific to the asset or liability. An adjustment to a Level 2 input that is significant to the entire measurement might result in a fair value measurement categorized within Level 3 of the fair value hierarchy if the adjustment uses significant unobservable inputs. Listed below are the factors that may require adjustments to Level 2 inputs:

a. The condition or location of the asset;
b. The extent to which inputs relate to items that are comparable to the asset or liability. For example, the adjustment to a quoted price of a liability that is held as an asset by another party to reflect elements that are relevant to the asset but not to the liability, such as third-party credit enhancements (for more information, see Chapter 10, Section 3.2); and
c. The volume or level of activity in the markets within which the inputs are observed.

To illustrate these provisions, let us assume that the reporting entity is required to measure the fair value of an apartment in a particular residential building. The reporting entity uses observable inputs (Level 2) of a transaction involving a similar apartment in the building. In this case, it may very well be that the observable transaction price will need to be adjusted in order to estimate the fair value. Thus, for example, adjustments may be required in respect of factors such as the size of the apartment, the directions that the apartment faces, the physical condition, the particular specification, the floor on which the apartment is located and so forth. It is likely that most of the said adjustments will not be observable (Level 3 input) and will involve subjectivity (as to the method of calculation, the sources from which inputs are obtained and so forth). In such a situation, the categorization of the valuation in its entirety will depend on the significance of the adjustments to the measurement in its entirety. It should be noted that one of the examples provided by the Standards refers to a situation where the reporting entity estimates the fair value of a building it holds by applying the market approach. According to the Standards, in this situation, a Level 2 input would be the price per square meter for the building derived from observable market inputs—for example, multiples derived from prices in observed transactions involving comparable buildings in similar locations. In this context, it should be noted that although sometimes the prices of comparable assets are transparent, inputs about current and representative income in comparable assets, the physical condition of those assets and even the method employed to measure their area are usually not. In such a situation, the extraction of comparable transactions' inputs will be subjective to a certain extent, and, in our view, it will be difficult to claim that these inputs are, indeed, observable inputs. Alternatively, even if the said inputs are considered Level 2, they may require additional processing or adjustment, which is usually based on unobservable inputs. It can be said that, practically speaking, substantially all real estate appraisals, which use the comparison approach, are categorized within Level 3 of the fair value hierarchy. This is due to differences between the asset and the comparable assets, which require making various unobservable adjustments (such as use of weights). Such differences include location, occupancy rate, physical condition and lessee mix, as well as other differences.

Another example referred to by the Standards in the context of Level 2 inputs (and in the context of a valuation of an operation using the multiples technique; for more information, see Section 3.2) is that of the valuation multiple (such as multiple of earnings, revenue or active users). The valuation multiple is derived from observable market inputs in similar transactions involving comparable businesses, taking into account operational, market, financial and nonfinancial factors. As in the case of the other example of Level 2 inputs provided by the Standards, in this theoretical example, it is important to note that the extraction of different multiples from the market transaction inputs will not always be transparent or one-to-one. For example, in order to calculate the earnings multiple, the reporting entity needs to calculate the representative earnings of the companies involved in the comparable transaction. Furthermore, reporting entities will almost always need to exercise judgment as to the adjustments they must make to the multiples in order to measure the fair value of the relevant enterprise, including how to apply weighting among the observable data included in the sample, how to account for changes in the market, how to exclude nonrecurring items and how to measure the fair value of excess assets and liabilities of the measured enterprise. Therefore, in practice, enterprise valuations, which use techniques such as DCF, multiples or NAV, will typically be categorized in their entirety within Level 3 of the fair value hierarchy.

B. Market-corroborated inputs

As mentioned above, Level 2 inputs include not only observable prices but also inputs that can be extracted relatively simply from market price level, such as extracting the expected volatility from the prices of options or extracting the yield to maturity, and the credit spreads from market prices of bonds. Thus, for example, if the reporting entity needs to estimate the fair value of a nontradable warrant and uses the implied volatility of the quoted price of tradable warrants for an identical period, then such implied volatility will be a Level 2 input.

Furthermore, Level 2 inputs also include market-corroborated inputs. These inputs are derived principally from, or corroborated by, observable market inputs through correlation or other means. In other words, market-corroborated inputs are not necessarily directly observable in the market or can be extracted in a simple or one-to-one manner from the market, but they can be determined through statistical tools. Indeed, in our view, the Standards require a relatively high level of reliability for the categorization of unobservable inputs as market-corroborated inputs (Level 2). Specifically, according to the Standards, if an asset or a liability has a defined contractual term, the input used must be observable for substantially the full term of the asset or the liability. To illustrate the use of market-corroborated inputs, let us assume that the reporting entity needs to measure the fair value of a three-year option on exchange-traded shares. It is also assumed that prices for one-year and two-year options on the shares are observable and that the reporting entity can derive the implied volatility of the shares for these periods from them. In this case, the implied volatility of the shares, derived through extrapolation to year 3, will be a Level 2 input. Furthermore, the extrapolated implied volatility should be corroborated by observable market data for substantially the full term of the option. This can be achieved, for example, by the implied volatility for three-year options on comparable entities' shares, provided that correlation to the one-year and two-year implied volatilities is established.

The conclusion from the above example may be that, in order to claim that unobservable inputs are market-corroborated inputs, a statistical analysis is not enough. Rather, results must prove sufficient statistical significance. The examples provided in the Standards indicate that when using extrapolation, reporting entities must ensure that potential and reasonable changes in the method employed to achieve the extrapolation will not be significant to the measurement in its entirety. Thus, for example, let us assume that the reporting entity needs to measure the fair value of a loan, which was extended to a particular borrower. The loan is repayable in a single installment after a 15-year period. For this purpose, the reporting entity opts to use the discount rate adjustment technique (for more information, see Section 3.4). The discount rate was extrapolated from two other loans of the borrower with characteristics (such as seniority, collaterals and financial covenants) that are identical to those of the measured loan, except for the fact that the said loans were extended for 2- and 4-year periods. In such a situation, bearing in mind the significant difference in the terms of the loans, it is definitely possible that reasonable changes in the extrapolation (e.g., changes in the appropriate credit spread or liquidity as a function of the term of the loan) will have a significant effect on the result of the fair value estimate. Therefore, in our view, the credit spread, the liquidity or the discount rate for a period of 15 years, as the case may be, will be categorized as a Level 3 input. Clearly, any further adjustments that the measurement may require, such as size adjustments (as a characteristic of the unit of account), may also result in the categorization within Level 3 of the fair value hierarchy.

8.7. Level 3 inputs

A. Inputs categorized within Level 3

Unlike Level 1 and Level 2 inputs, Level 3 inputs are unobservable inputs for the asset or liability, and therefore, they are the most subjective inputs. Level 3 inputs will be used to measure fair value to the extent that relevant observable inputs are not available (e.g., when there is little, if any, market activity for the asset or liability at the measurement date). However, the fair value measurement objective remains the same, that is, an exit price at the measurement date from the perspective of a market participant that holds the asset or owes the liability. Therefore, unobservable inputs will reflect the assumptions that market participants would use when pricing the asset or liability. Thus, for example, when Level 3 inputs are used, a reporting entity is not permitted to take into account a unique synergy of the reporting entity that is unavailable to other market participants.

In connection with the use of Level 3 inputs, the Standards emphasize the importance of taking into account assumptions about risk that market participants would take into account when pricing the asset or liability—for example, the risk inherent in a particular valuation technique used to measure fair value and the risk inherent in the inputs used. A measurement that does not include adjustment for risk would not represent a fair value measurement if market participants would include one when pricing the asset or liability—for example, in a case where there is significant measurement uncertainty due to a significant decrease in the volume or level of activity when compared with normal market activity, and the reporting entity has determined that the price in recent transactions does not represent fair value (for more information, see Chapter 7, Section 3).

A reporting entity shall develop unobservable inputs using the best information available under the circumstances, which might include the reporting entity's own inputs. This means that sometimes the starting point of developing unobservable inputs will be a reporting entity's own internal inputs, such as its forecasts or business plan. However, if reasonably available data indicate that other market participants would use different data (e.g., more conservative forecasts), the inputs used should be adjusted to reflect the inputs that market participants would have used.

One of the concerns noted in the explanatory notes of IFRS 13 in connection with the use of Level 3 inputs was that independent auditors or regulators would expect reporting entities to undertake unreasonable efforts in order to establish the assumptions from the perspective of market participants. However, the Standards state that a reporting entity need not undertake exhaustive efforts to obtain information about market participant assumptions. However, a reporting entity shall take into account all information about market participant assumptions that is reasonably available, and when such information is available, it shall not ignore it.

The Standards include several examples of Level 3 inputs. The most straightforward example of Level 3 inputs is that of the financial forecasts that are being used in order to estimate under a DCF technique the fair value of an enterprise (e.g., a cash-generating unit under IFRS), using the reporting entity's own inputs, provided there is no reasonably available information that indicates that market participants would use different assumptions. Such forecasts include, among other things, assumptions regarding future growth, profitability, working capital, capital investments and so forth. On a practical level and in substantially all cases, these forecasts are Level 3 inputs since they are not observable data. Furthermore, it is reasonable to assume that the discount rate used in the valuation (such as WACC) will be a Level 3 input as well. Therefore, the fair value obtained from the use of DCF techniques to measure the value of an enterprise will almost always be categorized in its entirety within Level 3 of the fair value hierarchy. As to the considerations to be taken into account when categorizing a fair value measurement achieved by using other approaches, such as the multiples technique, see Section 8.6. Another clear example of Level 3 inputs referred to by the Standards concerns the assumptions regarding the cash flows used by the reporting entity to estimate the fair value of a decommissioning and restoration liability (asset retirement obligation) assumed in a business combination (for more information, see Chapter 10, Section 4). Another example of Level 3 inputs under IFRS may include the assumptions that are sometimes needed to calculate the fair value of biological assets, as defined in IAS 41—*Agriculture*, specifically assumptions concerning unharvested crops, such as future crops, which depend on the weather and on other factors later on in the season.

B. Distinguishing between Level 2 inputs and Level 3 inputs

It should be noted that Level 2 inputs may also include unobservable data that was corroborated by market inputs (for more details, see Section 8.6), and which was developed by using various statistical methods. Sometimes, distinguishing between Level 3 inputs (that were calculated on the basis of market data and statistical methods) and Level 2 inputs (which are corroborated by market data) will by no means be easy and will require the reporting entity to exercise judgment. Some point to several qualitative factors that may indicate that an input is observable. These include support by market transactions, whether the input is proprietary, readily available, regularly distributed, transparent, verifiable or reliable. Additional factors include the identity of the provider and whether they are actively involved in the relevant market.

With regard to market-corroborated inputs, in our view, the guiding principles for this purpose should include the statistical significance of the results obtained, the extent of the results' sensitivity to reasonable changes in the extrapolation technique used to extract the input (or by using other acceptable techniques) and the question of whether observable inputs are available for substantially the full term of the measured asset or liability.

Thus, for example, let us assume that the reporting entity needs to estimate the fair value of a nontradable option to purchase a company's shares by using a valuation technique such as B&S. To this end, the reporting entity is also required to estimate the expected volatility of the share price over a period of three years. Unlike the implied volatility of the price of options for a similar period, or the implied volatility for other periods, which can be extrapolated reliably, the only relevant available data that can be used in order to develop the expected volatility of the share's price as above are the share's prices in the past. In the case in question, historical volatility does not typically represent the current expectations of market participants as to future volatility, even if this is the only data that can be obtained in order to price the option, and hence, such volatility is a Level 3 input. Therefore, in our view, the reporting entity should consider whether and how it should make adjustments to such volatility. In our view, the conclusion that projecting the future level of volatility based on historical volatility is a Level 3 input can also be supported based on the fact that the reporting entity is required to exercise considerable judgment as to the method of calculation of the standard deviation, as well as when making the necessary adjustments to reflect future periods. Thus, for example, the reporting entity is required to exercise judgment in relation to the period used to calculate the standard deviation in the past, in relation to the frequency of the sample (weekly standard deviation, daily standard deviation, etc.) and, of course, in relation to the adjustment required to reflect future periods. It is most definitely possible that reasonable changes in the technique used to calculate the standard deviation or changes in the adjustment technique used in respect of forward-looking information would result in relatively significant changes in the result of the measurement, and this conclusion is consistent with the categorization of this fair value measurement within Level 3 of the fair value hierarchy. Furthermore, in our view, the use of certain databases (such as a publicly available database comprising data on the level of earnings multiples in certain transactions or on the level of volatility in particular industries) does not mean that the obtained input (e.g., a multiple) will necessarily be considered an observable input, and therefore, it will not necessarily be categorized within Level 3. The reason is that the principal question that arises from the use of such databases has to do with the methods employed to develop the inputs that make up the database; another principal question is the availability of data to the data provider and whether or not the level of statistical significance indicates that the input is corroborated by market inputs. Thus, when there are several alternative ways (which significantly affect the result) for weighting or calculating the multiples, for selecting the period during which the multiples were estimated, for making required adjustments to the measured item or for selecting the representative input of the measured item (such as the representative profit), in our view, it is likely that this input will be considered a Level 3 input, despite the fact that many market data were used to calculate it.

Chapter 13

DISCLOSURE PROVISIONS

1. Overview

The Standards establish extensive disclosure requirements regarding fair value measurement. These requirements relate, among other things, to the valuation techniques used, the inputs used and the quality of these inputs (with an emphasis on Level 3 inputs, which are much more subjective); to the transfer between levels of the fair value hierarchy; and so forth.

In principle, reporting entities shall present the quantitative disclosures required by the Standards in a tabular format unless another format is more appropriate. Detailed illustrative examples were published as an appendix to the Standards; these examples illustrate, among other things, quantitative disclosure in a tabular format, which includes disaggregation into classes. The examples included in this section are based (with some changes) on the examples in the appendix to International Financial Reporting Standard (IFRS) 13.

2. The Scope of the Disclosure Requirements

Under IFRS, it should be mentioned that the disclosure section does not apply to certain fair value measurements, which are subject to IFRS 13's measurement provisions (for more information, see Chapter 2, Section 2.3).

The disclosure chapter of the Standards includes provisions that relate only to measurement of assets or liabilities. Therefore, when the reporting entity measures fair value, but not in the context of assets or liabilities (e.g., measuring the fair value of equity instruments issued as consideration as part of a transaction for the extinguishment of a financial liability with equity instruments, which is accounted for under IFRS in accordance with International Financial Reporting Interpretations Committee's Interpretation 19 (IFRIC 19)), in our view, such disclosure provisions will not apply. Furthermore, in our view, a similar conclusion applies to the measurement of fair value of the equity instruments of the reporting entity used as consideration in a business combination.

IFRS 13's explanatory notes clarify that the disclosure provisions apply only to subsequent measurements (regardless of whether those measurements are recurring or nonrecurring; see below), and they do not apply to fair value measured at initial recognition of assets or liabilities. This is also the case in the August 2018 amendments in Accounting Standards Codification (ASC) 820 described in Section 3. Thus, for example, the disclosure provisions do not apply to measurement of the fair value of financial instruments at initial recognition or to measurement of the fair value of assets and liabilities recognized in a business combination. In such situations, the relevant disclosure provisions for measurement at initial recognition, which are incorporated into the relevant Standards, such as IFRS 3 or ASC 805, will apply.

Furthermore, the Standards include relatively limited disclosure provisions that apply to fair value measurements carried out for disclosure purposes alone (for more information, see Section 6).

3. The Objective of the Disclosure

Originally, both IFRS 13 and ASC 820 stated the same objectives for the disclosure provisions. This objective was to provide the users of the reporting entity's financial statements with information that will help them assess both of the following:

a. For assets and liabilities measured at fair value, the valuation techniques and inputs used to develop those measurements. This information will help users of the reporting entity's financial statements to analyze the levels of reliability and uncertainty of the fair value balances presented in the statement of financial position and the extent to which such balances can be relied upon when making investment decisions.
b. For recurring fair value measurements using significant unobservable inputs (Level 3), the effect of the measurements on profit or loss or other comprehensive income for the period. Since Level 3 inputs are much more subjective, the disclosure requirements focus on the effect of fair value measurements categorized within this level for the purpose of periodic valuations of different items (such as investment property) on the reporting entity's comprehensive income for the period.

However, in August 2018 the Financial Accounting Standards Board (FASB) modified some aspects of ASC 820's disclosure requirements. Among other things, while IFRS 13's disclosure objectives remained the same, ASC 820's disclosure objective is now phrased slightly differently: to provide users of financial statements with information about assets and liabilities measured at fair value in the statement of financial position or disclosed in the notes to financial statements:

a. The valuation techniques and inputs that a reporting entity uses to arrive at its measures of fair value, including judgments and assumptions made by the entity;
b. The uncertainty in the fair value measurements as of the reporting date; and
c. How changes in fair value measurements affect an entity's performance and cash flows.

According to the objectives defined above, the Standards originally established a set of minimum disclosures a reporting entity must provide but guide the reporting entity to exercise judgment as to the level of detail necessary to satisfy the disclosure requirements and how much emphasis to place on each of the various requirements. Wherever necessary, disclosure of additional information may also be required to meet the above objectives, such as additional information about quantitative information disclosed. Following the August 2018 amendments, ASC 820 no longer refers to its list of disclosures as a minimum in order to promote the appropriate exercise of discretion by entities when considering fair value measurement disclosures and to clarify that materiality is an appropriate consideration of entities and their auditors when evaluating disclosure requirements. This seems to be an appropriate interpretation under IFRS as well.

As part of determining the format of disclosure, a reporting entity should decide how much emphasis to place on each of the various requirements and how much aggregation or disaggregation to undertake (for more information, see Section 5). Reporting entities need to exercise judgment regarding the disclosure requirements in order to avoid a situation where their disclosures are formal or cookie-cutter in nature while providing only partial information or even information that is irrelevant to users of the financial statements and omitting other important information.

4. Recurring and Nonrecurring Fair Value Measurements

As described above, some of the disclosure requirements apply only to recurring fair value measurements of assets and liabilities. Recurring fair value measurements of assets or liabilities are those that other Standards require or permit in the statement of financial position at the end of each reporting period. Prominent examples of recurring measurements under IFRS include periodic fair value measurements of investment property that is measured according to the fair value model, periodic fair value measurements of property, plant and equipment measured according to the revaluation model or (for both US Generally Accepted Accounting Principles (US GAAP) and IFRS) periodic fair value measurements of financial instruments classified into fair value through profit or loss or into fair value through other comprehensive income measurement category.

The second type of fair value measurements are referred to by the Standards as nonrecurring fair value measurements. Some of the disclosure requirements (disclosure requirements regarding the effect on comprehensive income) do not apply to those measurements for practical reasons. Nonrecurring fair value measurements of assets or liabilities are those that other Standards require or permit in the statement of financial position only under particular circumstances. Prominent examples of such measurements under IFRS include assets held for sale measured at fair value less costs to sell in accordance with IFRS 5—*Non-Current Assets Held for Sale and Discontinued Operations*.

It is important to emphasize that measurement of fair value only at initial recognition (e.g., at initial recognition of financial instruments or in a business combination) and fair value measurement less costs to sell to apply International Accounting Standard (IAS) 36—*Impairment of Assets* are excluded from the scope of the Standards' disclosure provisions (for more information, see Section 2).

5. Determining Appropriate Classes of Assets and Liabilities

The explanatory notes of IFRS 13 clarify that the disclosures were not designed to enable users of the financial statements to replicate the valuation techniques of the reporting entity. Therefore, the disclosure provided by a reporting entity is subject to aggregation. Determining appropriate classes of assets and liabilities for which disclosures about fair value measurements should be provided requires judgment.

The disclosures provided regarding assets and liabilities should be disaggregated into classes of assets and liabilities according to the following details:

a. Aggregation by the nature, characteristics, or risks, as follows:
   (1) Disaggregation by the nature of the item being measured—for example, disaggregation by types of items: investment property, derivative financial instruments, investments in hedge funds, investments in debt instruments, investments in equity instruments and so forth;

(2) Disaggregation by characteristics—for example, disaggregation by geographic location: investment property in Asia, Europe or the United States and so forth or disaggregation by location and use, such as investment property in the central part of the country that is designated for commercial use, investment property in the northern part of the country that is designated for office use and so forth;
(3) Disaggregation by risks—for example, disaggregating debt instruments by types of collaterals: commercial mortgage-backed securities, residential mortgage-backed securities, securities backed by other assets and so forth.

b. The level of the fair value hierarchy within which a fair value measurement is categorized (Level 1, 2 or 3) (for more information, see Chapter 12, Section 8.4).

A class of assets and liabilities will sometimes require greater disaggregation in the notes to the financial statements than the line items presented in the statement of the financial position. Reporting entities are required to ensure that they provide information sufficient to permit reconciliation to the line items presented in the statement of financial position. However, in our view, the aggregation in the notes to the financial statements of items that are presented separately in the statement of financial position is not permitted. Thus, for example, in our view, under IFRS information about fair value measurement of investment property and information about fair value measurement of investment property under construction should not be aggregated in the notes to the financial statements, if those items are presented separately in the statement of financial position.

Sometimes, another Standard specifies the class for an asset or a liability. Specifically, IFRS 7—*Financial Instruments*: *Disclosures* specifies classes of financial instruments. In such cases, a reporting entity may use such classes in providing the disclosures required in this Standard if that disclosure meets the objective defined above (providing information regarding the techniques and inputs used to measure fair value and information regarding the measurements' effect on the reporting entity's operating results). The number of classes may need to be greater for fair value measurements categorized within Level 3 of the fair value hierarchy because these measurements have a greater degree of uncertainty and subjectivity. For example, a reporting entity may need to provide separate disclosures by the type of technique used in the fair value measurements of such items.

ASC 820 states that, in addition, a reporting entity should provide additional information that will help users of its financial statements to evaluate the quantitative information disclosed. A reporting entity might disclose some or all of the following to comply with the disclosure subtopic:

a. The nature of the item being measured at fair value, including the characteristics of the item being measured that are taken into account in the determination of relevant inputs. For example, for residential mortgage-backed securities, a reporting entity might disclose the following: the types of underlying loans (e.g., prime loans or subprime loans), collateral, guarantees or other credit enhancements, seniority level of the tranches of securities, the year of issue, the weighted-average coupon rate of the underlying loans and the securities, the weighted-average maturity of the underlying loans and the securities, the geographical concentration of the underlying loans and information about the credit ratings of the securities.
b. How third-party information such as broker quotes, pricing services, net asset values (NAVs), and relevant market data was taken into account when measuring fair value.

6. Summary of Disclosure Requirements

For convenience purposes, the following table summarizes IFRS 13's disclosure requirements:

IFRS 13—Disclosure requirement	**Item measured at fair value (*)**						**Item is measured at cost, but its fair value is disclosed (*)**		
	Recurring			**Nonrecurring**					
	L1	**L2**	**L3**	**L1**	**L2**	**L3**	**L1**	**L2**	**L3**
Fair value at the end of the reporting period	V	V	V	V	V	V	V	V	V
Reasons for measurement				V	V	V			
Level within the fair value hierarchy	V	V	V	V	V	V	V	V	V
Transfers between levels of the fair value hierarchy	V	V	V						
The reporting entity's policy for determining when transfers between levels are deemed to have occurred	V	V	V						
Description of the valuation techniques and inputs used		V	V		V	V		V	V

IFRS 13—Disclosure requirement	**Item measured at fair value (*)**						**Item is measured at cost, but its fair value is disclosed (*)**		
	Recurring			**Nonrecurring**					
	L1	**L2**	**L3**	**L1**	**L2**	**L3**	**L1**	**L2**	**L3**
Description of the changes in the valuation techniques and the reasons for the changes		V	V		V	V		V	V
Quantitative information about significant unobservable inputs (Level 3)			V			V			
Reconciliation between opening and closing balances (including transfers between levels)			V						
Unrealized gains recognized in profit or loss			V						
Description of the valuation processes and the valuation policy			V			V			
A narrative (qualitative) description of the sensitivity to changes for unobservable inputs			V						
Quantitative sensitivity analysis of changes in fair value of financial assets and financial liabilities as a function of reasonably possible changes in unobservable inputs			V						
For nonfinancial assets, if the highest and best use of a nonfinancial asset differs from its current use, a reporting entity shall disclose that fact and why the nonfinancial asset is being used in a manner that differs from its highest and best use	V	V	V	V	V	V	V	V	V
Has the reporting entity applied the exception regarding measurement of netting positions of financial assets and financial liabilities (**)	V	V	V						

IFRS 13—Disclosure requirement	Item measured at fair value (*)						Item is measured at cost, but its fair value is disclosed (*)		
	Recurring			Nonrecurring					
	L1	L2	L3	L1	L2	L3	L1	L2	L3
For a liability measured at fair value and issued with inseparable third-party credit enhancements, disclosure of the existence of the credit enhancements and whether or not they are reflected in the fair value measurement of the liability	V	V	V	V	V	V	V	V	V

(*) L1, L2 and L3 refer to inputs categorized within Level 1, Level 2 and Level 3 of the fair value hierarchy, respectively.

(**) This exception is allowed only with respect to financial instruments measured at fair value every period.

For convenience purposes, the following similar table summarizes ASC 820's disclosure rules:

ASC 820—Disclosure requirement	Item measured at fair value						Item is measured at cost, but its fair value is disclosed			Required for nonpublic entities? (US GAAP only)
	Recurring			Nonrecurring						
	L1	L2	L3	L1	L2	L3	L1	L2	L3	
Fair value at the end of the reporting period	V	V	V	V	V	V	V	V	V	Yes
Reasons for measurement				V	V	V				Yes
Level within the fair value hierarchy	V	V	V	V	V	V	V	V	V	Yes
Transfers to or from Level 3 (Level 1 to 2 or the opposite is not required)	V	V	V							Yes

ASC 820—Disclosure requirement	**Item measured at fair value**						**Item is measured at cost, but its fair value is disclosed**			**Required for nonpublic entities? (US GAAP only)**
	Recurring			**Nonrecurring**						
	L1	**L2**	**L3**	**L1**	**L2**	**L3**	**L1**	**L2**	**L3**	
The reporting entity's policy for determining when transfers between levels are deemed to have occurred (GAAP difference)	Not required under US GAAP									
Description of the valuation techniques and inputs used		V	V		V	V		V	V	Yes
Description of the changes in the valuation techniques and the reasons for the changes		V	V		V	V		V	V	Yes
Quantitative information about significant unobservable inputs (Level 3)			V			V				Yes
Quantitative information about significant unobservable inputs (Level 3)—range and weighted average, including the manner in which the inputs were weighted (GAAP difference)			V			V				No, shall provide only the basic quantitate information
Reconciliation between opening and closing balances			V							Yes, modified (*)

ASC 820—Disclosure requirement	Item measured at fair value						Item is measured at cost, but its fair value is disclosed			Required for nonpublic entities? (US GAAP only)
	Recurring			Nonrecurring						
	L1	L2	L3	L1	L2	L3	L1	L2	L3	
Unrealized gains or losses recognized in earnings and in Other Comprehensive Income (OCI) (GAAP difference)			V							No
Description of the valuation processes and the valuation policy (GAAP difference)	Not required under US GAAP									
A narrative (qualitative) description of the uncertainty from the use of Level 3 inputs (GAAP difference)			V							No
Quantitative sensitivity analysis of changes in fair value of financial assets and financial liabilities as a function of reasonably possible changes in unobservable inputs (GAAP difference)	Not required under US GAAP									

ASC 820—Disclosure requirement	Item measured at fair value						Item is measured at cost, but its fair value is disclosed			Required for nonpublic entities? (US GAAP only)
	Recurring			Nonrecurring						
	L1	L2	L3	L1	L2	L3	L1	L2	L3	
For nonfinancial assets, if the highest and best use of a nonfinancial asset differs from its current use, a reporting entity shall disclose that fact and why the nonfinancial asset is being used in a manner that differs from its highest and best use	V	V	V	V	V	V	V	V	V	Yes
Has the reporting entity applied the exception regarding measurement of netting positions of financial assets and financial liabilities	V	V	V							Yes
For a liability measured at fair value and issued with inseparable third-party credit enhancements, disclosure of the existence of the credit enhancements (GAAP difference)	V	V	V	V	V	V	V	V	V	Yes

ASC 820—Disclosure requirement	Item measured at fair value						Item is measured at cost, but its fair value is disclosed			Required for nonpublic entities? (US GAAP only)
	Recurring			Nonrecurring						
	L1	L2	L3	L1	L2	L3	L1	L2	L3	
Additional disclosures on Fair Value (FV) measurement of investments in entities, based on reported NAV subject to the practical expedient (GAAP difference—not applicable under IFRS)	FV of such investments should not be categorized within L1/L2/L3. Specific disclosure requirements exist in ASC 820. Reconciliation of fair value of investments estimated based on reported NAV to the line items in the balance sheet is required (see Section 13).									Yes

(*) As can be seen above, nonpublic reporting entities are not required to disclose some of the information required by ASC 820, unless it is mandated by another Topic. The 2018 amendments state that, in lieu of the requirement to provide a full opening to closing balance reconciliation of Level 3 measurements, a nonpublic entity shall disclose separately changes during the period attributable to purchases, issues and transfers in and out of Level 3, separately. However, it is not required to provide information as to gains or losses for Level 3 items.

7. Disclosure Requirements for Assets and Liabilities Measured at Fair Value

The Standards establish disclosure requirements for each class of assets and liabilities measured at fair value subsequent to initial recognition. As mentioned above, while these are defined in IFRS 13 as minimal requirements, in many cases reporting entities will need to disclose additional information in order to meet the objective of the disclosure. In other cases, some of these requirements may provide information that is immaterial.

For some of the disclosure requirements listed below, the Standards distinguish between recurring and nonrecurring fair value measurements (for more information, see Sections 4 and 8). Furthermore, the Standards include a limited list of disclosure provisions that apply to fair value measurements that are implemented only for the purpose of the notes to the financial statements (for more details, see Section 10).

For all entities under IFRS 13, and for public entities only under ASC 820 (for more information about the requirements for nonpublic entities, see

Table 2 in Section 6), the following information should be disclosed for each class of assets and liabilities measured at fair value. However. It should be noted that the requirements below do not apply under ASC 820 for investments in certain entities measured based on their reported NAV per share or a similar metric, subject to the practical expedient in ASC 820 for such investments (for more information, see Section 13):

a. The fair value measurement at the end of the reporting period (for interpretations of the term "end of the reporting period", see Section 8); under ASC 820, derivative assets and liabilities should be reported on a gross basis in this regard, even if netted on the balance sheet.
b. For nonrecurring fair value measurements—the reasons for the measurement. For example, noting that a group of noncurrent assets and liabilities was classified as held for sale, with a reference to another note or to the summary of the relevant provisions; under ASC 820, derivative assets and liabilities should be reported on a gross basis in this regard, even if netted on the balance sheet.
c. The level of the fair value hierarchy within which the fair value measurements are categorized (for more information, see Chapter 12, Section 8.4); under ASC 820, derivative assets and liabilities should be reported on a gross basis in this regard, even if netted on the balance sheet.
d. IFRS 13 only—transfers between Level 1 and Level 2 of the fair value hierarchy—for assets and liabilities that are measured on a recurring basis and held as of the end of the reporting period (i.e., were not derecognized), a reporting entity shall disclose:

    (1) The amounts of any transfers between Level 1 and Level 2 of the fair value hierarchy; transfers into each level of the hierarchy are disclosed separately from transfers out of each level (i.e., offsetting is not permitted);
    (2) The reasons for the transfers (e.g., there is no longer an active market, or vice versa); and
    (3) The reporting entity's policy for determining when transfers between levels are deemed to have occurred (for more information, see Section 9).

e. For fair value measurements categorized within Level 2 and Level 3 of the fair value hierarchy, the disclosures are as follows:

    (1) A narrative description of the valuation technique(s) and the inputs used in the fair value measurement.

(2) If there has been a change in valuation technique, the reporting entity shall disclose that change and the reason(s) for making it.

(3) For fair value measurements categorized within Level 3 of the fair value hierarchy—a reporting entity shall provide quantitative information about the significant unobservable inputs used in the fair value measurement; for example, assumed discount rates, multiples, prices per square meter, adjustments due to factors such as illiquidity, counterparty credit risk, control premiums and so forth. ASC 820 requires the range and weighted average to be provided, in addition to describing the weighting method. It is also possible to provide mean or median instead of the weighted average, when appropriate. IFRS 13 does not contain this explicitly, but according to the examples provided by IFRS 13, in our view, such information can also be provided by noting a range and an average. Furthermore, according to IFRS 13's explanatory notes, when the reporting entity only uses inputs from prior transactions (or makes immaterial adjustments) in order to determine the fair value, it is not required to describe the specific assumptions but rather only the method of such measurement. If the required adjustments are material to the result of the fair value measurement and such adjustments are Level 3 inputs, then such assumptions should be disclosed. This means that under IFRS 13 and ASC 820, a reporting entity is not required to create quantitative information to comply with this disclosure requirement if quantitative unobservable inputs are not developed by the reporting entity when measuring fair value. However, when providing this disclosure, a reporting entity cannot ignore quantitative unobservable inputs that are significant to the fair value measurement and are reasonably available to the reporting entity.

f. Reconciliation from the opening balances to the closing balances—for recurring fair value measurements categorized within Level 3 of the fair value hierarchy, disclosing the reconciliation from the opening balances to the closing balances (of the total fair value) while providing separate disclosure of the changes during the period attributable to the following:

(1) Total gains or losses for the period recognized in profit or loss, and the line item(s) in profit or loss in which those gains or losses are recognized;

(2) Total gains or losses for the period recognized in other comprehensive income and the line item(s) in other comprehensive income in which those gains or losses are recognized;

(3) Purchases, sales, issues and settlements (each type of changes should be disclosed separately); and
(4) The amounts of any transfers into or out of Level 3 of the fair value hierarchy during the period (without offsetting transfers into Level 3 against transfers out of Level 3) and the reasons for those transfers. IFRS 13 only also requires the disclosure of the reporting entity's policy for determining when transfers between levels are deemed to have occurred (for more information, see Section 9).

Under ASC 820, derivative assets and liabilities could be reported on a gross or net basis in this regard.

g. Unrealized gains or losses for the period—for recurring fair value measurements categorized within Level 3 of the fair value hierarchy, a reporting entity is required to separate between the amount of gains or losses recognized in profit or loss in respect of items that were disposed of during the reporting period and the amount of the gains or losses for the period included in profit or loss that is attributable to the change in unrealized gains or losses relating to those assets and liabilities held at the end of the reporting period; the reporting entity shall note the line item(s) in profit or loss in which these unrealized gains or losses are recognized. The term "unrealized gains" refers to gains from items held by the reporting entity and that were not derecognized from its statement of financial position due to sale, settlement and so forth. Thus, for example, in the case of investment property under IFRS, the valuation gains or losses in the current period, which are attributable to assets that have not yet been sold, will be considered unrealized gains or losses. On the other hand, valuation gains or losses stemming from investment property assets that were sold and derecognized will be considered realized gains or losses. In our view, a similar principle will apply to financial assets and financial liabilities. It should also be noted that ASC 820 explicitly requires the reporting entity to include a similar disclosure as for unrealized gains recognized in OCI. In our view, this would also be appropriate under IFRS 13; under ASC 820, derivative assets and liabilities could be reported on a gross or net basis in this regard.
h. IFRS 13 only—a description of the valuation processes—for recurring and nonrecurring fair value measurements categorized within Level 3 of the fair value hierarchy, a description of the valuation processes used by the reporting entity. For example, how a reporting entity decides its valuation policies and procedures and analyzes changes in fair value measurements from period to period. The illustrative examples of IFRS

13 illustrate the type of relevant disclosures in the context of valuation procedures, such as:

(1) The identity of the reporting entity's employees who are in charge of the valuation policies and procedures, including the employees to whom they report and the controls put in place, including procedural aspects, such as discussion by management or the Financial Statements Review Committee (e.g., did the reporting entity use independent appraisers?);
(2) Frequency of calibration of valuation techniques and the methods employed in such calibrations (for more information, see Chapter 12, Section 5);
(3) The processes implemented to analyze changes in fair value from period to period;
(4) If the reporting entity used information received from third parties, such as pricing or quotations from brokers, how does the reporting entity assert that such information was prepared consistently with IFRS 13's principles?
(5) The methods applied to develop and establish the unobservable inputs used in the valuation.

In addition to the above list, in our view, other items that can be added include information regarding the procedures, frequency and sources of information reviewed by the reporting entity in order to decide when to carry out a new detailed valuation (regarding items measured at fair value, such as investment property or property, plant and equipment).

i. A qualitative description (narrative)—for recurring fair value measurements categorized within Level 3 of the fair value hierarchy, under IFRS 13 a reporting entity shall provide a narrative sensitivity analysis of the fair value measurement's sensitivity as a function of reasonably possible changes in unobservable inputs (Level 3) used in the valuation as at the measurement date. ASC 820 states that the narrative relates to uncertainty rather than sensitivity. The narrative description should include the following information:

(1) Fair value measurement's sensitivity to changes in those inputs, if a change in those inputs to a different amount might result in a significantly higher or lower fair value measurement. According to an illustrative example provided by IFRS 13, in our view, reporting entities are mainly required to identify the said unobservable assumptions and

to note how reasonable changes in each of these assumptions as at the reporting date will impact the fair value measurement in its entirety.

(2) If there are interrelationships between those inputs and other unobservable inputs used in the fair value measurement, a reporting entity shall also provide a description of these interrelationships and of how they might magnify or mitigate the effect of changes in the unobservable inputs on the fair value measurement.

(3) The required narrative description shall include, at a minimum, the unobservable inputs disclosed when complying with section e. above (i.e., all significant unobservable inputs identified).

IFRS 13 (but not ASC 820) also requires a quantitative sensitivity analysis with respect to financial instruments only, as described below.

j. IFRS 13 only—quantitative sensitivity analysis—for recurring fair value measurements that are categorized within Level 3 of the fair value hierarchy and relate only to financial assets and financial liabilities, a reporting entity shall include quantitative sensitivity analysis in respect of unobservable inputs (Level 3 assumptions). If changing one or more of the unobservable inputs to reflect reasonably possible alternative assumptions would change the fair value significantly, a reporting entity shall disclose the following:

(1) The fact that changing one or more unobservable inputs as mentioned above would result in a significant change to fair value.

(2) The effect of such changes, which reflect reasonably possible alternative assumptions. However, reporting entities are not required to take into account cross effects when preparing the sensitivity analysis. Rather, in our view, IFRS 13 requires a sensitivity analysis for each separate change in each of the analyzed unobservable inputs, with all other unobservable inputs held constant, even if there may be a potential correlation between the inputs.

(3) How the effect of a change to reflect reasonably possible alternative assumptions was calculated.

To examine the significance of reasonably possible changes in the unobservable assumptions, significance should be considered with respect to profit or loss, total assets or total liabilities or when changes in fair value are recognized in other comprehensive income—total equity.

Although there may be some overlap between the sensitivity analysis required for fair value of financial instruments and the sensitivity analysis required by IFRS 7, it should be noted that there are significant differences between such sensitivity analyses. The differences pertain, among other things, to aspects such as the value at risk (fair value compared to profit or loss), the scope of the tests (which IFRS 13 requires to apply only to Level 3 inputs) and the main objective of the sensitivity analyses. In IFRS 13, the goal is to provide disclosure to sensitivity to reasonable changes in unobservable assumptions under current market conditions, whereas in IFRS 7, the objective of the sensitivity analysis is to disclose sensitivity to future changes (other than measurement errors) in market risk factors. This difference can also be discerned in the clarifications for ASC 820 issued in August 2018.

8. The Meaning of the Term "End of the Reporting Period"

Some of the Standards' disclosure requirements refer to the end of the reporting period (for more information, see Section 7). Thus, for example, reporting entities are required to disclose the fair value amount as at the end of the reporting period, both for recurring and for nonrecurring fair value measurements. The application of this requirement may cause some practical difficulties, since sometimes the valuation does not measure fair value as at the end of the reporting period. Thus, for example, it may be that the reporting entity's policy is to revalue property, plant and equipment items at a different point during the reporting period rather than at the end of that period, or even less often, while depreciation expenses are recognized from this point onward. Some believe that in such a situation, the disclosure requirements shall apply to the fair value determined on the relevant valuation date. In other words, reporting entities are not required to conduct another valuation as of the end of the reporting period only to comply with the said disclosure requirement. In this sense, it should be noted that for nonrecurring measurements estimated at a date during the reporting period other than the end of the reporting period, ASC 820 explicitly states that a reporting entity shall clearly indicate that the fair value information presented is not as of the period's end as well as the date or period that the measurement was made.

9. Policy Regarding Transfers between Levels within the Fair Value Hierarchy

IFRS 13 includes disclosure requirements regarding transfers between Level 1 and Level 2 of the fair value hierarchy for recurring measurements. Both IFRS 13 and ASC 820 include disclosure requirements regarding transfers into or out of Level 3 of the fair value hierarchy for recurring measurement (for more information, see Section 7). For this purpose, reporting entities are required to consistently follow their policy for determining when transfers between levels of the fair value hierarchy are deemed to have occurred. The policy shall be identical for transfers to and from levels. According to IFRS 13 (only), the selected policy shall also be disclosed. Following are examples regarding possible types of such a policy:

a. The date of the event or change in circumstances that caused the transfer (e.g., the date on which an active market for the asset or the liability started, or ceased to exist). In such a situation, the transfer is carried out according to the value on the date of the change.
b. The beginning of the reporting period. In such a situation, the transfer is carried out according to the fair value at the beginning of the reporting period.
c. The end of the reporting period. In such a situation, the transfer is carried out according to the fair value at the end of the reporting period.

10. Disclosure Provisions That Apply to Fair Value Used Only for the Notes to the Financial Statements

The Standards include relatively limited disclosure provisions that apply to fair value measurements that are carried out for disclosure purposes only rather than for measurement purposes in the statement of financial position. A prominent example for such a situation is disclosing the fair value of investment property measured at amortized cost, as required in IFRS under IAS 40, or disclosure of the fair value of financial assets or financial liabilities that are measured at amortized cost, as required under IFRS 7 and ASC 825.

As to such fair value measurements, the following disclosure provisions will apply to each class of items:

a. The level of the fair value hierarchy within which the fair value measurements are categorized.
b. For Level 2 or Level 3 fair value measurements, a narrative description of the valuation technique and only a narrative description of the data used in the fair value measurement (i.e., there is no requirement to provide a quantitative disclosure of the unobservable assumptions). If there has been a change in the valuation technique, the reporting entity shall disclose that change and the reason(s) for making it.
c. Where relevant, if the highest and best use of a nonfinancial asset differs from its current use, a reporting entity shall disclose that fact and why the

nonfinancial asset is being used in a manner that differs from its highest and best use (for more information, see Chapter 9, Section 2).

11. Other Required Disclosures

In addition to the main disclosure requirements (for more information, see Section 7), the Standards establish several other specific disclosure requirements, as described below:

a. If the highest and best use of a nonfinancial asset differs from its current use, a reporting entity shall disclose that fact and why the asset is being used in a manner that differs from the highest and best use that was used as an assumption when measuring its fair value; this provision applies both to recurring and to nonrecurring fair value measurements (for more information, see Chapter 9, Section 2).
b. If a reporting entity makes an accounting policy choice to use the exception relating to the measurement of offsetting positions of financial assets and financial liabilities, it shall disclose that fact (for more information, see Chapter 11).
c. For a liability measured at fair value and issued with inseparable third-party credit enhancements, disclosure of the existence of those credit enhancements. IFRS 13 (only) also requires disclosure about whether these credit enhancements were reflected in the fair value measurement of the liability (for more information, see Chapter 10, Section 3.2).
d. ASC 820 (only) has specific provisions for the disclosures that apply with regard to investments in certain entities measured based on their reported NAV per share or a similar metric, subject to the practical expedient (for more information, see Section 13).

12. Disclosure Examples

12.1. Example of disclosure regarding fair value hierarchy categorization

The following example illustrates the disaggregation of assets into classes for disclosure purposes, including categorization based on levels of the fair value hierarchy (for more information, see Sections 5 and 7). The example also separates between recurring and nonrecurring fair value measurements. A similar disclosure will also be required in respect of the reporting entity's liabilities, with the required adjustments. It should be noted that the following disclosures were based on examples included in IFRS 13.

Note X—Fair Value

Breakdown of the assets measured at fair value in the statement of financial position, categorized within levels of the fair value hierarchy:

	Level 1	Level 2	Level 3	Total
As at December 31, 20XX		in CU thousands		
Recurring fair value measurements				
Investments in trading equity instruments[a]:				
Real estate industry	70	23	-	93
Gas and oil industry	45	-	-	45
Other	15	-	-	15
Total	130	23	-	153
Investments in other equity instruments[a]:				
Financial services industry	150	-	-	150
Energy industry	-	-	32	32
Healthcare industry	110	-	78	188
Private equity funds[b]	15	-	-	15
Total	275	-	110	385
Investments in debt instruments:				
Residential mortgage-backed debt	-	-	50	50
Commercial mortgage-backed debt	-	24	125	149
Government bonds	85	-	-	85
Corporate bonds of real estate companies	9	84	-	93
Corporate bonds of industrial companies	35	-	-	35
Other	15	-	-	15
Total	144	108	175	427
Investment in derivative instruments:				
Interest rate swaps	78	-	-	78
Foreign exchange swaps	-	24	15	39
Commodity future contracts	-	43	-	43
Commodity forward contracts	10	-	-	10
Total	88	67	15	170
Investment property:				
Commercial—Asia	-	-	31	31
Commercial—Europe	-	-	24	24
Residential	-	-	72	72
Land	-	-	15	15
Total	-	-	142	142
Total recurring fair value measurement	637	198	442	1,277

	Level 1	Level 2	Level 3	Total
Nonrecurring fair value measurements				
Noncurrent assets held for sale:				
Asset A	-	-	10	10
Disposal group held for sale[(c)]	-	-	681	681
Total held for sale items	-	-	691	691
Total nonrecurring fair value measurements	-	-	691	691

Comments:

(a) On the basis of its analysis of the nature, characteristics and risks of the securities, the reporting entity has determined that aggregating them by industry is appropriate.

(b) On the basis of its analysis of the nature, characteristics and risks of the investments, the reporting entity has determined that aggregating them within a single class is appropriate.

(c) In accordance with the provisions of IFRS 5, the value of assets and liabilities, which are classified as a disposal group and are attributed to a production line in the region of XXX, was written down from their carrying amount of CU 700,000 to their fair value (less costs to sell) of CU 681,000. The write-down resulted in a loss of CU 19,000, which was recognized in profit or loss for the period under the "other expenses" line item.

12.2. Example of disclosure in respect of reconciliation from opening to closing balances

Under disclosure requirements set by the Standards regarding Level 3 fair value measurements, the reconciliation from opening to closing balances should be disclosed (for more information, see Sections 5 and 7). The next example illustrates the application of this requirement. The example illustrates the details provided regarding the reporting entity's assets. A similar disclosure shall also be required in respect of the reporting entity's liabilities, with the required adjustments.

Note X—Fair Value

Reconciliation from opening to closing balances of fair value measurements of assets, which use significant unobservable inputs (Level 3):

	Investment in equity instruments		Investment in debt instruments measured at fair value		Investment property		
	Energy industry	Real estate industry	Energy industry	Real estate industry	Asia	Europe	Total
Balance as of January 1, 20XX	49	28	20	105	145	30	377
Transfers into Level 3	-	-	-	60[(a) (b)]	-	-	60
Transfers out of Level 3	-	-	-	(5)[(b) (c)]	-	-	(5)
Gains (losses) recognized in:							
Profit or loss[(d)]	-	-	5	(23)	7	5	(6)
Other comprehensive income[(e)]	3	1	-	-	-	-	4
Purchases, issues, sales and settlements:							
Purchases	1	3	-	-	-	18	22
Issues	-	-	-	-	-	-	-
Sales	-	-	-	-	(62)	(15)	(77)
Settlements	-	-	-	(12)	-	-	(12)
Balance as of December 31, 20XX	53	32	25	125	90	38	363

Comments:

(a) Transferred from Level 2 to Level 3 due to lack of observable market data, resulting from a decline in the volume of market activity for these securities.

(b) The reporting entity's accounting policy is to recognize transfers into and transfers out of Level 3 as of the date of the event or change in circumstances that caused the transfer.

(c) Transferred from Level 3 to Level 2 because observable market data became available for those securities.

(d) Out of a total loss of CU 6,000, which was recognized in profit or loss in 20XX, a loss of CU 4,000 is attributed to assets and liabilities that have not yet been derecognized from the statement of financial position. Out of the unrealized losses, a gain of CU 2,000 was recognized in the "gain or loss from change in fair value of investment property" line item in the statement of profit or loss, and a loss of CU 6,000 was recognized in the "finance expenses" line item.

(e) All gain amounts recognized in other comprehensive income in 20XX—totaling CU 4,000—are attributed to investments in equity instruments classified as at fair value through other comprehensive income and have not yet been sold; therefore, those amounts constitute unrealized gains. The said gains were recognized in the "change in the fair value of equity instruments designated as at fair value through other comprehensive income" line item within other comprehensive income.

12.3. Example for disclosure about valuation techniques and quantitative data used

The following note is an illustrative example of the required disclosure regarding valuation techniques used in fair value measurements and the quantitative information about unobservable inputs that are significant to the measurement in its entirety (for more information, see Sections 5 and 7). The example illustrates the details provided regarding the reporting entity's assets. A similar disclosure will also be required in respect of the reporting entity's liabilities, with the required adjustments.

Note X—Fair Value

Quantitative information about fair value measurements using unobservable inputs that are significant to the measurement in its entirety (Level 3):

Description of measured item	Fair value at December 31, 20XX	Valuation techniques	Description of unobservable inputs	Range (weighted average)
Investments in equity instruments:				
Healthcare industry	53	Discounted cash flows	a. Weighted average cost of capital (WACC)	7%–16% (12.1%)
			b. Long-term revenue growth rate	2%–5% (4.2%)
			c. Long-term operating margin	3%–12% (7%)
			d. Control premium[a]	10%–30% (20%)
		Multiples technique	a. EBITDA multiple[a]	10–13 (11.3)
			b. Revenue multiple[a]	1.5–2.0 (1.7)

Description of measured item	Fair value at December 31, 20XX	Valuation techniques	Description of unobservable inputs	Range (weighted average)
			c. Discount for lack of marketability[(a)]	5%–20% (15%)
			d. Control premium[(a)]	10%–30% (20%)
Private equity fund investments	25	Net asset value[(b)]	-	-
Investment property:				
Commercial—Asia	31	Discounted cash flows	a. Long-term net operating income margin	18%–32% (20%)
			b. Discount rate	7%–9% 8%
Commercial—Europe	27	Market comparable companies	a. Price per square meter (in thousands of Euros)	4,000–12,000 (8,500)
		Discounted cash flow	a. Long-term net operating income margin	15%–25% (18%)
			b. Discount rate	6%–10% (8%)

Note:

(a) Represents amounts that the reporting entity determined that market participants would take into account when pricing the measured item.

(b) The reporting entity has determined that the reported NAV received from the investment funds represents fair value at the end of the reporting period. See additional disclosure requirements under US GAAP in Section 13.

13. Disclosures for investments Subject to the NAV Practical Expedient (US GAAP Only)

ASC 820 requires specific disclosures for investments in certain entities that are measured using the practical expedient mentioned in Chapter 1, Section 4, whether these valuations were used on a recurring or nonrecurring basis during the period. Such fair value measurements are not subject to the regular requirements mentioned in Section 7.

The reporting entity shall disclose information that helps users of its financial statements to understand the nature and risks of these investments and whether the investments, if sold, are likely to be sold at amounts different from the NAV per share (or its equivalent, such as member units or an ownership interest in partners' capital to which a proportionate share of net assets is attributed). A reporting entity shall disclose, at a minimum, the following information for each class of investment:

a. The fair value measurement of the investments in the class at the reporting date and a description of the significant investment strategies of the investee(s) in the class;
b. For each class of investment that includes unredeemable investments in investees, but the reporting entity receives distributions through the liquidation of the underlying assets of the investees, the period over which the underlying assets are expected to be liquidated by the investees if the investee has communicated the timing to the reporting entity or announced the timing publicly. If the timing is unknown, the reporting entity shall disclose that fact;
c. The amount of the reporting entity's unfunded commitments related to investments in the class;
d. A general description of the terms and conditions upon which the investor may redeem investments in the class (e.g., quarterly redemption with 60 days' notice);
e. The circumstances under which an otherwise redeemable investment in the class (or a portion thereof) might not be redeemable (e.g., investments subject to a lockup or gate). Also, for those otherwise redeemable investments that are restricted from redemption as of the reporting entity's measurement date, the reporting entity shall disclose when the restriction from redemption might lapse if the investee has communicated that timing to the reporting entity or announced the timing publicly. If the timing is unknown, the reporting entity shall disclose that fact and how long the restriction has been in effect;
f. Any other significant restriction on the ability to sell investments in the class at the measurement date;
g. If a group of investments would otherwise meet the criteria for the practical expedient but the individual investments to be sold have not been identified (e.g., if a reporting entity decides to sell 20 percent of its investments in private equity funds but the individual investments to be sold have not been identified) so that the investments continue to qualify for the practical expedient, the reporting entity shall disclose its plans to sell and any remaining actions required to complete the sale(s).

Example—Disclosures for Investments Subject to the NAV Practical Expedient (US GAAP Only) (*)

	Fair value (in millions of CU)	Unfunded commitments	Redemption frequency (if currently eligible)	% of value not contractually redeemable (%)	Redemption notice period (in days)	Time to liquidation (years), when unredeemable
Equity long/short hedge funds	55	-	Quarterly	83	30–60	3–6, mostly 5
Event-driven hedge funds	45	-	Quarterly or annually	0	30–60	N/A
Real estate funds	35	20	Quarterly	100	30–45	7
Total	135	20				

(*) This table should be accompanied by additional qualitative disclosures, such as additional descriptions of the investment strategies, value estimation techniques (usually this would be expected to be reported based on NAV), brief descriptions of fund portfolio compositions, redemption limitations, restrictions on selling, general plans for selling and so forth.

www.ingramcontent.com/pod-product-compliance
Ingram Content Group UK Ltd.
Pitfield, Milton Keynes, MK11 3LW, UK
UKHW041831100926
8556IPUK00002B/113

9 781839 984198